Race and Slavery in the Middle East

RACE AND SLAVERY IN THE MIDDLE EAST

An Historical Enquiry

BERNARD LEWIS

OXFORD UNIVERSITY PRESS
New York Oxford

Oxford University Press

Oxford New York Toronto
Delhi Bombay Calcutta Madras Karachi
Petaling Jaya Singapore Hong Kong Tokyo
Nairobi Dar es Salaam Cape Town
Melbourne Auckland
and associated companies in
Berlin Ibadan

First published in 1990 by Oxford University Press, Inc.,
200 Madison Avenue, New York, New York 10016

First issued as an Oxford University Press paperback, 1992

Oxford is a registered trademark of Oxford University Press

Library of Congress Cataloging-in-Publication Data
Lewis, Bernard.
Race and slavery in the Middle East: an historical enquiry
Bernard Lewis
p. cm. Includes bibliographical references
ISBN 0-19-506283-3
ISBN 0-19-505326-5 (pbk.)
1. Slavery—Middle East—History.
2. Slavery and Islam—Middle East—History.
3. Race relations—Religious aspects—Islam.
4. Middle East—Race relations.
I. Title.
HT1316.L48 1990
306.3'62'0956—dc20
89-22913 CIP

2 4 6 8 10 9 7 5 3 1
Printed in the United States of America

Preface

The research presented in this book was first undertaken as part of a group project on tolerance and intolerance in human societies, for which I was asked to prepare a paper on the Islamic world. I began by examining this topic in conventional terms and collected data on the relations between different religions—that is, in the sense in which the words "tolerance" and "intolerance" have in the past normally been used. At a certain point it occurred to me that such an enquiry need no longer be bound by the habits and concerns of a previous generation, concerns which have lost their sharpness for many of us at the present time, at least in the Western world. But if these concerns have diminished or disappeared, they have been replaced by others no less acute. In the present climate of opinion what matters most in this respect is not creed, or even class, but race. This is seen as the ultimate basis of identity and of difference; and it is in this area that, in much of the world, the crucial test of tolerance or intolerance is now applied. I therefore turned to this problem and, in the course of my work, began to examine certain assumptions hitherto unquestioningly accepted by Western as well as Islamic scholars.

The group project on tolerance and intolerance was never completed. The material on Islam, however, aroused some interest, and I was stimulated to pursue it further by an invitation to lecture on the subject at a combined meeting of the three institutes of Anthropology, International Affairs, and Race Relations in London. The lecture was delivered in December 1969 and published in a slightly expanded form in the London monthly *Encounter* in August 1970. This was, in turn, further expanded and published as a small book in New York in 1971, entitled *Race and Color in Islam.*

The publication of a French translation in Paris in 1982 gave me the opportunity to make a number of substantial changes. In addition to correcting some errors, I added new documentation and discussed some further topics not touched upon in the earlier versions. I also appended a selection of relevant original sources, most of them translated from Arabic.

The study of race led inevitably, in the Islamic world as elsewhere, to the problem of slavery, by which both race relations and racial attitudes were profoundly affected. In preparing my successive earlier treatments of this topic, I was obliged to devote increasing attention to this aspect and to examine it in a Middle Eastern rather than in an Islamic context. In embarking, after an interval of years, on a new exploration of the theme, I decided to give the institution of slavery a more central position.

This immediately raised serious difficulties. One of them is the remarkable dearth of scholarly work on the subject. The bibliography of studies on slavery in the Greek and Roman worlds, or in the Americas, runs to thousands of items. Even for medieval Western Europe, where slavery was of relatively minor importance, European scholars have produced a significant literature of research and exposition. For the central Islamic lands, despite the subject's importance in virtually every area and period, a list of serious scholarly monographs on slavery—in law, in doctrine, or in practice—could be printed on a single page. The documentation for a study on Islamic slavery is almost endless; its exploration has barely begun.

Perhaps the main reason for the lack of scholarly research on Islamic slavery is the extreme sensitivity of the subject. This makes it difficult, and sometimes professionally hazardous, for a young scholar to turn his attention in this direction. In time, we may hope, it will be possible for Muslim scholars to examine and discuss Islamic slavery as freely and as openly as European and American scholars have, with the cooperation of scholars from other countries, been willing to discuss this unhappy chapter in their own past. But that time is not yet; meanwhile, Islamic slavery remains both an obscure and a highly sensitive topic, the mere mention of which is often seen as a sign of hostile intentions. Sometimes indeed it is, but it need not and should not be so, and the imposition of taboos on topics of historical research can only impede and delay a better and more accurate understanding. In this little book, I have tried to deal fairly and objectively with a subject of great historical and comparative importance and to do so without recourse to either polemics or apologetics.

The present volume incorporates most of what was said in my early treatments. This has, however, been extensively revised, expanded, and recast, and a considerable body of new material added, including several new chapters, making it a new book dealing with a related but different topic. I have also added a documentary appendix, translated, where necessary, from the original languages. Some of the documents included in the French edition have been omitted, as they are already available elsewhere in English in print. Others have been added, including several translated for this purpose.

There remains the pleasant task of thanking those who have, in various ways, contributed to the completion of this book. My thanks are due to the authorities of the Public Record Office, the India Office Records, and the British Library in London; the Topkapı Saray Museum in Istanbul; the Bibliothèque Nationale in Paris; and Mr. Arthur A. Houghton, for permission to reproduce documents and pictures in their possession. Crown copyright material in the Public Record Office and the India Office Records is reproduced by permission of the Controller of Her Majesty's Stationery Office.

I am indebted to David Goldenberg, John B. Kelly, Hava Lazarus-Yafeh, and Michel Le Gall for suggestions and help of various kinds. Above all, I would like to record my profound gratitude and appreciation to my assistant Leigh Faden, for her untiring and highly effective work in the preparation and numerous revisions of my text, to my research assistant Jonathan Berkey, whose scholarly knowledge and unstinting efforts in many ways lightened the labor of both research and writing and improved the quality of the results, and to both of them for preparing the index. Whatever faults and errors remain are entirely my own.

Princeton, N.J. B. L.
August 1989

Contents

Race and Slavery in the Middle East

1

Slavery

In 1842 the British Consul General in Morocco, as part of his government's worldwide endeavor to bring about the abolition of slavery or at least the curtailment of the slave trade, made representations to the sultan of that country asking him what measures, if any, he had taken to accomplish this desirable objective. The sultan replied, in a letter expressing evident astonishment, that "the traffic in slaves is a matter on which all sects and nations have agreed from the time of the sons of Adam . . . up to this day." The sultan continued that he was "not aware of its being prohibited by the laws of any sect, and no one need ask this question, the same being manifest to both high and low and requires no more demonstration than the light of day."[1]

The sultan was only slightly out of date concerning the enactment of laws to abolish or limit the slave trade, and he was sadly right in his general historic perspective. The institution of slavery had indeed been practiced from time immemorial. It existed in all the ancient civilizations of Asia, Africa, Europe, and pre-Columbian America. It had been accepted and even endorsed by Judaism, Christianity, and Islam, as well as other religions of the world.

In the ancient Middle East, as elsewhere, slavery is attested from the very earliest written records, among the Sumerians, the Babylonians, the Egyptians, and other ancient peoples.[2] The earliest slaves, it would seem, were captives taken in warfare. Their numbers were augmented from other sources of supply. In pre-classical antiquity, most slaves appear to have been the property of kings, priests, and temples, and only a relatively small proportion were in private possession. They were employed to till the fields and tend the flocks of their royal and priestly masters but otherwise seem to have played little role in economic production, which was mostly left to small farmers, tenants, and sharecroppers and to artisans and journeymen. The slave population was also recruited by the sale, abandonment, or kidnapping of small children. Free persons could sell themselves or, more frequently, their offspring into slavery. They could be enslaved for insolvency, as could be the persons offered by them as pledges. In some systems, notably that of Rome,[3] free persons could also be enslaved for a variety of offenses against the law.

Both the Old and New Testaments recognize and accept the institution of slavery. Both from time to time insist on the basic humanity of the slave, and the consequent need to treat him humanely. The Jews are frequently reminded, in both Bible and Talmud,[4] that they too were slaves in Egypt and should therefore treat their slaves decently. Psalm 123, which compares the worshipper's appeal to God for mercy with the slave's appeal to his master, is cited to enjoin slaveowners to treat their slaves with compassion.[5] A verse in the book of Job has even been interpreted as an argument against slavery as such: "Did not He that made me in the womb make him [the slave]? And did not One fashion us both?" (Job 31:15). This probably means no more, however, than that the slave is a fellow human being and not a mere chattel.[6] The same is true of the much-quoted passage in the New Testament, that "there is neither Jew nor Greek, there is neither bond nor free, there is neither male nor female; for ye are all one in Christ Jesus."[7] These and similar verses were not understood to mean that ethnic, social, and gender differences were unimportant or should be abolished, only that they conferred no religious privilege. From many allusions, it is clear that slavery is accepted in the New Testament as a fact of life.[8] Some passages in the Pauline Epistles even endorse it. Thus in the Epistle to Philemon, a runaway slave is returned to his master; in Ephesians 6, the duty owed by a slave to his master is compared with the duty owed by a child to his parent, and the slave is enjoined "to be obedient to them that are *your* masters, according to the flesh, in fear and trembling, in singleness of your heart, *as* unto Christ." Parents and masters are likewise enjoined to show consideration for their children and slaves.[9] All humans, of the true faith, were equal in the eyes of God and in the afterlife but not necessarily in the laws of man and in this world. Those not of the true faith—whichever it was—were in another, and in most respects an inferior, category. In this respect, the Greek perception of the barbarian and the Judeo-Christian-Islamic perception of the unbeliever coincide.

There appear indeed to have been some who opposed slavery, usually as it was practiced but sometimes even as such. In the Greco-Roman world, both the Cynics and the Stoics are said to have rejected slavery as contrary to justice, some basing their opposition on the unity of the human race, and the Roman jurists even held that slavery was contrary to nature and maintained only by "human" law. There is no evidence that either jurists or philosophers sought its abolition, and even their theoretical opposition has been questioned. Much of it was concerned with moral and spiritual themes—the true freedom of the good man, even when enslaved, and the enslavement of the evil freeman to his passions. These ideas, which recur in Jewish and Christian writings, were of little help to those who suffered the reality of slavery.[10] Philo, the Alexandrian Jewish philosopher, claims that a Jewish sect actually renounced slavery in practice. In a somewhat idealized account of the Essenes, he observes that they practiced a form of primitive communism, sharing homes and property and pooling their earnings. Furthermore,

> not a single slave is to be found among them, but all are free, exchanging services with each other, and they denounce the owners of slaves, not merely for their injustice in outraging the law of equality, but also for their impiety in annulling the statute of Nature, who mother-like bore and reared all men alike, and created them genuine brothers, not in mere name, but in very reality, though this kinship has been put to confusion by the triumph of malignant covetousness, which has wrought estrangement instead of affinity and enmity instead of friendship.[11]

This view, if it was indeed held and put into practice, was unique in the ancient Middle East. Jews, Christians, and pagans alike owned slaves and exercised the rights and powers accorded to them by their various religious laws. In all communities, there were men of compassion who urged slave-owners to treat their slaves humanely, and there was even some attempt to secure this by law. But the institution of slavery as such was not seriously questioned, and was indeed often defended in terms of either Natural Law or Divine Dispensation. Thus Aristotle defends the condition of slavery and even the forcible enslavement of those who are "by nature slaves, for whom to be governed by this kind of authority is beneficial";[12] other Greek philosophers express similar ideas, particularly about enslaved captives from conquered peoples.[13] For such, slavery is not only right; it is also to their advantage.

The ancient Israelites did not claim that slavery was beneficial to the slaves, but, like the ancient Greeks, they felt the need to explain and justify the enslavement of their neighbors. In this, as in other matters, they sought a religious rather than a philosophical sanction and found it in the biblical story of the curse of Ham. Significantly, this curse was restricted to one line only of the descendants of Ham, namely, the children of Canaan, whom the Israelites had subjugated when they conquered the Promised Land, and did not affect the others.[14]

The Qur'ān, like the Old and the New Testaments, assumes the existence of slavery. It regulates the practice of the institution and thus implicitly accepts it. The Prophet Muḥammad and those of his Companions who could afford it themselves owned slaves; some of them acquired more by conquest.[15]

But Qur'anic legislation, subsequently confirmed and elaborated in the Holy Law,[16] brought two major changes to ancient slavery which were to have far-reaching effects. One of these was the presumption of freedom; the other, the ban on the enslavement of free persons except in strictly defined circumstances.

The Qur'ān was promulgated in Mecca and Medina in the seventh century, and the background against which Qur'anic legislation must be seen is ancient Arabia. The Arabs practiced a form of slavery, similar to that which existed in other parts of the ancient world. The Qur'ān accepts the institution, though it may be noted that the word *ʿabd* (slave) is rarely used, being more commonly replaced by some periphrasis such as *mā malakat aymānukum,* "that which your right hands own." The Qur'ān recognizes the basic inequality between master and slave and the rights of the former over the latter (XVI:71; XXX:28). It also recognizes concubinage (IV:3; XXIII:6; XXXIII:50–52; LXX:30). It urges, without actually commanding, kindness to the slave (IV:36; IX:60; XXIV:58) and recommends, without requiring, his liberation by purchase or manumission. The freeing of slaves is recommended both for the expiation of sins (IV:92; V:92; LVIII:3) and as an act of simple benevolence (II:177; XXIV:33; XC:13). It exhorts masters to allow slaves to earn or purchase their own freedom. An important change from pagan, though not from Jewish or Christian, practices is that in the strictly religious sense, the believing slave is now the brother of the freeman in Islam and before God, and the superior of the free pagan or idolator (II:221).[17] This point is emphasized and elaborated in innumerable *ḥadīth*s (traditions), in which the Prophet is quoted as urging considerate and sometimes even equal treatment for slaves, denouncing cruelty, harshness, or even discourtesy, recommending the liberation of slaves, and reminding the Muslims that his apostolate was to free and slave alike.[18]

Though slavery was maintained, the Islamic dispensation enormously improved the position of the Arabian slave, who was now no longer merely a chattel but was also a human being with a certain religious and hence a social status and with certain quasi-legal rights. The early caliphs who ruled the Islamic community after the death of the Prophet also introduced some further reforms of a humanitarian tendency. The enslavement of free Muslims was soon discouraged and eventually prohibited. It was made unlawful for a freeman to sell himself or his children into slavery, and it was no longer permitted for freemen to be enslaved for either debt or crime, as was usual in the Roman world and, despite attempts at reform, in parts of Christian Europe until at least the sixteenth century. It became a fundamental principle of Islamic jurisprudence that the natural condition, and therefore the presumed status, of mankind was freedom, just as the basic rule concerning actions is permittedness: what is not expressly forbidden is permitted; whoever is not known to be a slave is free.[19] This rule was not always strictly observed. Rebels and heretics were sometimes denounced as infidels or, worse, apostates, and reduced to slavery, as were the victims of some Muslim rulers in Africa, who proclaimed jihad against their neighbors, without looking closely at their religious beliefs, so as to provide legal cover for their enslavement. But by and large, and certainly in the central lands of Islam, under regimes of high civilization, the rule was honored, and free subjects of the state, Muslim and non-Muslim alike, were protected from unlawful enslavement.

Since all human beings were naturally free, slavery could only arise from two circumstances: (1) being born to slave parents or (2) being captured in war. The latter was soon restricted to infidels captured in a jihad.

These reforms seriously limited the supply of new slaves. Abandoned and unclaimed children could no longer be adopted as slaves, as was a common practice in antiquity,[20] and free persons could no longer be enslaved. Under Islamic law, the slave population could only be recruited, in addition to birth and capture, by importation, the last either by purchase or in the form of tribute from beyond the Islamic frontiers. In the early days of rapid conquest and expansion, the holy war brought a plentiful supply of new slaves, but as the frontiers were gradually stabilized, this supply dwindled to a mere trickle. Most wars were now conducted against organized armies, like those of the Byzantines or other Christian states, and with them prisoners of war were commonly ransomed or exchanged.[21] Within the Islamic frontiers, Islam spread rapidly among the populations of the newly acquired territories, and even those who remained faithful to their old religions and lived as protected persons (*dhimmī*s) under Muslim rule could not, if free, be legally enslaved unless they had violated the terms of the *dhimma,* the contract governing their status, as for example by rebelling against Muslim rule or helping the enemies of the Muslim state or, according to some authorities, by withholding payment of the *Kharāj* or the *Jizya,* the taxes due from *dhimmī*s to the Muslim state.

In the Islamic empire, the humanitarian tendency of the Qur'ān and the early caliphs was to some extent counteracted by other influences. Notable among these was the practice of the various conquered peoples and countries which the Muslims encountered after their expansion, especially in provinces previously under Roman law. This law, even in its Christianized form, was still very harsh in its treatment of slaves. Perhaps equally important was the huge increase in the slave population resulting first from the conquests themselves, and then from the organization of a great network of importation. These led to a fall in the cash value and hence the human value of slaves, and to a general adoption of a harsher tone and severer rules. But even after this stiffening of attitudes and laws, Islamic practice still represented a vast improvement on that inherited from antiquity, from Rome, and from Byzantium.

Slaves were excluded from religious functions or from any office involving jurisdiction over others. Their testimony was not admitted at judicial proceedings. In penal law, the penalty for an offense against a person, a fine or bloodwit, was, for a slave, half of that for a freeman. While maltreatment was deplored, there was no fixed *sharī'a* penalty. In what might be called civil matters, the slave was a chattel with no legal powers or rights whatsoever. He could not enter into a contract, hold property, or inherit. If he incurred a fine, his owner was responsible. He was, however, distinctly better off, in the matter of rights, than a Greek or Roman slave, since Islamic jurists, and not only philosophers and moralists, took account of humanitarian considerations. They laid down, for example, that a master must give his slave medical attention when required, must give him adequate upkeep, and must support him in his old age. If a master defaulted on these and other obligations to his slave, the qadi could compel him to fulfill them or else either to sell or to emancipate the slave. The master was forbidden to overwork his slave, and if he did so to the point of cruelty, he was liable to a penalty which was, however, discretionary and not prescribed by law. A slave could enter into a contract to earn his freedom, in which case his master had no obligation to pay for his upkeep. While in theory the slave could not own property, he could be granted certain rights of ownership for which he paid a fixed sum to his master.

A slave could marry, but only by consent of the master. Theoretically, a male slave could marry a free woman, but this was discouraged and in practice prohibited. A master could not marry his own slave woman unless he first freed her.

Islamic law provides a number of ways in which a slave could be set free. One was manumission, accomplished by a formal declaration on the part of the master and recorded in a certificate which was given to the liberated slave.[22] The manumission of a slave included the offspring of that slave, and the jurists specify that if there is any uncertainty about an act of manumission, the slave has the benefit of the doubt. Another method is a written agreement by which the master grants liberty in return for a fixed sum. Once such an agreement has been concluded, the master no longer has the right to dispose of his slave, whether by sale or gift. The slave is still subject to certain legal disabilities, but in most respects is virtually free. Such an agreement, once entered into, may be terminated by the slave but not by the master. Children born to the slave after the entry into force of the contract are born free. The master may bind himself to liberate a slave at some specified future time. He may also bind his heirs to liberate a slave after his death. The law schools differ somewhat on the rules regarding this kind of liberation.

In addition to all these, which depend on the will of the master, there are various legal causes which may lead to liberation, independently of the will of the master. The commonest is a legal judgment by a qadi ordering a master to emancipate a slave whom he has maltreated. A special case is that of the *umm walad,* a slave woman who bears a son to her master, and thereby acquires certain irrevocable legal rights.[23]

Non-Muslim subjects of the Muslim state, that is, *dhimmī*s, were in practice allowed to own slaves; and Christian and Jewish families who could afford it owned and employed slaves in the same way as their Muslim counterparts. They were not permitted to own Muslim slaves; and if a slave owned by a *dhimmī* embraced Islam, his owner was legally obliged to free or sell him. Jews and Christians were of course not permitted to have Muslim concubines, and were indeed usually debarred by their own religious authorities—not always effectively—from sexual access to their slaves.[24] Jewish slaves, acquired through privateering in the Mediterranean and slave raiding in Eastern Europe, were often redeemed and set free by their local co-religionists.[25] The vastly more numerous Christian slaves—apart from West Europeans, whose ransoms could be arranged from home—were for the most part doomed to remain. Sometimes, Christian and Jewish slaveowners tried to convert their domestic slaves to their own religions. Jews were indeed required by rabbinic law to try to persuade their slaves to accept conversion with circumcision and ritual immersion. A form of semi-conversion, whereby the slave accepted some basic commandments and observances, but not the full rigor of the Mosaic law, was widely practiced. According to Jewish law, a converted or even semi-converted slave could not be sold to a Gentile. If the owner in fact so sold him or her, the slave was to be set free. Conversely, a slave who refused even semi-conversion was, after a stipulated interval of time, to be sold to a Gentile.[26] Muslim authorities, both jurists and rulers, took different views of this. Conversion from Islam was of course a capital offense, and some jurists held that only conversion to Islam was lawful. Others, however, saw no objection to conversion between non-Muslim religions, provided that the converted slaves had reached the age of reason and changed their religion of their own free will.[27]

Though a free Muslim could not be enslaved, conversion to Islam by a non-Muslim slave did not require his liberation. His slave status was not affected by his Islam, nor was that of a Muslim child born to slave parents.

There were occasional slave rebellions and, from the rules and regulations about runaway slaves, it would appear that such escapes were not infrequent. Slaves from neighboring countries might have some chance of returning to their homes, and examples are known of European slaves in the Ottoman lands escaping to Europe, where some indeed wrote memoirs or accounts of their captivity.[28] The chances of a slave from the steppe-lands or from Africa finding his way back were remote.

As we have seen, the slave population was recruited in four main ways: by capture, tribute, offspring, and purchase.

Capture: In the early centuries of Islam, during the period of the conquest and expansion, this was the most important source.[29] With the stabilization of the frontier, the numbers recruited in this way diminished, and eventually provided only a very small proportion of slave requirements. Frontier warfare and naval raiding yielded some captives, but these were relatively few and were usually exchanged. In later centuries, warfare in Africa or India supplied some slaves by capture. With the spread of Islam, and the acceptance of *dhimmī* status by increasing numbers of non-Muslims, the possibilities for recruitment by capture were severely restricted.

Tribute: Slaves sometimes formed part of the tribute required from vassal states beyond the Islamic frontiers. The first such treaty ever made, that of the year 31 of the Hijra (= 652 A.D.), with the black king of Nubia, included an annual levy of slaves to be provided from Nubia.[30] This may indeed have been the reason why Nubia was for a long time not conquered. The stipulated delivery of some hundreds of male and female slaves, later supplemented by elephants, giraffes, and other wild beasts, continued at least until the twelfth century, when it was disrupted by a series of bitter wars between the Muslim rulers of Egypt and the Christian kings of Nubia.[31] Similar agreements, providing for the delivery of a tribute of slaves, were imposed by the early Arab conquerors on neighboring princes in Iran and Central Asia, but were of briefer duration.[32]

Offspring: The recruitment of the slave population by natural increase seems to have been small and, right through to modern times, insufficient to maintain numbers. This is in striking contrast with conditions in the New World, where the slave population increased very rapidly. Several factors contributed to this difference, perhaps the most important being that the slave population in the Islamic Middle East was constantly drained by the liberation of slaves—sometimes as an act of piety, most commonly through the recognition and liberation, by a freeman, of his own offspring by a slave mother. There were also other reasons for the low natural increase of the slave population in the Islamic world. They include

1. Castration. A fair proportion of male slaves were imported as eunuchs and thus precluded from having offspring. Among these were many who otherwise, by the wealth and power which they acquired, might have founded families.
2. Another group of slaves who rose to positions of great power, the military slaves, were normally liberated at some stage in their career, and their offspring were therefore free and not slaves.
3. In general, only the lower orders of slaves—menial, domestic, and manual workers—remained in the condition of servitude and transmitted that condition to their descendants. There were not many such descendants—casual mating was not permitted and marriage was not encouraged.
4. There was a high death toll among all classes of slaves, including great military commanders as well as humble menials. Slaves came mainly from remote places, and, lacking immunities, died in large numbers from endemic as well as epidemic diseases. As late as the nineteenth century, Western travelers in North Africa and Egypt noted the high death rate among imported black slaves.[33]

Purchase: This came to be by far the most important means for the legal acquisition of new slaves. Slaves were purchased on the frontiers of the Islamic world and then imported to the major centers, where there were slave markets from which they were widely distributed. In one of the sad paradoxes of human history, it was the humanitarian reforms brought by Islam that resulted in a vast development of the slave trade inside, and still more outside, the Islamic empire. In the Roman world, the slave population was occasionally recruited from outside, when a new territory was conquered or a barbarian invasion repelled, but mostly, slaves came from internal sources. This was not possible in the Islamic empire, where, although slavery was maintained, enslavement was banned. The result was an increasingly massive importation of slaves from the outside. Like enslavement, mutilation was forbidden by Islamic law. The great numbers of eunuchs needed to preserve the sanctity of palaces, homes, and some holy places had to be imported from outside or, as often happened, "manufactured" at the frontier. In medieval and Ottoman times the two main sources of eunuchs were Slavs and Ethiopians (Ḥabash, a term which commonly included all the peoples of the Horn of Africa). Eunuchs were also recruited among Greeks (Rūm), West Africans (Takrūrī, pl. Takārina), Indians, and occasionally West Europeans.[34]

The slave population of the Islamic world was recruited from many lands. In the earliest days, slaves came principally from the newly conquered countries—from the Fertile Crescent and Egypt, from Iran and North Africa, from Central Asia, India, and Spain. Most of these slaves had a cultural level at least as high as that of their Arab masters, and by conversion and manumission they were rapidly absorbed into the general population. As the supply of slaves by conquest and capture diminished, the needs of the slave market were met, more and more, by importation from beyond the frontier. Small numbers of slaves were brought from India, China, Southeast Asia, and the Byzantine Empire, most of them specialists and technicians of one kind or another. The vast majority of unskilled slaves, however, came from the lands immediately north and south of the Islamic world—whites from Europe and the Eurasian steppes, blacks from Africa south of the Sahara. Among white Europeans and black Africans alike, there was no lack of enterprising merchants and middlemen, eager to share in this profitable trade, who were willing to capture or kidnap their neighbors and deliver them, as slaves, to a ready and expanding market. In Europe there was also an important trade in slaves, Muslim, Jewish, pagan, and even Orthodox Christian, recruited by capture and bought for mainly domestic use.[35]

Central and East European slaves, generally known as Saqāliba (i.e., Slavs),[36] were imported by three main routes: overland via France and Spain, from Eastern Europe via the Crimea, and by sea across the Mediterranean. They were mostly but not exclusively Slavs. Some were captured by Muslim naval raids on European coasts, particularly the Dalmatian. Most were supplied by European, especially Venetian, slave merchants, who delivered cargoes of them to the Muslim markets in Spain and North Africa. The Saqāliba were prominent in Muslim Spain and to a lesser extent in North Africa but played a minor role in the East. With the consolidation of powerful states in Christian Europe, the supply of West European slaves dried up and was maintained only by privateering and coastal raiding from North Africa.

Black slaves were brought into the Islamic world by a number of routes—from West Africa across the Sahara to Morocco and Tunisia, from Chad across the desert to Libya, from East Africa down the Nile to Egypt, and across the Red Sea and Indian Ocean to Arabia and the Persian Gulf. Turkish slaves from the steppe-lands were marketed in Samarkand and other Muslim Central Asian cities and from there exported to Iran, the Fertile Crescent, and beyond. Caucasians, of increasing importance in the later centuries, were brought from the land bridge between the Black Sea and the Caspian and were marketed mainly in Aleppo and Mosul.

By Ottoman times, the first for which we have extensive documentation, the pattern of importation had changed.[37] At first, the expanding Ottoman Empire, like the expanding Arab Empire of earlier times, recruited its slaves by conquest and capture, and great numbers of Balkan Christians were forcibly brought into Ottoman service. The distinctively Ottoman institution of the *devşirme,* the levy of boys from the Christian village population, made it possible, contrary to previous Islamic law and practice, to recruit slaves from the subject peoples of the conquered provinces.[38] The *devşirme* slaves were not servants or menials, however, but were groomed for the service of the state in military and civil capacities. For a long time, most of the grand viziers and military commanders of the Ottoman forces were recruited in this way. In the early seventeenth century, the *devşirme* was abandoned; by the end of the seventeenth century, the Ottoman advance into Europe had been decisively halted and reversed. Sea raiders operating out of North African ports continued to bring European captives, but these did not significantly add to the slave populations. Pretty girls disappeared into the harem; men often had the choice of being ransomed or joining their captors—a choice of which many availed themselves. The less fortunate, like the Muslim captives who fell to the European maritime powers, served in the galleys.[39]

The slave needs of the Ottoman Empire were now met from new sources. One of these was the Caucasians—the Georgians, Circassians, and related peoples, famous for providing beautiful women and brave and handsome men. The former figured prominently in the harems, the latter in the armies and administrations of the Ottoman and also the Persian states. The supply of these was reduced but not terminated by the Russian conquest of the Caucasus in the early years of the nineteenth century. Another source of supply was the Tatar khanate of the Crimea, whose raiders every year rode far and wide in Central and Eastern Europe, carrying off great numbers of male and female slaves. These were brought to the Crimea and shipped thence to the slave markets in Istanbul and other Turkish cities. This trade came to an end with the Russian annexation of the Crimea in 1783 and the extinction of Tatar independence.[40]

Deprived of most of their sources of white slaves, the Ottomans turned more and more to Africa, which in the course of the nineteenth century came to provide the overwhelming majority of slaves used in Muslim countries from Morocco to Asia. According to a German report published in 1860,

> the black slaves, at that time, were recruited mainly by raiding and kidnapping from Sennaar, Kordofan, Darfur, Nubia, and other places in inner Africa; the white mostly through voluntary sale on the part of their relatives in the independent lands of the Caucasus (Lesghi, Daghestani, and Georgian women, rarely men). Those offered for sale were already previously of servile status or were slave children by birth.[41]

The need, from early medieval times onward, to import large and growing numbers of slaves led to a rapid increase, in all the lands beyond the frontiers of the Islamic world, of both slave raiding and slave trading—the one to procure and maintain an adequate supply of the required commodity, the other to ensure its efficient distribution and delivery. In the ancient world, where most slaves other than war captives were of local provenance, slave trading was a simple and mostly local affair, often combined with other articles of commerce. In the Islamic world, where slaves were transported over great distances from their places of origin, the slave trade was more complex and more specialized, with a network of trade routes and markets extending all over the Islamic world and far beyond its frontiers and involving commercial relations with suppliers in Christian Europe, in the Turkish steppe-lands, and in black Africa. In every important city there was a slave market, usually called *Sūq al-Raqīq*. When new supplies were brought, government inspectors usually took the first choice, then officials, then private persons. It would seem that slaves were not normally sold in open markets but in decently covered places—a practice which continued in some areas to the nineteenth, in others till the twentieth, century.[42]

There is a fair amount of information on slave prices, most of it too heterogeneous in date and provenance to provide more than a general impression. The best-documented data come from medieval Egypt and show a remarkable consistency in price levels. Slave girls averaged twenty dinars (gold pieces), corresponding, at the rate of gold to silver current at that time, to 266 dirhams (silver pieces). Other medieval data show somewhat higher prices. Black slaves seem to have cost from two to three hundred dirhams; black eunuchs, at least two or three times as much. Female black slaves were sold at five hundred dirhams or so; trained singing girls or other performers, at ten or even twenty thousand. White slaves, mainly for military purposes, were more expensive. Prices of three hundred dirhams are quoted for Turks near the source in Central Asia, and much higher prices elsewhere. In Baghdad they fetched four to five hundred dirhams, while a white slave girl could be sold for a thousand dinars or more.[43] The mid-nineteenth-century German report from Turkey quotes prices of four thousand to five thousand piasters, or two hundred to three hundred dollars, as the current price in Istanbul for a "trained, strong, black slave," while "for white slave girls of special beauty, fifty thousand piasters and more are paid."[44] In general, eunuchs fetched higher prices than other males, younger slaves were worth more than older slaves, and slave women, whether for work or pleasure, were more expensive than males. Olufr Eigilsson, an Icelandic Lutheran pastor who was carried off to captivity with his family and many of his flock when his native village was raided by Barbary Corsairs in 1627 and who wrote an account of his adventures, notes that his young maidservant was sold for seven hundred dollars and later resold for a thousand.[45]

Slaves were employed in a number of functions—in the home and the shop, in agriculture and industry, in the military, as well as in specialized tasks. The Islamic world did not operate on a slave system of production, as is said of classical antiquity, but slavery was not entirely domestic either. Slave laborers of various kinds were of some importance in medieval times, especially where large-scale enterprises were involved, and they continued to be into the nineteenth century. The most important slaves, however, those of whom we have the fullest information, were domestic and commercial, and it is they who were the characteristic slaves of the Muslim world. They seem to have been mainly blacks, with some Indians, and some whites. In later times, for which we have more detailed evidence, it would seem that while the slaves often suffered appalling privations from the moment of their capture until their arrival at their final destination, once they were placed with a family they were reasonably well treated and accepted in some degree as members of the household. In commerce, slaves were often apprenticed to their masters, sometimes as assistants, sometimes advancing to become agents or even business partners.

The slave and also the liberated ex-slave played an important part in domestic life. Eunuchs were required for the protection and maintenance of harems, as confidential servants, as palace staff, and also as custodians of mosques, tombs, and other sacred places. Slave women were required mainly as concubines and as menials. A Muslim slaveowner was entitled by law to the sexual enjoyment of his slave women. While free women might own male slaves, they had of course no equivalent right.

The economic exploitation of slaves, apart from some construction work, took place mainly in the countryside, away from the cities, and like almost everything else about rural life is sparsely documented. The medieval Islamic world was a civilization of cities. Both its law and its literature deal almost entirely with townspeople, their lives and problems, and remarkably little information has come down to us concerning life in the villages and the countryside. Sometimes a dramatic event like the revolt of the Zanj in southern Iraq or an occasional passing reference in travel literature sheds a sudden light on life in the countryside. Otherwise, we remain ignorant of what was happening outside the cities until the sixteenth century, when for the first time the surviving Ottoman archives make it possible to follow in some detail the life and activities of rural populations—and the exploration of this material has still barely begun. The common view of Islamic slavery as primarily domestic and military may therefore reflect the bias of our documentation rather than the reality. There are occasional references, however, to large gangs of slaves, mostly black, employed in agriculture, in the mines, and in such special tasks as the drainage of marshes. Some, less fortunate, were hired out by their owners for piecework. These working slaves had a much harder life. The most unfortunate of all were those engaged in agricultural and other manual work and large-scale enterprises, such as for example the Zanj slaves used to drain the salt flats of southern Iraq, and the blacks employed in the salt mines of the Sahara and the gold mines of Nubia. These were herded in large settlements and worked in gangs. Large landowners, or crown lands, often employed thousands of such slaves. While domestic and commercial slaves were relatively well-off, these lived and died in wretchedness. Of the Saharan salt mines it is said that no slave lived there for more than five years. The cultivation of cotton and sugar, which the Arabs brought from the East across North Africa and into Spain, most probably entailed some kind of plantation system. Certainly, the earliest relevant Ottoman records show the extensive use of slave labor in the state-maintained rice plantations.[46] Some such system, for cultivation of cotton and sugar, was taken across North Africa into Spain and perhaps beyond. While economic slave labor was mainly male, slave women were sometimes also exploited economically. The pre-Islamic practice of hiring out female slaves as prostitutes is expressly forbidden by Islamic law but appears to have survived nonetheless.[47]

The military slaves were in a sense the aristocrats of the slave population. By far the most important among these were the Turks imported from the Eurasian steppe, from Central Asia, and from what is now Chinese Turkistan. A similar position was occupied by Slavs in medieval Muslim Spain and North Africa and, later, by slaves of Balkan and Caucasian origin in the Ottoman Empire. Black slaves were occasionally employed as soldiers, but this was not common and was usually of brief duration.

Certainly the most privileged of slaves were the performers. Both slave boys and slave girls who revealed some talent received musical, literary, and artistic education. In medieval times most singers, dancers, and musical performers were, at least in origin, slaves. Perhaps the most famous was Ziryāb, a Persian slave at the court of Baghdad who later went to Spain, where he became an arbiter of taste and is credited with having introduced asparagus to Europe. Not a few slaves and freedmen have left their names in Arabic poetry and history.

In a society where positions of military command and political power were routinely held by men of slave origin or even status and where a significant proportion of the free population were born to slave mothers, prejudice against the slave as such, of the Roman or American type, could hardly develop. Where such prejudice and hostility appear—and they are often expressed in literature and other evidence—they must be attributed to racial more than to social distinction. The developing pattern of racial specialization in the use of slaves must surely have contributed greatly to the growth of such prejudice.

2

Race

During the last half century or so, the word "race," in most Western languages, has undergone substantial and significant changes of meaning. Much confusion and misunderstanding have been caused by the failure to recognize these changes, still more by the survival of earlier meanings when new ones have already been generally accepted. As late as the midcentury, the word "race" was still commonly used in Europe, and occasionally in the United States, to designate what we would nowadays call an ethnic group, that is to say, a group defined primarily by linguistic and other cultural, historical, and in some sense geographical criteria. In Britain the word was generally, even officially, used to designate the four components that made up the common British nationality.[1] Similarly, India was inhabited by a great variety of so-called races, speaking different but closely related languages and sharing a common civilization. Sometimes, the term "race" was used in a broader and looser sense, to denote a group of peoples, speaking related languages. It was in this sense that philologists and ancient historians spoke of the Semites, the Indo-Europeans, and other linguistically defined families of peoples.

As so often happens, social scientists took a word of common but imprecise usage and gave it a precise technical meaning. For the anthropologist, a race was a group of people sharing certain visible and measurable characteristics, such as hair, pigmentation, skull measurements, height, and other physical features. Races thus consisted of such categories as whites, blacks, Mongols, and the like. These might be sub-divided—thus, for example, whites could be classed as Nordic, Alpine, or Mediterranean. This kind of race, though obviously overlapping to some extent with ethnic groupings, was independent of ethnic features. Different races could share a culture. Different cultures could divide a race. By the strictly physical definition, even members of the same family, with different genes, could belong to different races.

In current American usage, which has now spread to most other countries, the word "race" is used exclusively to denote such major divisions as white, black, Mongolian, and the like.[2] It is no longer applied to national, ethnic, or cultural entities, such as the English or the Irish, the Germans or the Slavs, or even the Japanese, who are now seen as being part of a much larger racial grouping found in East Asia.

In this modern sense, race was of minor importance in antiquity. Where modern scholarship has discerned racial tension and hostility, it has been in the earlier sense of race as an ethnic or national group, such as the Egyptians, the Assyrians, the Israelites, and others defined by language, culture, and religion. Though the ancient civilizations of the Middle East show considerable diversity, there is no great racial difference between their peoples. In friezes and other pictorial representations, aliens are distinguished by their garb, their hair, their beards, and their accoutrements, rather than by physical features. The nose alone—used rather in the manner of a modern cartoonist—seems to have provided the ancient artist with a physical symbol of national identity.[3] No doubt there were differences of predominant physical type between, say, Egyptians and Assyrians, but these were no greater than the differences between the different peoples of Europe. In anthropological terms, the major peoples of the Middle East who have left their mark in history—the Egyptians, the Sumerians and Akkadians, the Israelites, the Aramaeans, the Hittites, the Medes, and the Persians and even, later, the Greeks and the Romans—exhibited no marked contrasts of racial type.

Like every other society known to human history, the ancient Middle Eastern peoples harbored all kinds of prejudices and hostilities against those whom they regarded as "other." But the "other" was primarily someone who spoke another language (the prototypal barbarian) or professed another religion (the Gentile or heathen or—in Christian and Islamic language—the infidel). There are many hostile references to the "others"—among Jews about Gentiles and heathens, among Greeks about barbarians, among Romans about almost everybody. It would be easy to assemble a fine collection of ethnic slurs from Greek and Latin literature—but they are ethnic, not racial, slurs. When Juvenal, irked by the Syrian presence in Rome, complains that the Orontes had overflowed into the Tiber or when Ammianus Marcellinus, who was himself a Syrian, said of the Saracens, meaning the Bedouin, that he did not find them desirable either as friends or as enemies, they were making cultural, not racial, statements.[4] This and other similar anti-Arab remarks, and the attitude which they express, did not prevent an Arab chieftain from becoming the Roman Emperor Philip or a Syrian local priest from becoming the Emperor Heliogabalus.

Other races were of course known. The ancient Egyptians were closely acquainted with their black southern neighbors and sometimes portray them, in words or pictures, with characteristic Negroid features. But there is no evidence that they regarded them as inferior for that reason. The much-cited inscription of Pharaoh Sesostris III, in the nineteenth century B.C., barring, or rather restricting, access by blacks to Egyptian territory, is a normal security precaution on a vulnerable frontier, where many wars had been fought. It is no more a sign of racial prejudice than are numerous similar restrictions on numerous other frontiers.[5] The Persians, Greeks, and later Romans had some occasional contacts with China, and rather more with Ethiopia, which was a known part of the civilized world even in biblical times. But these countries were very remote, and contacts with them were few. Ethiopia and China were both respected, and there is no real evidence in Jewish, Greek, or Roman sources of lower esteem for darker skins or higher esteem for lighter complexions.[6] Nor were there slave races. Foreigners, especially if barbarians, were enslavable. The ancients, like the rest of humanity, believed foreigners to be inferior. Conquest confirmed that belief and, through the universal rule of enslaving the conquered, provided it with practical application. Classical writers, from Aristotle onward, stated the general principle that there are races suited by nature to slavery, but although there are occasional references to this or that people as fitting this description, these are only passing examples of wit or spite, in no sense amounting to any kind of scientific or philosophical statement.[7]

The advent of Islam created an entirely new situation in race relations. All the ancient civilizations of the Middle East and of Asia had been local, or at most regional. Even the Roman Empire, despite its relatively larger extent, was essentially a Mediterranean society. Islam for the first time created a truly universal civilization, extending from Southern Europe to Central Africa, from the Atlantic Ocean to India and China. By conquest and by conversion, the Muslims brought within the bounds of a single imperial system and a common religious culture peoples as diverse as the Chinese, the Indians, the peoples of the Middle East and North Africa, black Africans, and white Europeans. Nor was this coming together of races limited to a single rule and a single faith. The Muslim obligation of pilgrimage, which requires that every adult Muslim, at least once in his lifetime, must go on a journey to the holy places in Mecca and Medina, brought travelers from the remotest corners of the Muslim world, covering vast distances, to join with their fellow believers in common rites and rituals at the very center of the Islamic faith and world. The pilgrimage, probably the most important factor of individual, personal mobility in pre-modern history, combined with the better-known forces of conquest, commerce, and concubinage to bring about a great meeting and mixing of peoples from Asia, Europe, and Africa.

At different times and places, Muslims have responded to the challenge of racial encounter and cohabitation in a variety of ways. These responses are reflected, in sometimes striking contrast, in both old and recent literature. One view of Muslim racial attitudes, widely accepted in the modern West, is expressed in a famous passage in Arnold Toynbee's *Study of History,* documented, like so much in that massive work, with a personal experience:

> For instance, the Primitive Arabs who were the ruling element in the Umayyad Caliphate called themselves "the swarthy people," with a connotation of racial superiority, and their Persian and Turkish subjects "the ruddy people," with a connotation of racial inferiority: that is to say, they drew the same distinction

> that we draw between blondes and brunettes but reversed the values which we assign to the two shades of white. Gentlemen may prefer blondes; but brunettes are the first choice of Allah's "Chosen people." Moreover, the Arabs and all other White Muslims, whether brunettes or blondes, have always been free from colour-prejudice *vis-à-vis* the non-White races; and, at the present day, Muslims still make that dichotomy of the human family which Western Christians used to make in the Middle Ages. They divide Mankind into Believers and Unbelievers who are all potentially Believers; and this division cuts across every difference of Physical Race. This liberality is more remarkable in White Muslims today than it was in the White Western Christians in our Middle Ages; for our medieval forefathers had little or no contact with peoples of a different colour, whereas the White Muslims were in contact with the Negroes of Africa and with the dark-skinned peoples of India from the beginning and have increased that contact steadily, until nowadays Whites and Blacks are intermingled, under the aegis of Islam, throughout the length and breadth of the Indian and the African Continent. Under this searching test, the White Muslims have demonstrated their freedom and race-feeling by the most convincing of all proofs: they have given their daughters to black Muslims in marriage.[8]

The Arabs, that is to say, as swarthy whites, felt superior to the fairer-skinned peoples to the north of them but were entirely free from any feeling of color prejudice directed against their darker southern neighbors. Prejudice against those of fairer skin, clearly, is felt to be no more than an amusing paradox. What counts is prejudice against those of darker skin, and since this is lacking, the Arabs and Islam may be pronounced free from infection.

Similar views are expressed in a number of other writings, and date back, it would seem, to the nineteenth century, and more especially to the American Civil War, which brought the linked issues of race and slavery into sharp focus before world opinion. The freedom of the Islamic world—as opposed to Western Christendom—from racial prejudice and discrimination rapidly became commonplace.

The Middle East is an ancient land of myths in which the mythopoeic faculty—the ability to create myths, to believe in them, and to make others believe—has by no means died out. It would be wise to subject any widely held assumption regarding this area to critical scrutiny.

Even the reader whose acquaintance with Arabic literature goes no further than *The Thousand and One Nights* may feel some doubts about the validity of this picture of an interracial utopia. His doubts might begin at the very beginning—with the framework story. King Shahzāmān, it will be recalled, left home to visit his brother King Shahriyār but turned back to collect something which he had forgotten. Arriving unexpectedly at his palace at midnight, he found his wife sleeping in his bed and attended by a male black slave, who had fallen asleep by her side. The king, enraged by this sight, killed both offenders with his sword as they lay in bed and then resumed his journey to visit his brother. There the situation was even worse. While King Shahriyār went hunting, not only his wife but twenty female members of his household came out and were (to repeat the Victorian translator's discreet usage) "attended" by twenty male black slaves:

> The King's wife, who was distinguished by extraordinary beauty and elegance, accompanied them to a fountain, where they all disrobed themselves, and sat down together. The King's wife then called out, O Mes'ood! and immediately a black slave came to her, and embraced her, she doing the like. So also did the other slaves and women; and all of them continued revelling together until the close of the day.[9]

King Shahzāmān and King Shahriyār were clearly white supremacists, with sexual fantasies, or rather nightmares, of a sadly familiar quality. This resemblance in *The Thousand and One Nights* to certain aspects of the old American South is confirmed if we look more closely into that work. Blacks appear frequently in the stories that make up the *Nights*. Where they do, it is almost invariably in a menial role—as porters, household servants, slaves, cooks, bath attendants, and the like—rarely, if ever, rising above this level in society. Perhaps even more revealing in its way is the story of the good black slave who lived a life of virtue and piety, for which he was rewarded by turning white at the moment of his death.[10]

We thus have two quite contradictory pictures before us—the first contained in the *Study of History,* the second reflected in that other great imaginative construction, *The Thousand and One Nights*. The one depicts a racially egalitarian society free from prejudice or discrimination; the other reveals a familiar pattern of sexual fantasy, social and occupational discrimination, and an unthinking identification of lighter with better and darker with worse.

Both versions are impressively documented from Islamic sources. The cause of racial equality is sustained by the almost unanimous voice of Islamic religion—both the exhortations of piety and the injunctions of the law. And yet, at the same time, the picture of inequality and injustice is vividly reflected in the literature, the arts, and the folklore of the Muslim peoples. In this, as in so much else, there is a sharp contrast between what Islam says and what Muslims—or at least some Muslims—do.

What, then, are the realities? There is a distinction which it is important to make in any discussion of Islam. The word "Islam" is used with at least three different meanings, and much misunderstanding can arise from the failure to distinguish between them. In the first place, Islam means the religion taught by the Prophet Muḥammad and embodied in the Muslim revelation known as the Qur'ān. In the second place, Islam is the subsequent development of this religion through tradition and through the work of the great Muslim jurists and theologians. In this sense it includes the mighty structure of the Sharīʿa, the holy law of Islam, and the great corpus of Islamic dogmatic theology. In the third meaning, Islam is the counterpart not of Christianity but rather of Christendom. In this sense Islam means not what Muslims believed or were expected to believe but what they actually did—in other words, Islamic civilization as known to us in history. In discussing Muslim attitudes on ethnicity, race, and color, I shall try to deal to some extent at least with all three but to make clear the distinction between them.

3

Islam in Arabia

The ultimate Islamic text is the Qur'ān, and any enquiry into Islamic beliefs and laws must begin there. There are only two passages in the Qur'ān which have a direct bearing on race and racial attitudes. The first of these occurs in chapter XXX, verse 22, and reads as follows:

> Among God's signs are the creation of the heavens and of the earth and the diversity of your languages and of your colors. In this indeed are signs for those who know.

This is part of a larger section enumerating the signs and wonders of God. The diversity of languages and colors is adduced as another example of God's power and versatility—no more.

The second quotation, chapter XLIX, verse 13, is rather more specific:

> O people! We have created you from a male and a female and we have made you into confederacies and tribes[1] so that you may come to know one another. The noblest among you in the eyes of God is the most pious, for God is omniscient and well-informed.

It will be clear that the Qur'ān expresses no racial or color prejudice. What is perhaps most significant is that the Qur'ān does not even reveal any awareness of such prejudice. The two passages quoted show a consciousness of difference; the second of them insists that piety is more important than birth. The point that is being made, however, is clearly social rather than racial—against tribal and aristocratic rather than against racial pride.

In the Qur'ān, the question of race is obviously not a burning issue. It became a burning issue in later times, as can be seen from the elaboration on these texts by subsequent commentators and by the collectors of tradition.

The evidence of the Qur'ān on the lack of racial prejudice in pre-Islamic and the earliest Islamic times is borne out by such fully authenticated fragments of contemporary literature as survive. As in the Qur'ān, so also in the ancient Arabian poetry, we find an awareness of difference—the sentiment of an Arab as against a Persian, Greek, or other identity. We do not, however, find any clear indication that this was felt in racial terms or went beyond the normal feeling of distinctness which all human groups have about themselves in relation to others.

On the specific question of color, ancient Arabian literature is very instructive. The early poets used a number of different words to describe human colors, a much wider range than is customary at the present time. They do not correspond exactly to those that we use now and express a different sense of color—one more concerned with brightness, intensity, and shade than with hue. Human beings are frequently described by words which we might translate as black, white, red, olive, yellow, and two shades of brown, one lighter and one darker. These terms are usually used in a personal rather than an ethnic sense and would correspond to such words as "swarthy," "sallow," "blonde," or "ruddy" in our own modern usage more than to words like "black" and "white." Sometimes they are used ethnically but even then in a relative rather than an absolute sense. The Arabs, for example, sometimes describe themselves as black in contrast to Persians, who are red, but at other times as red or white in contrast to the Africans, who are black. The characteristic color of the Bedouin is variously stated as olive or brown.

In early Arabic poetry and historical narrative, the Persians are sometimes spoken of as "the red people," with a suggestion of ethnic hostility. This seems to date back to pre-Islamic times—to Arab resistance to Persian imperial penetration in Arabia and Arab reaction to the disdain which the civilized Persians showed for the semi-barbarous tribes on their desert frontier.[2] After the Arab conquest of Iran, the roles were reversed; the Arabs were now the imperial masters, and the Persians their subjects. In this situation, the term "red people" acquired a connotation of inferiority and was used in particular reference to the non-Arab converts to Islam. Redness is similarly ascribed to the conquered natives of Spain, to the Greeks, and to other Mediterranean peoples of somewhat lighter skin than the Arabs.[3]

As between Arabs and Africans the situation is more difficult to assess. There are verses, indeed many verses, attributed to pre-Islamic and early Islamic poets which would suggest very strongly a feeling of hatred and contempt directed against persons of African birth or origin. Most if not all of these, however, almost certainly belong to later periods and reflect later problems, attitudes, and preoccupations.

References to black people in pre-Islamic Arabia have usually been taken to mean Ethiopians—commonly called Ḥabash, the Arabic name from which our word "Abyssinian" is derived. Ḥabash was probably used for the peoples of the Horn of Africa and their immediate neighbors. Apart from a few

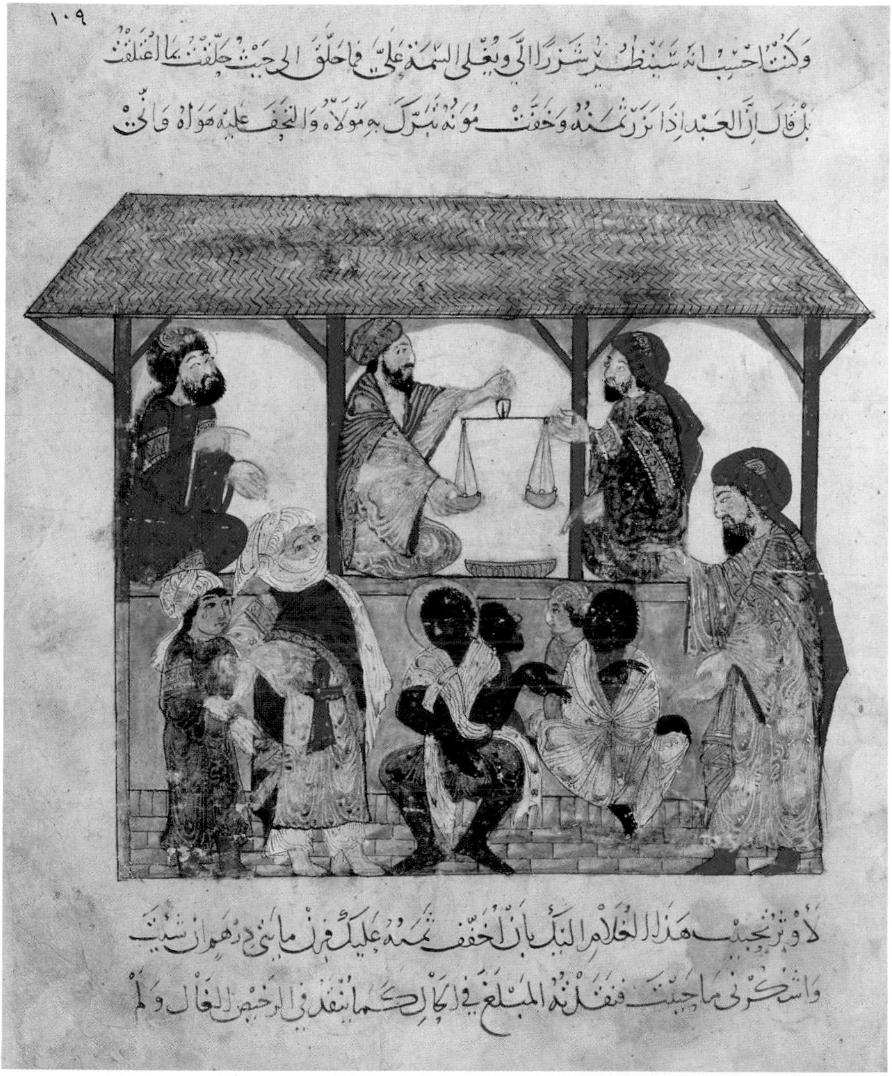

1. The slave market in Zabid, in the Yemen.
Baghdad, 1237

2. A slave bringing food.
Probably Syria, 1222.

3. The story of the two foxes. A prince hunting with falcon, cheetah, and huntsman.
Herat, ca. 1490–1500.

4. The birth of the Persian hero Rustam, with women and black servants in attendance.
Egypt, 1510.

5. A merchant with attendants and packhorse driver.
Tabriz, Iran, ca. 1530.

6. An Ottoman prince and grand vizier with attendants.
Istanbul, 1597.

7. The heir apparent Mehmed at the Ibrahim Pasha Palace, with eunuchs.
Istanbul, 1597.

8. The funeral of the sultan's mother, Nur Banu, with eunuchs in the background.
Istanbul, 1597.

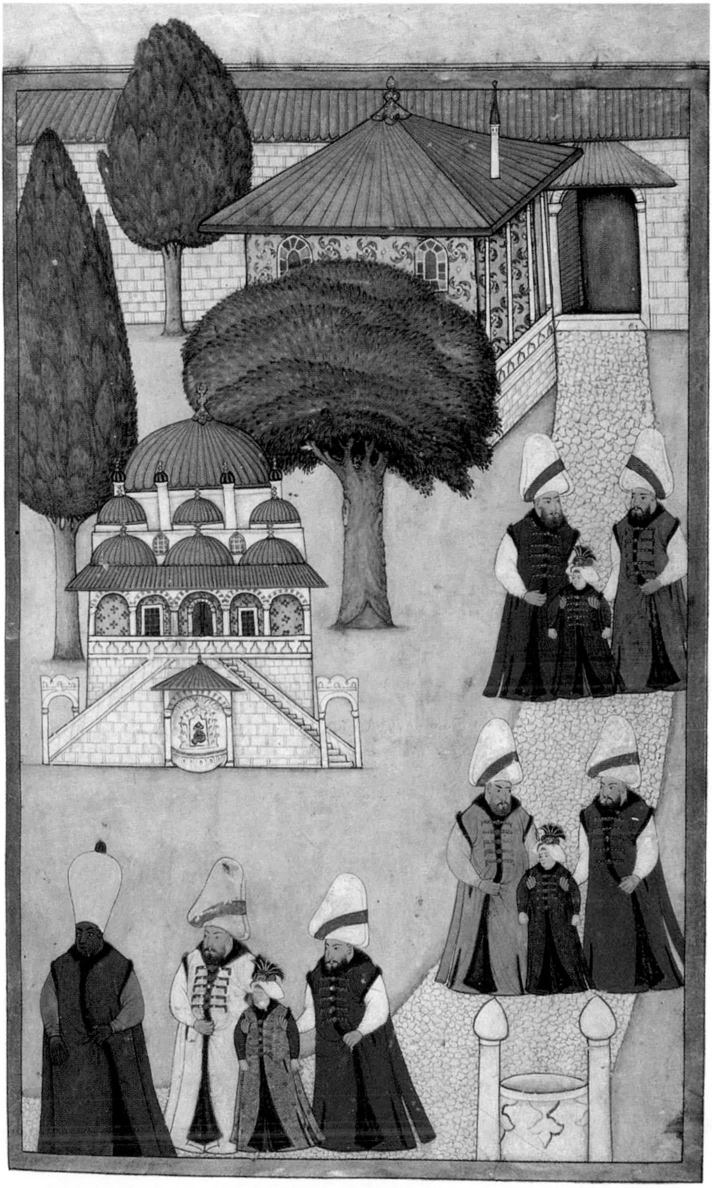

9. The chief black eunuch conducts the young prince to the circumcision ceremony.
Istanbul, ca. 1720–1732.

10. Princes, pages, and eunuchs at an evening party by the Golden Horn.
Istanbul, ca. 1720–1732.

11. Isfandiyar slaying the black sorceress.
Iran, early sixteenth century.

12. Iskandar fighting the Zanjis (Habashis).
Qazvin, ca. 1590–1594.

13. Mihrasb and Tahrusiyye watching Darab fighting the Zanjis. The body of Tanbalus is floating in the water.
Mughal, India, ca. 1580–1585.

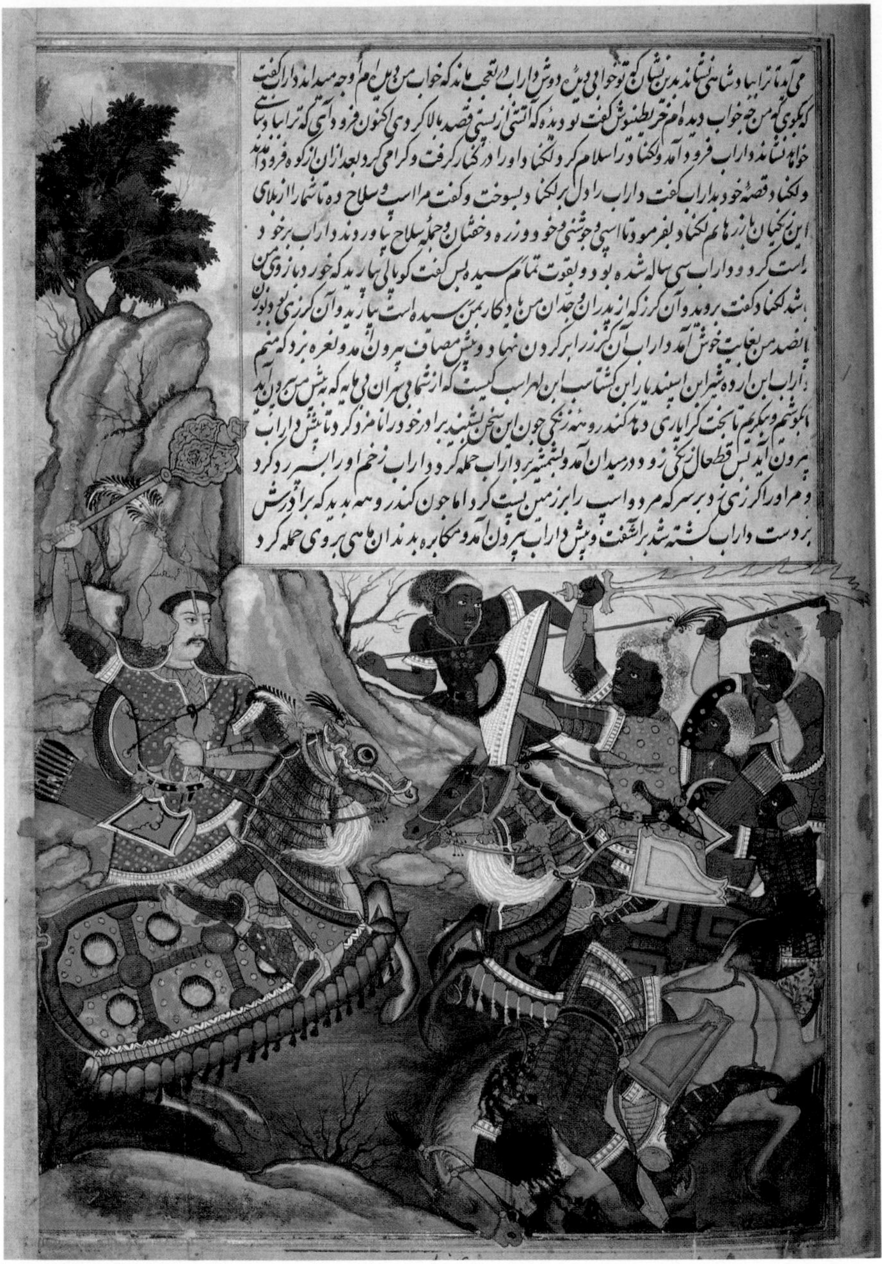

14. Darab going into battle against the Zanjis.
Mughal, India, ca. 1580–1585.

15. Darab receiving homage from the defeated Zanjis.
Mughal, India, ca. 1580–1585.

وبرطون ويرم مهلع ديخاكا راضى وليكى طونچقردى
تمّان كيدى دوزدى ابوجهل ايله كورشدوتدى بربريله

اوست ويوقار واولديلر اخرالامراني ديخى بصلى خلايق
چاغرشديلر آفريزقلدديلر ابوجهلى وكديار ايتديلردجون

16. A black slave wrestles with Abu Jahl, an Arab *sayyid*.
    Istanbul, 1594–1595.

محترم ننه اولدیکی کندو وطنو کردن رحلت قلد و کوزیول
تعین کروب دکن زحمتن چکوب بوملك مشرف ایلد و کوزردی

آندا اصحاب اولولری سوزه کلدیلر حضرت رسالتك احوالررند
قریشك حضرت رسولله مناظره لرند حضرت رسول جبشه

17. The Ethiopian king with some of the Prophet's Companions, who are bringing greetings.
Istanbul, 1594–1595.

18. Bilal and other Companions of the Prophet. Istanbul, 1594–1595.

19. Iskandar shooting a duck from a boat, with boatmen.
Tabriz, Iran, 1526.

20. Magicians.
Istanbul, fifteenth century.

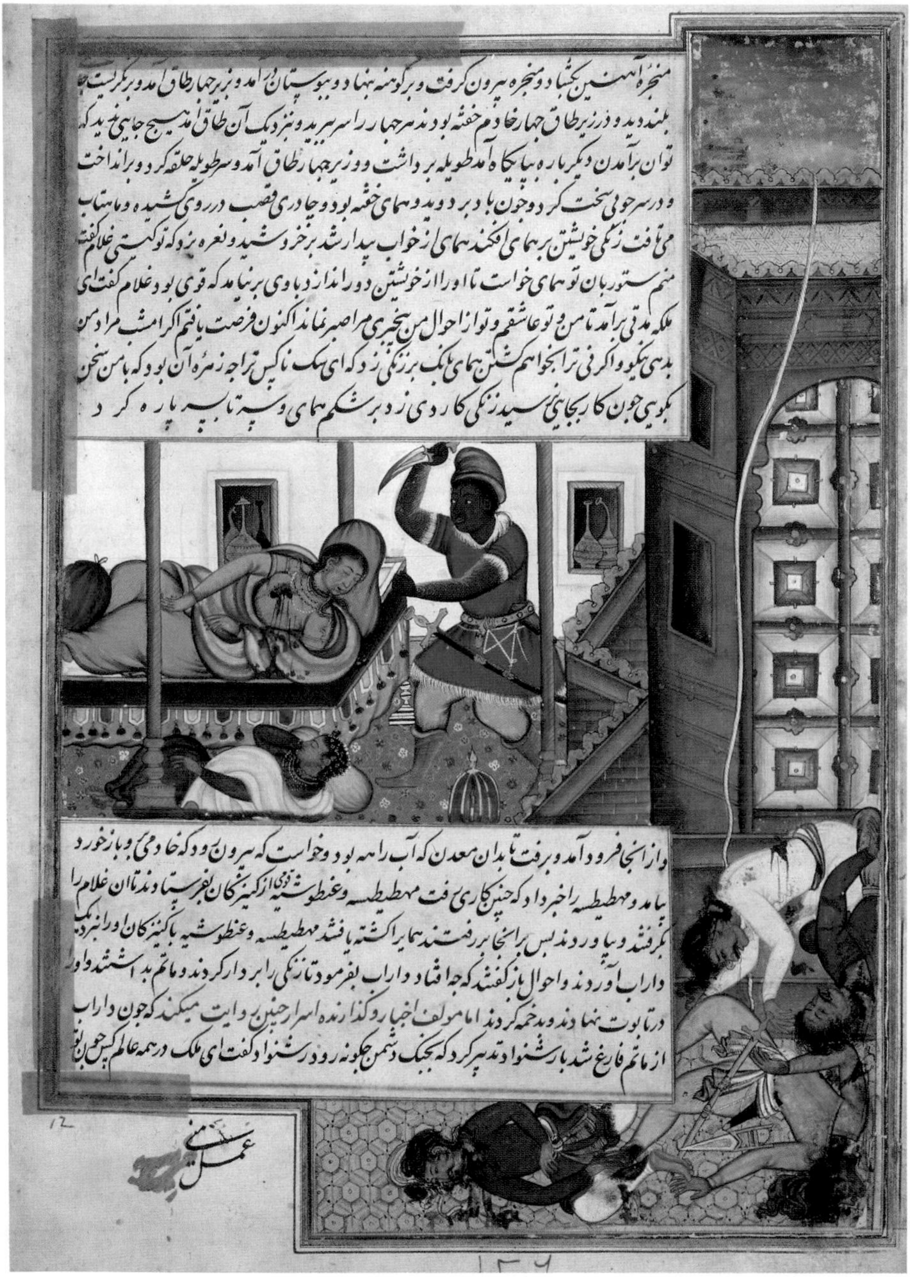

21. Humay's groom, who had a secret passion for her, murdering her at night when she would not submit to him.
Mughal, India, ca. 1580–1585.

22. "The woman who discovered her maidservant having improper relations with an ass."
Tabriz, Iran, ca. 1530.

23. “The old man who upbraided the Negro and the girl for flirting.”
Mughal, India, 1629

24. A woman of the Sudan.
Istanbul, ca. 1793.

questionable references to Nubians, no other specific ethnic term relating to an African people is used in the most ancient Arabic sources; such terms do not appear until after the great waves of Islamic conquest had carried the Arabs out of Arabia and made them masters of a vast empire in southwest Asia and northern Africa.

Ethiopians were active in Arabia in the sixth century as allies of the Byzantines in the great struggle for power and influence between the Christian Roman Empire on the one hand and the Persian Empire on the other. An Ethiopian expedition seems to have crossed the Red Sea in about 512 A.D. to help the Christians in southern Arabia. After fighting a victorious campaign they returned home, leaving garrisons behind them. These were, however, overwhelmed in a local reaction. The Ethiopians returned in about 525 A.D. to restore their authority and protect the Christians. Having done this, they once again withdrew, leaving the country in the hands of a local puppet ruler. Later, he was overthrown by a group of Ethiopian deserters who had remained in the country. Their leader, who now became king, was Abraha, a former slave of a Byzantine merchant in the Ethiopian port of Adulis. The Ethiopians tried unsuccessfully to remove him and then agreed to grant him some form of recognition. He probably led the Ethiopian force which advanced northward from the Yemen and attacked Mecca, at that time a Yemenite trading post on the West Arabian caravan route to Syria.[4] The attempt, which seems to have been part of a campaign against the Persians, failed, and in about 570 the Persians sent a naval expedition which brought the Yemen under their control.

Some Ethiopians remained in Arabia, mostly as slaves—that is to say, as captives—or as mercenaries. These were at times of some importance, as is attested by the Arabic sources and also by ancient Ethiopic loanwords in classical Arabic. The early poets also made frequent references to Ethiopians serving the Arab tribesmen as shepherds and herdsmen.

Apart from some inscriptions there is no contemporary internal historical evidence on Arabia on the eve of the birth of the Prophet Muḥammad. There is, however, a great deal of poetry and narrative, committed to writing in later (that is, Islamic) times. Although very detailed and informative, it needs careful critical scrutiny in that it often tends to project back into the pre-Islamic Arabian past the situations and attitudes of the very different later age in which the texts were compiled and written. This consideration applies particularly to the poems and traditions relating to blacks, whose situation changed radically after the great Arab conquests, as did also the attitude of the Arabs toward them.

The normal fate of captives in antiquity was enslavement, and Ethiopians appear together with Persians, Greeks, and others among the foreign slave population of seventh-century Arabia. The proportion of black slaves is unknown; but from lists of the slaves and freedmen of the Prophet and of some of his Companions, it would seem that they formed a minority. Slave women were normally and lawfully used as concubines; and it was not unusual for a man to have a free, noble Arab as father and a slave concubine as mother. In such a case, according to ancient Arabian custom, he was a slave unless he was recognized and liberated by his father.

Arab poetry and legend have preserved the names of several famous figures in ancient Arabia who are said to have been born to Ethiopian mothers and who in consequence were of dark complexion. The most famous of these was the poet and warrior ʿAntara, whose father was of the Arab tribe of ʿAbs and whose mother was an Ethiopian slave woman called Zabība. He is considered one of the greatest Arabic poets of the pre-Islamic period. Already in early times he became the subject of a series of tales and legends. As the son of a slave mother, he was by ancient custom himself a slave. A relatively early account tells how he gained his freedom. One day his tribe, the ʿAbs, were attacked by raiders from a hostile tribe, who drove off their camels.

> The ʿAbs pursued and fought them, and ʿAntara, who was present, was called on by his father to charge. "ʿAntara is a slave," he replied, "he does not know how to charge—only to milk camels and bind their udders." "Charge!" cried his father, "and you are free." And ʿAntara charged.[5]

If we are to accept the verses ascribed to him, ʿAntara, once free, despised those who were still slaves and, proud of his part-Arab descent, looked down on the "jabbering barbarians" and "skin-clad, crop-eared slaves" who lacked this advantage. Later, in the shortened form ʿAntar, his name appears as the hero of a famous Arab romance of chivalry, covering the wars against Persia, Byzantium, the Crusaders, and various other enemies. On one campaign, against the blacks, the hero penetrates farther and farther into Africa until he reaches the empire of Ethiopia and discovers, in true fairy-tale style, that his mother, the slave girl Zabība, was the granddaughter of the emperor.

All this is clearly fiction; but even the early historical accounts of ʿAntara are questionable, and only a very small part of the poetry extant in his name can be ascribed to him with any certainty. The greater part, and especially the verses in which he complains of the insult and abuse which he suffered because of his blackness, is of later composition and is probably the work of later poets of African origin. Some of these verses do indeed recur in collections ascribed to later poets of African or part-African birth. And it is not uncommon to find the same verses ascribed to more than one of these poets. A famous verse ascribed only to ʿAntara runs:

> I am a man,
> of whom one half ranks with the best of ʿAbs.
> The other half I defend with my sword.[6]

This may mean no more than that his mother was a slave, without reference to race or color. There are, however, other verses ascribed to him, indicating that his African blood and dark skin marked him as socially inferior and exposed him to insult and abuse. For example:

> Enemies revile me for the blackness of my skin,
> but the whiteness of my character effaces the blackness.[7]

In another poem, he is even quoted as insulting his own mother:

> I am the son of a black-browed woman
>   like the hyena that thrives on an abandoned camping ground
> Her leg is like the leg of an ostrich, and her hair
>   is like peppercorns
> Her front teeth gleam behind her veil like lightning
>   in curtained darkness.[8]

Similar complaints are ascribed to other figures of the pre-Islamic and early Islamic period, including, for example, a tribal chief called Khufāf ibn Nadba, a contemporary of the Prophet. The son of an Arab father and a black slave mother, Khufāf was a man of position and a chief in his tribe. A verse ascribed to him remarks that his tribe had made him chief "despite this dark pedigree."[9]

These stories and verses almost certainly belong to a later period and reflect a situation which did not yet exist at that time. This is indicated by the very fact that such men as ʿAntara, Khufāf, and others could rise to the social eminence they attained, something which would have been very difficult a century later. In pre-Islamic and early Islamic Arabia, there would have been no reason whatever for Arabs to regard Ethiopians as inferior or to regard Ethiopian ancestry as a mark of base origin. On the contrary, there is a good deal of evidence that Ethiopians were regarded with respect as a people on a level of civilization substantially higher than that of the Arabs themselves. A slave as such was of course inferior—but the black slave was no worse than the white. In this respect pagan and early Islamic Arabia seems to have shared the general attitude of the ancient world, which attached no stigma to blackness and imposed no restrictions on black freemen.[10]

There were many contacts between Arabs and Ethiopians, both in Arabia and in Africa, and during the career of the Prophet several of his Meccan Companions were able, for a while, to find refuge in Ethiopia from the persecution of their pagan compatriots. Many prominent figures of the earliest Islamic period had Ethiopian women among their ancestresses, including no less a person than the Caliph ʿUmar himself, whose father, al-Khaṭṭāb, had an Ethiopian mother. Another was ʿAmr ibn al-ʿĀṣ, the conqueror of Egypt and one of the architects of the Arab Empire. There were several others of Ethiopian descent among the Companions of the Prophet.[11] One of the most famous was Bilāl ibn Rabāḥ. Born a slave in Mecca, he was an early and devoted convert to Islam and was acquired and manumitted by Abū Bakr, the Prophet's father-in-law and eventual successor as first caliph. He is remembered chiefly as the first muezzin, when the call to prayer was instituted shortly after the Prophet's arrival in Medina. He was also the personal attendant of the Prophet and is variously described in the sources as his mace bearer, his steward, his adjutant, and his valet.[12] Another Companion was Abū Bakra, literally, "the Father of the Pulley," an Ethiopian slave in Ṭā'if. He acquired this nickname by letting himself down with a pulley during the Muslim siege of Ṭā'if, and joining the Muslims. He was accepted and manumitted by the Prophet and later settled in Basra, where he died in about 672 A.D.

During the period immediately following the death of the Prophet in 632 A.D., the great Islamic conquests took the new faith to vast areas of Asia and also of Africa. A new situation was created, and many changes can be observed in the literature of the time.

The first of these is the narrowing, specializing, and fixing of color terms applied to human beings. In time almost all disappear apart from "black," "red," and "white"; and these become ethnic and absolute instead of personal and relative. "Black," overwhelmingly, means the natives of Africa south of the Sahara and their offspring. "White"—or occasionally (light) "red"—means the Arabs, Persians, Greeks, Turks, Slavs, and other peoples to the north and to the east of the black lands. Sometimes, in contrast to the white Arabs and Persians, the northern peoples are designated by terms connoting dead white, pale blue, and various shades of red or ruddy. In some contexts the term "black" is extended to include the Indians and even the Copts; but this is not normal usage.[13]

Together with this specialization and fixing of color terms comes a very clear connotation of inferiority attached to darker and more specifically black skins. A story is told concerning the Arab conquest of Egypt which, if authentic, may well be the last surviving example of the older attitude. The story tells how a certain Arab leader called ʿUbāda ibn al-Sāmit took a party of Muslims to meet the Muqawqis, the great Christian functionary who at one point led the defenders of Egypt. ʿUbāda (the chronicler tells us) was "black," and when the Arabs came to the Muqawqis and entered his presence, ʿUbāda led them. The Muqawqis was frightened by his blackness and said to them: "Get this black man away from me and bring another to talk to me."

The Arabs insisted that ʿUbāda was the wisest, best, and noblest among them and was their appointed leader, whom they obeyed and to whose judgment they deferred. The Muqawqis asked:

> "How can you be content that a black man should be foremost among you? It is more fitting that he should be below you."
>
> "Indeed no," they replied, "for though he is black, as you see, he is still the foremost among us in position, in precedence, in intelligence and in wisdom, for blackness is not despised among us."

The Muqawqis asked ʿUbāda to speak gently to him, because speaking harshly would increase the dread already inspired by his blackness. The narrative concludes with ʿUbāda stepping forward and saying to the Muqawqis: "I have heard what you say. Among the men I command there are a thousand, all of them black, indeed blacker and more frightening than I. If you saw them, you would be very frightened indeed."[14]

There are two interesting points about this story. The first is that the black man appears as a figure of terror rather than of contempt, though that element is not entirely lacking. The second, and far more important, is that ʿUbāda is not an African or even of African descent but (as the chroniclers are careful to point out) a pure and noble Arab. Here "black" is still a personal and relative term describing an individual's complexion and not an ethnic absolute denoting the distinguishing marks of a race. "Blackness is not despised among us" means no more than that persons of dark complexion are not considered inferior to those of light complexion. The episode of the noble but swarthy 'Ubāda occurred at the very beginning of Arab expansion. Under the patriarchal caliphs and still more under the Umayyad caliphs in the late seventh and early eighth centuries, we find ample evidence of a radical change of attitudes.

4

Prejudice and Piety, Literature and Law

The evidence for the growth of anti-black prejudice comes in the main from two groups of sources. The first of these is literary, especially poetry and anecdote. Several Arabic poets, of the pre-Islamic and early Islamic periods, are described as "black" and are known collectively, to the literary tradition, as *aghribat al-ʿArab*—"the crows of the Arabs."[1] Some of them—mostly pre-Islamic—were Arabs of swarthy complexion; others were of mixed Arab and African parentage. For the latter, and still more for the pure Africans, blackness was an affliction. In many verses and narratives, they are quoted as suffering from insult and discrimination, as showing resentment at this, and yet in some way as accepting the inferior status resulting from their African ancestry.

One such was the poet Suḥaym (d. 660), born a slave and of African origin. His name, obviously a nickname, might be translated as "little black man." In one poem he laments:

> If my color were pink, women would love me
> But the Lord has marred me with blackness.[2]

In another he defends himself (in striking anticipation of William Blake's famous line, "But I am black, but O! my soul is white"):

> Though I am a slave my soul is nobly free
> Though I am black of color my character is white.[3]

In the same mood:

> My blackness does not harm my habit, for I am like
> musk; who tastes it does not forget.

I am covered with a black garment, but under it there
is a lustrous garment with white skirts.[4]

These lines are also attributed to Nuṣayb ibn Rabāḥ (d. 726), probably the most gifted of these black poets.[5] He was very conscious of his birth and color, for which he endured many insults. On one occasion the great Arab poet Kuthayyir said mockingly:

I saw Nuṣayb astray among men
his color was that of cattle.
You can tell him by his shining blackness
even if he be oppressed, he has the dark face of an oppressor.[6]

Challenged by his friends to reply, Nuṣayb refused with dignity. For one thing, he said, God had given him the gift of poetry to use for good; he would not misuse it for satire. For another, "all he has done is call me black—and he speaks truth." Then Nuṣayb said, of his own color:

Blackness does not diminish me, as long as I
have this tongue and this stout heart.
Some are raised up by means of their lineage; the
verses of my poems are my lineage!
How much better a keen-minded, clear-spoken
black than a mute white!

But all the same:

If I am jet-black, musk too is very dark—and
there is no medicine for the blackness of my skin.[7]

A black contemporary of Nuṣayb, similarly attacked, responded less meekly. All that we know of al-Ḥayquṭān is that he was a black slave, who lived in the Umayyad period. The name denotes a kind of bird, something like a partridge, and was presumably a slave name or nickname. No less a person than the famous Arab poet and satirist Jarīr (d. ca. 729) chose al-Ḥayquṭān as the butt of his wit. Jarīr, we are told, encountered al-Ḥayquṭān on a festival day, wearing a white shirt over his black skin. This prompted the poet to improvise a line of verse, likening him to a donkey's penis wrapped in papyrus. Al-Ḥayquṭān responded with a long ode, beginning:

Though my hair is woolly and my skin coal-black,
My hand is open and my honor bright[8]

After proclaiming the greatness and glory of the Ethiopians and taunting the Arabians with their previous fear of Ethiopian conquest, he ends by returning Jarīr's insult in kind. Alluding to an accusation sometimes brought against the tribe of Kulayb, to which Jarīr belonged, he concluded:

Are you not of Kulayb, and is not your mother a ewe?
Fat sheep are both your pride and your shame.[9]

Some of these made careers as court poets. One such was a second Nuṣayb, known as Nuṣayb al-Asghar, the Younger (d. 791). In the course of a panegyric ode addressed to the Caliph Hārūn al-Rashīd, he remarks of himself:

> Black man, what have you to do with love?
> Give over chasing white girls if you have any sense.
> An Ethiop black like you
> has no means of access to them.[10]

Probably the best known of the early black poets in Arabic was Abū Dulāma (d. ca. 776), a slave who became the court poet—and jester—of the first Abbasid caliphs. The name means, literally, "Father of Blackness." In his verses, the acceptance of inferiority is unmistakable. To amuse his master, Abū Dulāma makes fun of his own appearance, of his aged mother, and of his family:

> We are alike in color; our faces are black and
> ugly, our names are shameful.[11]

The Arab anthologists tell us something about the lives of these men. Several anecdotes show Nuṣayb ibn Rabāḥ's awareness of his color problem. In an autobiographical fragment, he remarks that before he went on his first journey to Egypt, he consulted his sister, a wise woman. She reminded him that he combined the disadvantages of being black and ridiculous in men's eyes. He then recited some of his verses, and she was persuaded that their merits gave him some prospect of success.[12]

A rather different story tells how Nuṣayb lunched one day with the Umayyad Caliph ʿAbd al-Malik and, after obtaining the caliph's promise of safety, said to him:

> My color is pitch-black, my hair is woolly, my appearance repulsive. I did not attain the favor which you have vouchsafed me by the honor of my father, or my mother, or my tribe. I attained it only by my mind and my tongue. I adjure you by God, O Commander of the Faithful, do not cut me off from that by which I have attained my position with you.[13]

The point of the story is that the poet chooses an opportunity and uses his wit to secure immunity from execution. But the passage vividly illustrates the association already accepted at this time of blackness, ugliness, and inferior station.

The same theme occurs in stories of the black poet Dā'ūd ibn Salm (d. ca. 750), known as Dā'ūd the Black (al-Adlam) and famous for his ugliness. On one occasion, it is said, together with an Arab called Zayd Ibn Jaʿfar, he was arrested and brought before a judge in Mecca, on a charge of flaunting luxurious clothes. The two accused received very different treatment. The handsome Arab, says the chronicler, was released; the ugly black was flogged.

> The judge said: "I can stand this from Ibn Jaʿfar, but why should I stand it from you? Because of your base origin, or your ugly face? Flog him, boy!—and he flogged him."[14]

Another story tells of a misadventure of the famous singer Saʿīd ibn Misjaḥ (d. ca. 705–15), considered the greatest musician of his time. Seeking a lodging in Damascus, he managed to get himself accepted by one of a group of young men, the others being reluctant. He accompanied them to a singing girl's house; and when lunch was served he withdrew, saying, "I am a black man. Some of you may find me offensive. I shall therefore sit and eat apart." They were embarrassed but arranged for him to take his food (and later his wine) separately. Then slave girl singers appeared, and Saʿīd ibn Misjaḥ praised their performance. Singers and owners alike were affronted by the impudence of "this black man" in daring to praise the girls, and he was warned by the other companions to mend his manners. Later his identity was revealed and then all vied in seeking the company of the famous singer.[15] These episodes show both the nature and the limits of social discrimination against the dark-skinned.

After the eighth century, there are few identifiable black poets in Arabic literature, and their blackness is not a significant poetic theme. There were a few poets in the black lands converted to Islam who composed in Arabic; but most black African Muslims preferred to use Arabic for scholarship, as European Christians used Latin, and their own languages for poetry. In the central lands, though the flow of black, as of other, slaves continued into the twentieth century, the school of self-consciously black poets came to an end. Few of the slaves were sufficiently assimilated or educated to compose poetry in Arabic, while the few Arabic poets of African or part-African ancestry were too assimilated to see themselves as black and therefore other.[16]

The whole question of blackness was discussed in a special essay by Jāḥiẓ of Basra (ca. 776–869), one of the greatest prose writers in classical Arabic literature and said by some of his biographers to be of partly African descent.[17] Entitled "The Boast of the Blacks against the Whites,"[18] the essay purports to be a defense of the dark-skinned peoples—and especially of the Zanj, the blacks of East Africa—against their detractors, refuting the accusations commonly brought against them and setting forth their qualities and achievements, with a wealth of poetic illustration. They are strong, brave, cheerful, and generous—and not, as people say, "because of weakness of mind, lack of discernment, and ignorance of consequences." Another false charge is stupidity. To those who ask, "How is it that we have never seen a Zanjī who had the intelligence even of a woman or of a child?" the answer, says Jāḥiẓ, is that the only Zanj they knew were slaves of low origin and from outlying and backward areas. If they judged by their experience of Indian slaves, would they have any notion of Indian science, philosophy, and art? Obviously not—and the same is true of the black lands. Jāḥiẓ also defends the equality of blacks as marriage partners and notes the paradox that discrimination against them first arose after the advent of Islam: "It is part of your ignorance," he makes the blacks say, "that in the time of heathendom [i.e., in pre-Islamic Arabia] you regarded us as good enough to marry your women, yet when the justice of Islam came, you considered this wrong." Another point is that the blacks are more numerous than the whites—certainly true, since Jāḥiẓ, along with some other Arabic authors of the ninth and tenth centuries, includes the Copts, the Berbers, and the inhabitants of India, Southeast Asia, and China. A curious quotation follows: "There are more blacks than whites, more rocks than mud, more sand than soil, more salt water than sweet water." In conclusion, Jāḥiẓ argues against the common equation of blackness with ugliness, and insists that black is beautiful—in nature, in the animal kingdom, and in man. In any case, blackness is not a curse or punishment, as is commonly alleged, but a result of natural conditions:

> This exists in all things. Thus we see that locusts and worms on plants are green, and we see that the louse is black on a young man's head, white if his hair whitens, red if it is dyed.

Jāḥiẓ was a great humorist and satirist, and the reader of his defense of the blacks may sometimes wonder whether its intention is wholly serious. This doubt is strengthened if one compares the essay with his remarks about blacks in his other writings. Despite his putative African ancestry, he expresses—or perhaps cites—negative views of the Zanj:

> We know that the Zanj are the least intelligent and the least discerning of mankind, and the least capable of understanding the consequences of actions.[19]

> Like the crow among mankind are the Zanj for they are the worst of men and the most vicious of creatures in character and temperament.[20]

> They [the Shuʿūbiyya] maintain that eloquence is prized by all people at all times—even the Zanj, despite their dimness, their boundless stupidity, their obtuseness, their crude perceptions and their evil dispositions, make long speeches.[21]

The last passage gives a clue to what might be Jāḥiẓ's purpose. The Shuʿūbiyya were a faction of non-Arab Muslims, mostly Persians, who protested against Arab privilege and superiority in the Islamic Empire and objected to the central position accorded to Arabic culture. A characteristic form of Shuʿūbī polemic was to laud the achievements and capacities of their own peoples and decry those of the Arabs. Jāḥiẓ was a fervent defender of the Arabs and the Arabic cultural tradition against all comers, and especially against the Persians, who, alone among the conquered peoples, offered a serious challenge to Arab supremacy. His defense of the blacks, though in part intended seriously, may perhaps also be understood as a parody of Shuʿūbiyya tracts, intended to throw ridicule on Persian pretensions by advancing similar arguments on behalf of the lowly and despised Zanj.[22]

While however there may be some question about Jāḥiẓ's intentions, there can be none about those of some later writers, who, from the tenth century onward, produced a series of books offering not indeed a boast but rather a defense of the black peoples and an answer to the insults and charges leveled against them. An obvious question that arises is why such an anti-defamation campaign should have been thought necessary. No such defenses have come down to us from the ancient world, whether Middle Eastern or Greco-Roman, no doubt for the good reason that there were no such accusations to answer.

The case against prejudice was succinctly stated by the famous statesman and man of letters al-Ṣāḥib ibn ʿAbbād (938–95), who remarks that men may be praised or blamed, rewarded or punished for their deeds, in which they have choice: "But since God created tallness and shortness and the blackness of the Zanj and the whiteness of the Greeks, it is not right that men should be blamed or punished for these qualities, since God neither enjoined nor forbade them."[23]

Books written in defense of the blacks in the Islamic Middle Ages were usually chiefly concerned with the Ethiopians. There are a few such books; they have survived in only a few copies, and none of them has as yet been printed. One of the earliest, written by Jamāl al-Dīn Abu'l-Faraj ibn al-Jawzī (d. 1208 A.D.), is entitled *The Lightening of the Darkness on the Merits of the Blacks and the Ethiopians.* In this the author attempts to defend both groups against the various accusations made against them. In a striking passage, he explains another of his purposes:

> I have seen a number of outstanding Ethiopians whose hearts were breaking because of their black color. So I let them know that respect is based on the performance of good deeds, and not on beautiful forms. I therefore composed for them this book, which deals with a good number of Ethiopians and Blacks.[24]

A second work, based in part on the previous one and written by the famous Egyptian polyhistor Jalāl al-Dīn al-Suyūṭī (d. 1505 A.D.) is *The Raising of the Status of the Ethiopians.* Another, by a sixteenth-century author, is entitled *The Colored Brocade on the Good Qualities of Ethiopians.* A similar work in Turkish was written by an Ethiopian protégé of the chief black eunuch, who was brought to Istanbul, studied there, and rose to high rank as a judge in the Ottoman service. There were also other, earlier works of the same type, but these have not survived.

The books that have come down to us follow the same main pattern. They discuss the origins of the blacks and deal with the reasons for their blackness, rejecting hostile myths concerning this. They set forth the good qualities of blacks and also draw attention to blackness itself as a good quality in certain plants, stones, and animals. They insist that whites cannot claim superior merit because of their whiteness but must earn it by piety and good deeds. Most of them then discuss Ethiopians among the slaves and freedmen of the Prophet's Companions who fled from Arabia, the words of Ethiopic origin in the Qur'ān and more generally in Arabic, utterances of the Prophet concerning Ethiopians, and the like. There are also collections of anecdotes illustrating good and pious deeds by blacks, though here the usual theme is that simple piety is better than sophisticated wickedness, with the black used as the example of simplicity as much as of piety.[25]

Another type of information on racial attitudes may be found in religious literature, specifically that which by apt quotation seeks to condemn racial prejudice and discrimination. During the centuries which followed the death of the Prophet, pious Muslims collected vast numbers of what are known as *ḥadīth*s, that is to say, traditions concerning Muḥammad's actions and utterances. A very large proportion of these are certainly spurious—but this, while it may nullify their value as evidence of the Prophet's own views, still leaves them as important evidence on the development of attitudes during the period in which they were manufactured. A number of these traditions deal with questions of race and color. There are some which specifically condemn one or another race. Thus the Prophet is quoted as saying of the Ethiopian: "When he is hungry he steals, when he is sated he fornicates."[26] This is undoubtedly spurious, but is also well known in early and modern times as an Arabic proverb about the Zanj.[27] Similar traditions, equally spurious, are cited disparaging the Persians, the Turks, and other parties to the struggles of early Islamic history. Sometimes these traditions have an eschatological content, as for example when the Prophet predicts that the Kaʿba, the sanctuary in Mecca, will be destroyed by "black-skinned, short-shanked men," who will tear it apart and thus begin the destruction of the world.[28]

Such traditions are few, and most of them are not regarded as authentic. A larger body of accepted traditions survives, the general purport of which is to deplore racial prejudice and to insist on the primacy of piety. One of the commonest is the phrase ascribed to the Prophet, "I was sent to the red and the black"—an expression taken to embrace the whole of mankind.[29] With the passage in the Qur'ān already quoted as point of departure, the manufacturers of tradition—for these too are almost certainly spurious—have as their purpose to insist that true merit is to be found in piety and good deeds and that these take precedence over gentle, noble, or even purely Arab birth.

These traditions, and those opposed to them, clearly reflect the great struggles in the early Islamic Empire between the pure Arab conquistador aristocracy, claiming both ethnic and social superiority, and the converts among the conquered, who could claim neither ethnic nor family advantage and perhaps for that reason insisted on the primacy of religious merit.

Here I may draw attention to a rhetorical device very common in classical Arabic usage—an argument by the absurd. It is, however, very different from that device which we call the *reductio ad absurdum*. The purpose of the *reductio ad absurdum* is to demonstrate the falsity of an argument by stating it in its most extreme and therefore absurd form. The Arabic rhetorical device to which I refer has the opposite purpose—not to disprove but to emphasize and reaffirm; it is thus not a *reductio ad absurdum,* but rather a *trajectio ad absurdum* (if I may coin a rhetorical term). A principle is asserted and an extreme, even an absurd, example is given—but the purpose is to show that the principle still applies even in this extreme and absurd formulation.

One cannot but be struck by the number of times the black—as also the Jew and the woman—is used to point this type of argument in both classical and modern times. Thus, in asserting the duty of obedience, of submission to legitimate authority, however unlikely the form in which it appears, Muslim jurists cite a dictum attributed to the Prophet: "Obey whoever is put in authority over you, even if he be a crop-nosed Ethiopian slave."[30] This combination of qualities is clearly intended to indicate the ultimate improbability at once in physical, social, and racial terms.

A different point is made in the same way in a late anecdote, the purpose of which is to emphasize the importance of humane treatment for slaves. An Arab had a black slave woman, who tended his sheep. Angered when she allowed a wolf to take one of them, he slapped her face. She complained; and the Prophet, hearing of the matter, ruled that the compensation due for the slap was her freedom. The owner objected that she was "black and barbarous" and understood nothing of the faith. "The Prophet asked her: 'Where is God?' She replied: 'In heaven.' The Prophet said: 'She is a believer; free her.' "[31]

Some traditions use the same rhetorical device in relation to the choice of a wife:

> Do not marry women for their beauty, which may destroy them, or for their money, which may corrupt them, but for religion. A slit-nosed black slave-woman, if pious, is preferable.[32]

Piety must overcome inclination, though it cannot redirect it.

This theme also occurs in stories about Abū Dharr, an early Muslim hero who is often cited as a model of piety and humility. As examples of his humility it is mentioned that he married a black woman, "for he wanted a wife who would lower him and not exalt him," and that he was willing to pray behind an Ethiopian.[33] The point is most forcibly made by the famous Ibn Ḥazm (994–1064), who observes that

> God has decreed that the most devout is the noblest[34] even if he be a Negress's bastard, and that the sinner and unbeliever is at the lowest level even if he be the son of prophets.[35]

The sentiment is impeccably pious and egalitarian—yet somehow the formulation does not entirely carry conviction. Significantly, Ibn Ḥazm makes this remark in the introduction to a treatise on Arab genealogy, in which he tries to demonstrate the importance and dignity of this science. In another somewhat equivocal tradition, an Ethiopian says to the Prophet, "You Arabs excel us in all, in build, color, and in the possession of the Prophet. If I believe, will I be with you in Paradise?" The Prophet answers, "Yes, and in Paradise the whiteness of the Ethiopian will be seen over a stretch of a thousand years."[36]

The moral of this and of countless other anecdotes and sayings of the same kind is that piety outweighs blackness and impiety outweighs whiteness. This is not the same as saying that whiteness and blackness do not matter. Indeed, the contrary is implied in such tales as that of the pious black who turns white, and the parallel stories of white evildoers who turn black.[37] A vivid example occurs in the *Risālat al-Ghufrān,* a vision of heaven and hell by the Syrian poet Abu'l-ʿAlā' al-Maʿarrī (973–1057). In paradise the narrator meets an exceedingly beautiful houri, who tells him that in life she was Tawfīq the Negress, who used to fetch books for copyists in the Academy of Baghdad.

"But you were black," he exclaims, "and now you have become whiter than camphor!"—to which she replies by quoting a verse: "If there were a mustard-seed of God's light among all the blacks, the blacks would become white."[38] The same association of light with good is shown in the Muslim hagiographic literature, which depicts the Prophet himself as of white or ruddy color. Similar descriptions are given of his wife ʿĀ'isha, his son-in-law ʿAlī and his descendants, and even his predecessors, the prophets Abraham, Moses, and Jesus.[39]

From both the expressions and the denunciations of racial prejudice, in both general and religious literature, it is clear that a major transformation had taken place. In ancient Arabia, as elsewhere in antiquity, racism—in the modern sense of that word—was unknown. The Islamic dispensation, far from encouraging it, condemns even the universal tendency to ethnic and social arrogance and proclaims the equality of all Muslims before God. Yet, from the literature, it is clear that a new and sometimes vicious pattern of racial hostility and discrimination had emerged within the Islamic world.

5

Conquest and Enslavement

This great change of attitude, within a few generations, can be attributed in the main to three major developments.

The first of these is the fact of conquest—the creation by the advancing Arabs of a vast empire in which the normal distinctions inevitably appeared between the conquerors and the conquered. At first, Arab and Muslim were virtually the same thing and the distinction could be perceived as religious. But as conversions to Islam proceeded very rapidly among the different conquered peoples, a new class came into existence—the non-Arab converts to Islam, whose position in some ways resembled that of the native Christians in the latter-day European empires. According to the doctrines of Islam—repeatedly reaffirmed by the pious exponents of the Faith—the non-Arab converts were the equals of the Arabs and could even outrank them by superior piety. But the Arabs, like all other conquerors before and since, were reluctant to concede equality to the conquered; and for as long as they could, they maintained their privileged position. Non-Arab Muslims were regarded as inferior and subjected to a whole series of fiscal, social, political, military, and other disabilities. They were known collectively as the *mawālī* (sing. *mawlā*), a term the primary meaning of which was "freedman." Many indeed were brought to Islam by way of capture, enslavement, and manumission—a process reflected in a famous if spurious *ḥadīth,* according to which the Prophet said:

> Will you not ask me why I laugh? I have seen people of my community who are dragged to Paradise against their will. They asked, "O Prophet of God, who are they?" He said, "They are non-Arab people whom the warriors in the Holy War have captured and made to enter Islam."[1]

Already in antiquity, some Greek philosophers had argued that slavery was beneficial to the barbarian slave, in that it initiated him to a better and more civilized way of life. The religious version of this—of slavery as a road to the blessings of Islam—later became a commonplace.[2] But the earliest converts who came by this road encountered difficulties.

A Spanish-Arab author, Ibn ʿAbd Rabbihi (860–940), describes the attitude of the early Arabs to the non-Arab *mawālī:*

> Nāfiʿ ibn Jubayr ibn Muṭʿim gave precedence to a *mawlā* to lead him in prayer. People spoke to him about this, and he said: "I wished to be humble before God in praying behind him."
>
> The same Nāfiʿ ibn Jubayr, when a funeral passed by, used to ask who it was. If they said: "A Qurashī," he would say: "Alas for his kinsfolk!" If they said: "A *mawlā,*" he would say: "He is the property of God, Who takes what He pleases and leaves what He pleases."
>
> They used to say that only three things interrupt prayer—a donkey, a dog, and a *mawlā.* The *mawlā* did not use the *kunya* [part of an Arab name, consisting of *Abū*—father of—followed by another personal noun, usually but not always that of his son] but was addressed only by his personal name and by-name. People did not walk side by side with them, nor allow them precedence in processions. If they were present at a meal, they stood while the others sat, and if a *mawlā,* because of his age, his merit or his learning, was given food, he was seated at the end of the table, lest anyone should fail to see that he was not an Arab. They did not allow a *mawlā* to pray at funerals if an Arab was present, even if the only Arab present was an inexperienced youth. The suitor for a *mawlā* woman did not address himself to her father or brother, but to her patron, who gave her in marriage or refused, as he pleased. If her father or brother gave her in marriage without the patron's approval, the marriage was invalid, and if consummated was fornication not wedlock.
>
> It is related that ʿĀmir ibn ʿAbd al-Qays, known for his piety, asceticism, austerity and humility, was addressed in the presence of ʿAbdallah ibn ʿĀmir, the governor of Iraq, by Ḥumrān, the *mawlā* of the Caliph ʿUthman ibn ʿAffan. Ḥumrān accused ʿĀmir of reviling and abusing the Caliph. ʿĀmir denied this, and Ḥumrān said to him: "May God not multiply your kind among us!" To this ʿĀmir replied: "But may God multiply your kind among us!" ʿĀmir was asked: "Does he curse you and do you bless him?" "Yes," he replied, "for they sweep our roads, sew our boots, and weave our clothes!"
>
> ʿAbdallah ibn ʿĀmir, who was leaning, sat bolt upright, and said: "I didn't think that you, with your virtue and your asceticism, knew about these things." To which ʿĀmir replied: "I know more than you think I know!"[3]

The struggle for equal rights of the non-Arab converts was one of the main themes of the first two centuries of Islam. Another theme of comparable importance was the struggle of the half-breeds for equality with the full-breeds. The Arab conquerors, despite the teachings of Islam and against the protests of the pious, had, perhaps inevitably, ruled as a sort of conquistador tribal aristocracy. Only true Arabs could belong, meaning those who were of free Arab ancestry on both their father's and mother's side. Exercising the immemorial rights of the conqueror, the Arabs took concubines among the daughters of the conquered; but their offspring by these slave women were not considered full Arabs, and were not admitted to the highest positions of power. Almost until the end of the Umayyad Caliphate, all the caliphs were the sons of free Arab mothers; and it is clear that Umayyad princes who were the sons of non-Arab slave women were not for one moment considered as possible candidates for the succession. Even a gifted leader and commander like Maslama[4] neither saw himself nor was seen by others as a possible claimant to the caliphate.

This kind of discrimination is well attested in Arabic literature; so too is the resentment of its victims. As this class of victims—the sons of Arab fathers and non-Arab mothers—became more numerous and more important, their resentments became more dangerous. At one time it was argued—principally by nineteenth-century European scholars reflecting the preoccupation of their time and place with struggles for national freedom—that the great upheavals of the mid-eighth century were due to a rising tide of Persian revolt against Arab domination and that the Abbasid revolution marked their victory. This theory, and the accompanying idea of a new Persian ascendancy, is not supported by the evidence. On the contrary, all the indications are that the Arab ascendancy continued for some time after the advent of the Abbasid caliphs. The caliphs themselves and all their senior officials and commanders were still Arabs, Arabic was the sole language of government, and Arabs still continued to enjoy important social and economic privileges in the empire.[5]

Nevertheless, major changes had been taking place. According to a saying attributed to the Prophet, "the ruin of the Arabs will come when the sons of the daughters of Persia grow to manhood."[6] The tradition is certainly spurious, but like many such spurious traditions it reflects, very accurately, the issues and concerns of the time. Those who challenged and in time unseated the Arab conquistador aristocracy were not the subject peoples, still traumatized by conquest and politically inert. The challengers were their own sons, half-Arab and therefore only half-privileged, increasing in numbers and in power, and ever less willing to accept the disabilities and humiliations imposed upon them by their full-blooded half-brothers. As with most major revolutionary changes, the equalization of the half-Arabs began before the revolution and was not accomplished until some time after its political completion. The last two Umayyad caliphs were the sons of slave mothers; the first Abbasid, the son of a free Arab woman.[7] But the second Abbasid caliph, and those who came after him, were the sons of foreign concubines. The army of Khorāsān, to which the Abbasids owed their victory and for a while their survival, was an Arab, not a Persian, army—but an Arab army half-Persianized by generations of residence and intermarriage.[8]

The term commonly used by the ancient Arabs for the offspring of mixed unions was *hajīn,* a word which, like the English "mongrel" and "half-breed," was used both of animals and of human beings. For example, *hajīn* would indicate a horse whose sire was a purebred Arab and whose dam was not. It had much the same meaning when applied to human beings, denoting a person whose father was Arab and free and whose mother was a foreign slave. The term *hajīn* in itself is social rather than racial in content, expressing the contempt of the highborn for the baseborn, without attributing any specific racial identity to the latter. Non-Arabs, of whatever racial origin, were of course baseborn but so too were many Arabs who, for one reason or another, were not full and free members of a tribe. Full Arabs—those born of two free Arab parents—ranked above half-Arabs, the children of Arab fathers and non-Arab mothers (the opposite case was inadmissible). Half-Arabs, in turn, ranked above non-Arabs, who were, so to speak, outside the system.

Among the ancient Arabs there was an elaborate system of social gradations. A man's status was determined by his parentage, family, clan, sept, and tribe and the rank assigned to them in the Arab social order. All this is richly documented in poetry, tradition, and a vast genealogical literature. A more difficult question is how far the ancient Arabs recognized and observed social distinctions among the various non-Arab peoples and races who supplied much, though not all, of the slave population of Arabia. According to ʿAbduh Badawī, "there was a consensus that the most unfortunate of the *hajīn*s and the lowest in social status were those to whom blackness had passed from their mothers."[9]

At his discretion, the free father of a slave child could recognize and liberate him and thus confer membership in the tribe. Under the Islamic dispensation such recognition became mandatory. In pre-Islamic custom, however, the father retained the option; according to Badawī and the sources cited by him, Arab fathers at that time were reluctant to recognize the sons of black mothers.

This is probably an accurate description of the social attitudes of the Bedouin aristocracy of conquest that emerged after the great expansion of the Arabs in the seventh century and for a while dominated the new Islamic Empire, which they created in the lands of the Middle East and North Africa.

Among these two groups, the non-Arab converts and the half-breed Arabs, color as such does not seem to have been a significant issue. The literature preserves the memory of a bitter struggle in which the three parties are Arabs, half-Arabs, and non-Arabs. The identity of the non-Arab component seems to have been of secondary importance, at least to the Arabs, though it may have meant more among the non-Arabs themselves. The significance of an African origin as distinct from other possible non-Arab origins lay in its visibility. The son of an Arab father and a Persian or Syrian mother would not look very different from the son of two Arab parents. The difference was in effect social and depended on social knowledge. The son of an African mother, however, was usually recognizable at sight and therefore more exposed to abuse and discrimination. "Son of a black woman" was a not infrequent insult addressed to such persons, and "son of a white woman" was accordingly used in praise or boasting.[10]

Even the Caliph ʿUmar, said to have been the grandson of an Ethiopian woman, was attacked retrospectively on this account. An early Arab author, Muḥammad ibn Ḥabīb, tells us that one day, during the lifetime of the Prophet, a man insulted ʿUmar and called him "Son of a black woman," whereupon God revealed the Qur'anic verse, "O believers! People should not mock other people who may be better than they are" (XLIX: 11).[11] The story, which occurs in a rather brief chapter on great men who were the sons of Ethiopian women, is almost certainly a pious invention, but not the less interesting for that. It is probably a reply to Shiʿite propaganda against ʿUmar, which made some play with his Ethiopian ancestress to discredit him.[12]

A second factor of importance was the wider range of experience which conquest brought to the Arabs. Before Islam, their acquaintance with Africa was substantially limited to Ethiopia, a country with a level of moral and material civilization significantly higher than their own. During the lifetime of the Prophet, the good reputation of the Ethiopians was further increased by the kindly welcome accorded to Muslim refugees from Mecca. After the conquests, however, there were changes. Advancing on the one hand into Africa and on the other into Southwest Asia and Southern Europe, the Arabs encountered fairer-skinned peoples who were more developed and darker-skinned peoples who were less so. No doubt as a result of this they began to equate the two facts.

Coupled with this expansion was the third major development of the early Islamic centuries—slavery and the slave trade.[13] The Arab Muslims were not the first to enslave black Africans. Even in Pharaonic times Egyptians had already begun to capture and use black African slaves, and some are indeed depicted on Egyptian monuments.[14] There were black slaves in the Hellenistic and Roman worlds—but they seem to have been few and relatively unimportant, and regarded no differently from other slaves imported from remote places.[15] The massive importation of black slaves and the growth of ethnic, even racial specialization in the slave population date from after the Arab expansion in Africa and were an indirect and unintended consequence of one of the most important humanitarian advances brought by the Islamic dispensation.

Inevitably, the large-scale importation of African slaves influenced Arab (and therefore Muslim) attitudes to the peoples of darker skin whom most Arabs and Muslims encountered only in this way.

This changing attitude affected even freemen of African ancestry—even descendants of the Companions of the Prophet. Thus ʿUbaydallāh, the son of Abū Bakra,[16] was appointed governor of Sīstān in 671 and again in 697. Already by that time blackness had become a reproach; and a poet, in a satire against him, said:

> The blacks do not earn their pay
>   by good deeds, and are not of good repute
> The children of a stinking Nubian black—
>   God put no light in their complexions!

Even the caliph, who had appointed him, remarked: "The black man is lord of the people of the East."[17] The descendants of Abū Bakra had acquired a prominent social position in Basra and had forged themselves an Arab pedigree. This was rejected by the Caliph al-Mahdī (reigned 775–85 A.D.), who compelled them to revert to the status of freedmen of the Prophet.

The low status of black slaves is illustrated by a number of anecdotes. An Arab, seeking to avoid civil war among the Muslims, swears that "he would prefer to be a mutilated Ethiopian slave tending broody goats on a hilltop until death overtakes him, rather than that a single arrow should be shot between the two sides."[18] An early chronicler, Jahshiyārī, in a history of ministers and secretaries, tells an anecdote about a certain ʿAbd al-Ḥamīd (d. ca. 750), the secretary of the last Umayyad caliph. The caliph had received the gift of a black slave from a provincial governor. He was not greatly pleased with this gift and instructed his secretary to write a letter of thanks and disparagement. ʿAbd al-Ḥamīd, we are told, wrote: "Had you been able to find a smaller number than one and a worse color than black you would have sent that as a gift."[19] Jahshiyārī's purpose in telling this story is not to insult blacks but to illustrate the readiness of wit of ʿAbd al-Ḥamīd—but the story vividly reflects a common attitude.

To the Muslims—as to the people of every other civilization known to history—the civilized world meant themselves. They alone possessed enlightenment and the true faith; the outside world was inhabited by infidels and barbarians. Some of these were recognized as possessing some form of religion and a tincture of civilization. The remainder—polytheists and idolators—were seen primarily as sources of slaves, to be imported into the Islamic world and molded in Islamic ways, and, since they possessed no religion of their own worth the mention, as natural recruits for Islam. For these peoples, enslavement was thus a benefaction and was indeed often accepted as such. This attitude is exemplified in the story of a pagan black king who is tricked and kidnapped by Muslim guests whom he has befriended and sold into slavery in Arabia. Meeting them again years later, he shows contempt but no resentment, since they had been the means of bringing him to Islam.[20] The notion that slavery is a divine boon to mankind, by means of which pagan and barbarous peoples are brought to Islam and civilization, occurs very frequently in later writers.

6

Ventures in Ethnology

The ancient Arabs, like every other people known to history, divided the world into themselves and others. For the ancient Greeks, the outsider was the barbarian, a term with a connotation of language and culture; for the Israelites, he was the Gentile, with a connotation of belief and worship. Modern societies make many distinctions, but the only one that is universally and officially accepted is between the citizen and the alien—a term that for some seems to combine the worst features of the barbarian and the unbeliever.

In ancient Arabia, those who were not Arabs were *ʿAjam,* a term which included the Persians, the Greeks, the Ethiopians, the Nabataeans, and the various other peoples with whom the ancient Arabs had contact. Later it was specialized to mean the Persians, though it continued in occasional use in the broader sense. In modern Turkish, by a curious development of an earlier usage, *ajemi* (in modern Turkish orthography, *acemi*) has acquired the meaning of "clumsy" or "inept."[1]

The ancient Arabs showed an acute awareness of ethnic, but very little consciousness of racial, differences. At first, their main concern was not with the difference between Arabs and non-Arabs but rather between the different tribes into which they themselves were divided. A conventional genealogical table of eponymous tribal ancestors divided the Arab tribes into two main groups, the Northern and the Southern. These terms related not to their current position in Arabia, where the so-called Southern tribes were often in the Syrian and Iraqi borderlands (to the north of the so-called Northern tribes), but to their presumed ancestry.

Tribal loyalty was intense, to the larger league or confederacy of tribes of presumed common ancestry, to the individual tribe, and even to the clan or sept within the tribe to which one belonged. These tribal loyalties gave rise to severe feuding and sometimes warfare and to bitter controversies which spilled over into the political life of the caliphate and even the religious life of Islam. Much of early Arab historiography, at least until the mid-ninth century, is concerned with tribal rivalries. Ancient Arab literature, for longer than that, is dominated by inter-tribal polemics, and the invectives which tribal spokesmen hurled at one another.[2]

The Arab expansion, and the creation of a far-flung empire in which the Arabs were a dominant but small minority among the vast non-Arab population, did not at first change, but rather intensified, this situation. The Arabs, with much larger prizes at stake, continued their feuding, in clans, in tribes, and in confederacies. These involved the growing number of half-breed Arabs; in addition, the non-Arab converts to Islam, enrolled as *mawālī* in one tribe or another, shared in their alliances and enmities.[3]

The involvement of the half-Arabs at the higher levels of Arab society paved the way for the non-Arab converts to Islam, many of whom by now shared the language and culture as well as the religion of the conquerors. By the ninth century Arabic literature—now written by men of diverse origins—reveals two significant developments: on the Arab side, a dawning awareness that they had lost their exclusive primacy and a tendency to seek compensation for that loss in a kind of social and cultural snobbery unrelated to the realities of power; among the non-Arabs, a growing assertiveness of their own distinctive ethnic, even national traditions and accomplishments, often accompanied by the denigration of the Arabs as primitives and nomads, in all but religion inferior to the peoples they had fortuitously conquered. These sentiments are expressed in the writings of a school of thought known as the Shuʿūbiyya.[4] This tendency was stronger at the extremities of the Islamic world, in Persia in the East and Spain in the West,[5] weaker in the Fertile Crescent and North Africa, where Arabic finally replaced the previous languages and where the various peoples eventually adopted an Arab identity.[6]

It was inevitable, in a society of such acute ethnic awareness, that attention should be given, by scholars and others, to ethnic relationships, characteristics, differences, and presumed aptitudes. The numerous writings dealing with these matters may be considered under three headings, which we may call literary, practical, and scientific.

The earliest attempts at a classification of ethnic groups in Arabic Islamic literature derive from Genesis 10, dealing with Noah's three sons—Shem, Ham, and Japhet—and the lines of filiation of the various nations and peoples whom they engendered. This biblical ethnology is not in the Qur'ān, and has no special place in the Islamic religious tradition. It was transmitted to the Muslims by Jews and Christians and converts from these religions, and this origin was generally recognized.[7] It appears in early Arabic historical literature in a variety of forms, often with considerable differences.[8] An interesting feature of the Arab versions is the attempt to fit the data in Genesis 10 into a larger framework, including on the one hand the Arabian tribes and their eponymous ancestors, and on the other such other peoples as the Persians, the Turks, the Romans, and the Slavs, familiar to the Arabs but not yet visible on the Pentateuchal horizon. All agree that the Arabs are descendants of Shem, and the blacks—sometimes including the Copts and Berbers—of Ham; most agree in assigning the Turks and Slavs to Japhet. There is, however, disagreement about the Persians and the Byzantines, the two civilized peoples with whom the Arabs had the longest and most intimate acquaintance. Some assign them to Japhet, making them kinsmen of the Turks and Slavs. Others, however, assign them to Shem, thus making them kinsmen of the Arabs. Some writers of Persian background tried to incorporate such Persian mythological heroes as Ferīdūn and Jamshīd in the biblical ethnology. Centuries later, Turkish genealogists attempted the same for the Turkish tribes of inner Asia.[9]

Most of these accounts are concerned only with classification and filiation and make no attempt at characterization. There are, however, exceptions, and in some versions characters and even functions are assigned to the various lines of descent. In an adaptation of the biblical story, the descendants of Ham are condemned to be slaves and menials. Some also assign specific roles to the descendants of Shem and of Japhet, the former to be prophets and nobles (*sharīf*), the latter to be kings and tyrants. These arguments are not pursued, and neither the literary nor the religious tradition appears to attach much importance to them.[10]

The discussion of ethnic characters and aptitudes seems to have begun with a ninth-century Arabic translation of a pre-Islamic Persian text, the *Letter of Tansar.*[11] This includes, naturally enough, an assertion of the superior merit of the Persians. Interestingly, their superiority lies in that they combine the best features of all the different peoples who are their neighbors:

> Our people are the most noble and illustrious of beings. The horsemanship of the Turk, the intellect of India, and the craftsmanship and art of Greece, God (blessed be His realm) has endowed our people with all these, more richly than they are found in the other nations separately. He has withheld from them the ceremonies of religion and the serving of kings which He gave to us. And He made our appearance and our colouring and our hair according to a just mean, without blackness prevailing, or yellowness or ruddiness; and the hair of our beards and heads neither too curly like the negro's nor quite straight like the Turk's.[12]

An Iraqi Arab author, writing in about 902–3, presents the same idea in a more elaborate form, in relation to his own people and country:

> A man of discernment said: The people of Iraq have sound minds, commendable passions, balanced natures, and high proficiency in every art, together with well-proportioned limbs, well-compounded humors, and a pale brown color, which is the most apt and proper color. They are the ones who are done to a turn in the womb. They do not come out with something between blonde, buff, blanched, and leprous coloring, such as the infants dropped from the wombs of the women of the Slavs and others of similar light complexion; nor are they overdone in the womb until they are burned, so that the child comes out something between black, murky, malodorous, stinking, and crinkly-

> haired, with uneven limbs, deficient minds, and depraved passions, such as the Zanj, the Ethiopians, and other blacks who resemble them. The Iraqis are neither half-baked dough nor burned crust but between the two.[13]

Such ideas appear to have been current at the time. Thus Ibn Qutayba (828–89) remarks of the blacks that

> they are ugly and misshapen, because they live in a hot country. The heat overcooks them in the womb, and curls their hair. The merit of the people of Babylon is due to their temperate climate.[14]

Earlier in the ninth century, Jāḥiẓ had observed in passing: "If the country is cold, they are undercooked in the womb."[15]

The arguments of the Shuʿūbiyya and the Arab response to them gave rise to an extensive literary discussion of national characteristics, differences, and aptitudes. Jāḥiẓ devoted separate essays to the Turks[16] and the blacks[17] and in a number of places developed something like a set of rules for the classification and description of ethnic groups. By the tenth and eleventh centuries, a period of Iranian cultural renaissance, these became matters of frequent discussion; and the literature of the time preserves a rich variety of anecdote and debate.[18] At the center of the debate are the Arabs and Persians, by now established as the two major ethnic groups within Islam, more or less on a footing of equality. Third in line are the Rūm, or Romans. In classical Arabic usage this denotes the Christian Byzantine Empire and also includes the large and important communities of Orthodox Christians living in the Islamic lands. The Yūnān, the ancient Greeks, are seen as a separate group, but, generally, as the predecessors of the Rūm. The Romans of ancient Rome do not normally make a separate appearance in these discussions. Next in line come India and China—remoter and less familiar but recognized as areas of relatively advanced, albeit idolatrous, civilization. After them come the barbarous peoples beyond the outer perimeter—in the North, the Turks and the Slavs; in the far West, the Franks; in the South, the various peoples of black Africa. These peoples are seen as eventual converts and in the meantime as being useful as slaves.[19]

Several authors, from Jāḥiẓ onward, attempt to classify various peoples by their skills and aptitudes and sometimes differentiate carefully between the two. According to Jāḥiẓ, the Chinese excel in the arts, the Greeks in philosophy and science, the Arabs in language and poetry, the Persians in government and statecraft, the Turks in warfare.[20] A century later, Abū Sulaymān is quoted as giving a slightly different version:

> Wisdom descended upon the heads of the Byzantines, the tongues of the Arabs, the hearts of the Persians, the hands of the Chinese.[21]

In time, certain conventional descriptions emerged, which became the common stereotypes for various national groups. Arabs had generosity and courage; Persians, statecraft and civility; Greeks were philosophers and artists; Indians, magicians and conjurers; while the dexterous Chinese were makers of furniture and gadgets. Blacks were hardworking and somewhat simple but gifted with exuberance and a sense of rhythm. Turks were impetuous fighting men.[22] With mostly minor changes, these become standard in the discussion of the various ethnic groups both inside and outside the world of Islam.

In addition to the characteristics of specific groups, the discussion also dealt with some broader and more general questions. Are all ethnic groups equal in their potential, or are some more gifted than others? If one nation excels all others in a certain field, is it because of an inherited talent (or as some put it, a divine gift), or is it because, for historical and cultural reasons, it had chosen to specialize in that area? Some writers argue strongly that so-called national characteristics, even including such racial characteristics as blackness, are really a response to environment and that any other ethnic group finding itself in the same situation would respond in the same way.

Ibn Khaldūn (1332–1406), surely the greatest historian and social thinker of the Middle Ages, devotes a whole chapter to the influence of climate on human character. Even the merriment which, in common with many other Arab writers, he attributes to blacks is, in his view, climatic and not genetic in origin. Joy and mirth, he explains, are induced by heat. Just as the heat given off by alcohol makes the drinker merry and the warm air of the bath causes the bather to sing, so too does the heat of his homeland incline the black to mirth and exuberance.[23]

At the far end of the Islamic world, Ṣāʿid al-Andalusī (d. 1070), a qadi in the Muslim city of Toledo, attempted a general classification and characterization of civilized nations. Defining them as those nations that had cultivated science and learning, he enumerated eight nations: the Indians, Persians, Chaldees, Greeks, Romans, Egyptians, Arabs, and Jews. Ṣāʿid's "nations" are as much religious as national. His Arabs include non-Arab Muslims; his Romans include Arabic-speaking Christians. The others, apart from the Jews, are all pagan.

For Ṣāʿid, only these eight peoples have contributed to civilization. Some others, such as the Chinese and the Turks, he allows to have achieved distinction in other respects; the rest of mankind he dismisses contemptuously as the Northern and the Southern barbarians, "who are more like beasts than like men." He has a few well-chosen words to say about each.

> For those who live furthest to the north between the last of the seven climates and the limits of the inhabited world, the excessive distance of the sun in relation to the zenith line makes the air cold and the atmosphere thick. Their temperaments are therefore frigid, their humors raw, their bellies gross, their color pale, their hair long and lank. Thus they lack keenness of understanding and clarity of intelligence, and are overcome by ignorance and dullness, lack of discernment, and stupidity. Such are the Slavs, the Bulgars, and their neighbors. For those peoples on the other hand who live near and beyond the

> equinoctial line to the limit of the inhabited world in the south, the long presence of the sun at the zenith makes the air hot and the atmosphere thin. Because of this their temperaments become hot and their humors fiery, their color black and their hair woolly. Thus they lack self-control and steadiness of mind and are overcome by fickleness, foolishness, and ignorance. Such are the blacks, who live at the extremity of the land of Ethiopia, the Nubians, the Zanj and the like.

Even the most ignorant peoples, Ṣāʿid goes on to explain, if they are sedentary, have some kind of monarchical government and some kind of religious law. The only people "who diverge from this human order and depart from this rational association are some dwellers in the steppes and inhabitants of the deserts and wilderness, such as the rabble of Bujja, the savages of Ghana, the scum of Zanj, and their like."[24] Ṣāʿid does not use such language when speaking of the fairer-skinned barbarians of Europe.

With the exception of one group, writers on these matters do not normally attempt to lay down rules, or even offer guidance, on the suitability of various races for different tasks and occupations. The one exception is the extensive practical literature on slaves. There is a considerable body of writing, extending over almost a thousand years and written in Arabic, Persian, and Turkish, offering what one might call consumer guidance for those who deal in slaves and those who buy them.[25]

The earliest writings of this kind, dating from the tenth century, are physiological, giving guidance on how to judge a slave's state of health from outward signs, and physiognomical, on how to judge his character from his face. Before long, however, writers on how to choose and use slaves offer information and advice on ethnological matters also. Ibn Buṭlān, an eleventh-century Christian physician in Baghdad, wrote a sort of slavetrader's vade mecum, which is the first of a series of such works.[26] He reviews the range of slaves available in the markets of the Middle East, and considers the different kinds, black and white, male and female, classifying them according to their racial, ethnic, and regional origins and indicating which groups are best suited to which tasks. Similar advice on these matters is offered by a number of later writers, sometimes in separate handbooks, sometimes in chapters or sections of books dealing with larger topics.

The statements made in these books about different races usually consist of conventional and stereotyped wisdom, but they also contain some interesting ethnographic information, notably about the peoples of the Caucasus, the Turkish peoples of the Eurasian steppe and of inner Asia, and the black peoples of eastern as well as of sub-Saharan Africa. By Ottoman times, they even include the Christian peoples of Europe, from among whom the Ottomans and the North African states drew a large part of their slave populations. The Russians, for example, we learn from various authorities, are handsome, blond, and charming, hardworking and obedient, dishonest and unchaste. In earlier times, says one authority, the Russians were famous for their laziness, so that a single Tatar could capture many Russians. But today (mid-sixteenth century) the situation is reversed, and the Russians have subjugated most of the Tatar lands. This is no doubt a reference to the advance of Muscovy and the capture of Kazan, the Tatar capital, by the Czar Ivan the Terrible in 1552. The Franks too, according to the same authority, are handsome, charming, and serviceable, sometimes indeed excellent, but unlike other slaves they are not willing to become Muslims.[27]

In addition to literary essays and practical advice, there is a considerable body of scholarly literature, providing detailed factual information about the different races of mankind, both inside and outside the Islamic ecumene. The Arab exploration of black Africa, the vast expansion of the slave trade in these lands, and ultimately the spread of Islam, all helped to produce a rich Arabic literature of human geography, which constitutes the most important source of information on tropical Africa in the pre-colonial period. The Arab geographers' descriptions of the homelands from which their slaves were brought throw much light on relationships and attitudes.

7

The Discovery of Africa

Muslim geographers—and to a much lesser extent Muslim historians—have something to say about all these various peoples beyond the frontiers of the Islamic ecumene. About Western Europe—remote and, in their perspective, unimportant—they knew little and cared less, and it was not until Ottoman times that Muslim writers began to pay some attention to European peoples and states.[1] Even then, it is very little. Medieval Muslim writers have rather more to say about the Slavic and Turkic peoples in the Eurasian steppe, immediately to the north of the lands of Islam. But it was with black Africa that the Muslim lands, from Morocco across to Arabia, developed the closest and most intimate relations.[2]

In the earliest Arabic references, black Africans are either Ḥabash or Sūdān, the former designating the Ethiopians and their immediate neighbors in the Horn of Africa, the latter (an Arabic word meaning "black") denoting blacks in general. It sometimes includes Ethiopians, but not Egyptians, Berbers, or other peoples north of the Sahara. Later, after the Arab expansion into Africa, other and more specific terms are added, the commonest being Nūba, Bujja (or Beja), and Zanj. Nūba, "from Nubia," usually designates the Nilotic and sometimes also the Hamitic peoples south of Egypt, that is, roughly in the present area of the republic of the Sudan; the Bujja were nomadic tribes between the Nile and the Red Sea; Zanj, a word of disputed origin, is used specifically of the Bantu-speaking peoples in East Africa south of the Ethiopians and sometimes more loosely of black Africans in general.[3] The term *Bilād al-Sūdān*—"lands of the blacks"—is applied in classical Arabic usage to the whole area of black Africa south of the Sahara, from the Nile to the Atlantic and including such West African black states as Ghana and Songhay. Sometimes it is even extended to the countries of South and Southeast Asia, inhabited by relatively dark-skinned people.

Some authors distinguish carefully between the different groups of black Africans; others tend to lump them together under the general heading of Sūdān, blacks. The Zanj are the least respected; the Ethiopians, the most. The Nūba and Bujja occupy an intermediate position. Some geographical writers distinguish between different African races on grounds of color, noting that some, such as the Ethiopians, are of lighter complexion; others, such as the Zanj, of darker. The term Ifrīqiya, an Arabic borrowing from the Latin "Africa," is used in classical Arabic only of the Maghrib, usually just the eastern Maghrib.

From the ninth century onward, Arab and other Muslim writers provide information about the movement of slaves from the black lands toward the North and the East—across the Red Sea and Indian Ocean to Arabia, Iraq, and Iran, down the Nile to Egypt, and across the Sahara to the slave markets of North and Northwest Africa.

"They export black slaves," says Yaʿqūbī (ninth century), speaking of Zawīla, "belonging to the tribes of Mīra, Zaghāwa, Maruwa, and other black races who are near to them and whom they capture. I hear that the black kings sell blacks without pretext and without war."[4]

"To the Zanj," says Muṭahhar ibn Ṭāhir al-Maqdisī (tenth century), "food and clothing are exported; from them come gold, slaves, and coconuts."[5]

"The Zanj," says Idrīsī (1110–65),

> are in great fear and awe of the Arabs, so much so that when they see an Arab trader or traveler they bow down and treat him with great respect, and say in their language: "Greeting, O people from the land of the dates!" Those who travel to this country steal the children of the Zanj with dates, lure them with dates, and lead them from place to place, until they seize them, take them out of the country, and transport them to their own countries. The Zanj people have great numbers but little gear. The ruler of the island of Kish in the sea of ʿUmān raids the Zanj country with his ships and takes many captives.

In a detailed account of West Africa, he notes that the Moroccan merchants in Takrūr "bring wood, copper, and beads, and take away gold ore and [castrated] slaves."[6] "From this country," says Ibn Baṭṭūta (1304–77), speaking of Tagadda in West Africa, "come excellent slavegirls, eunuchs, and fabrics dyed with saffron." When he left Tagadda for the North, on September 11, 1353, he traveled "with a large caravan which included six hundred women slaves."[7]

Muslim authors sometimes discuss the ethnic origins and native lands of their black slaves. They have some slight information about Nubia, with which arrangements for the regular supply of slaves to Egypt were set up at an early date. About the Zanj they know rather less. Ibn Khurradādhbih (820–912/13), the earliest original Muslim geographer whose work is extant, mentions the Zanj country as one of those from which goods—unspecified, but presumably slaves—reached Aden. He records only two facts about the land of the Zanj: that it is on the Eastern Ocean, and that anyone who goes there will inevitably get the itch.[8] Ibn Qutayba (d. 889) notes that the blacks live on fish and for this reason sharpen their teeth like needles, so that the fish should not stick to them. In another work he observes that the Zanj have the best-smelling mouths of all mankind, even though they do not brush their teeth; this is because they have much saliva.[9]

On the blacks in general, Masʿūdī (d. 956) quotes Galen, who, he says:

> mentions ten specific attributes of the black man, which are all found in him and in no other; frizzy hair, thin eyebrows, broad nostrils, thick lips, pointed teeth, smelly skin, black eyes, furrowed hands and feet, a long penis and great merriment. Galen says that merriment dominates the black man because of his defective brain, whence also the weakness of his intelligence.[10]

This description is repeated, with variations, by later writers. Most geographers speak of the nudity, paganism, cannibalism, and primitive life of the black peoples. Of the neighbors of the Bujja, Maqdisī had heard that

> there is no marriage among them; the child does not know his father, and they eat people—but God knows best. As for the Zanj, they are people of black color, flat noses, kinky hair, and little understanding or intelligence.[11]

A Persian treatise on world geography, written in 982 A.D., devotes barely five out of two hundred pages to the black lands:

> As regards southern countries, all their inhabitants are black on account of the heat of their climate. Most of them go naked. In all their lands and provinces, gold is found. They are people distant from the standards of humanity.

On the Zanj: "Their nature is that of wild animals. They are extremely black." Of Zabaj: "This country and its inhabitants are all like the Zanj, but they are somewhat nearer to humanity." On the Sūdān:

> Most of them go about naked. Egyptian merchants carry there salt, glass and lead, and sell them for the same weight in gold. A group of them wanders in this region of theirs, camping at the places where they find more gold ore. In the southern parts there is no more populous country than this. The merchants steal their children and bring them with them. Then they castrate them, import them into Egypt, and sell them. Among themselves there are people who steal each other's children and sell them to the merchants when the latter arrive.[12]

The attitude to black Africans remains on the whole negative. Some Muslim authors give balanced and factual accounts, based on personal knowledge, of the black kingdoms; a few even write pious treatises to defend the dark peoples against their detractors. Such defense was clearly felt to be necessary, because of the survival of old prejudices.[13] Even the great geographer Idrīsī, in concluding his account of the first climate (geographical zone) with some general remarks on its inhabitants, repeats the old clichés about furrowed feet and stinking sweat and ascribes "lack of knowledge and defective minds" to the black peoples. Their ignorance, he says, is notorious; men of learning and distinction are almost unknown among them, and their kings only acquire what they know about government and justice from the instruction of learned visitors from farther north. The thirteenth-century Persian writer Naṣīr al-Dīn Ṭūsī remarks that the Zanj differ from animals only in that "their two hands are lifted above the ground" and continues, "Many have observed that the ape is more teachable and more intelligent than the Zanjī."[14] A century later, a similar point was made by Ibn Khaldūn. Distinguishing between white slaves and black slaves he remarks:

> Therefore, the Negro nations are, as a rule, submissive to slavery, because [Negroes] have little [that is essentially] human and have attributes that are quite similar to those of dumb animals, as we have stated.[15]

As Muslim power and the Islamic religion advanced farther into black Africa and a succession of black kingdoms became an accepted part of the House of Islam, such extravagant accounts of African manners and customs became less and less frequent.[16] But the perception remained, disputed but widespread, that African Muslims were somehow different from other Muslims and that Africa was a legitimate source of slaves. A unique letter, preserved by an Egyptian historian, vividly illustrates how black African Muslims must have felt. The letter, dated 794 A.H. (= 1391–92 A.D.), was sent by the black king of Bornu, now in northern Nigeria, to the sultan of Egypt. The king, his family, and his people were free Muslims and therefore by Muslim law not enslavable. To strengthen this status, he claims that his tribe was founded by an Arab, of the Prophet's tribe of Quraysh. Yet despite this, Arab tribesmen "have devastated all our land, all the land of Bornu . . . they took free people among us captive, of our kin among Muslims . . . they have taken our people as merchandise." These raiders carried off free women, children, and infirm men. Some they kept as slaves for their own use; the rest they sold to slave dealers in Egypt, Syria, and elsewhere. The king urges the sultan of Egypt to send orders to his governors, judges, and inspectors of markets, to search out these captives and restore them to freedom and Islam.[17]

No answer to this letter has been preserved; and it is unlikely that the sultan of Egypt, whose power did not extend to the Western Sudan, would have been able to do much about it, even had he wished. The enslavement of free Muslims was of course totally forbidden by the Sharīʿa, and from time to time voices were raised, urging the slaveraiders to desist from this offense and to direct their efforts against pagans in other places. But the practice continued, especially in Africa.

8

In Black and White

The Qur'ān gives no countenance to the idea that there are superior and inferior races and that the latter are foredoomed to a subordinate status; the overwhelming majority of Muslim jurists and theologians share this rejection. There are some early traditions, and early juridical opinions and rulings citing them, which assign a privileged status to the Arabs, as against other peoples within the Islamic community. The Caliph ʿUmar is even quoted, improbably, as saying that no Arab could be owned. Some pagan Arabs were in fact enslaved by the early caliphs and even by the Prophet himself, and the idea of Arab exemption from the normal rules regarding enslavement was not approved by later jurists.[1]

Such an opinion did indeed reflect the social realities in the early centuries of the Islamic Empire, created by Arab conquests. By the ninth century, however, this privileged status had for all practical purposes ended. Some jurists, citing early traditions and the Qur'ān itself, totally reject the idea of Arab or any other ethnic privilege. Even those who grant some limited acceptance to the idea, do so on the basis of kinship with the Prophet and reduce it to a kind of social prestige, of limited practical significance. At no time did Muslim theologians or jurists accept the idea that there may be races of mankind predisposed by nature or foredoomed by Providence to the condition of slavery.

Such ideas were, however, known from the heritage of antiquity and found echoes in Muslim writings, the more so when they began to correspond to the changing realities of Muslim society. Aristotle, in his discussion of slavery, had observed that while some are by nature free, others are by nature slaves. For such, the condition of slavery is both "beneficial and just," and a war undertaken to reduce them to that condition is a just war.[2]

This idea, along with others from the same source, was taken up and echoed by a few Muslim Aristotelians.[3] Thus the tenth-century philosopher al-Fārābī lists, among the categories of just war, one the purpose of which is to subjugate and enslave those whose "best and most advantageous status in the world is to serve and be slaves" and who nevertheless refuse to accept slavery.[4] The idea of natural slavery is mentioned, though not developed, by some other Aristotelian philosophers. Al-ʿĀmirī, for example, follows Aristotle in comparing the natural superiority of master to slave with the equally natural superiority of man to woman.[5]

Aristotle does not specify which races he has in mind, merely observing that barbarians are more slavish (*doulikoteroi*) than Greeks, and Asiatics more so than Europeans. That, according to Aristotle, is why they are willing to submit to despotic government—that is, one that rules them as a master (*despotes*) rules his slaves.[6] By the tenth and eleventh centuries, some Muslim philosophers were more specific. The great physician and philosopher Avicenna (980–1037) notes as part of God's providential wisdom that he had placed, in regions of great heat or great cold, peoples who were by their very nature slaves, and incapable of higher things—"for there must be masters and slaves."[7] Such were the Turks and their neighbors in the North and the blacks in Africa. Similar judgments were pronounced by his contemporary, the Ismaili theologian Ḥamīd al-Dīn al-Kirmānī (d. 1021), who was chief of missions of the Fatimid Caliphate in Cairo. In a philosophical work, he dismisses "the Turks, Zanj, Berbers, and their like" as "by their nature" without interest in the pursuit of intellectual knowledge and without desire to understand religious truth.[8]

By this time, the great majority of Muslim slaves were either Turks or blacks, and Aristotle's doctrine of natural slavery, brought up to date, provided a convenient justification of their enslavement.

Another attempt to justify the enslavement of a whole race, this time in religious rather than philosophical terms and restricted to the dark-skinned people of Africa, is the Muslim adaptation of the biblical story of the curse of Ham.[9] In the biblical version (Genesis 9:1–27) the curse is servitude, not blackness, and it falls on Canaan, the youngest son of Ham, and not on his other sons, including Kush, later seen as ancestor of the blacks. The rationale of the story is obvious—the slaves of the Israelites were their near kinsmen the Canaanites, and a religious (i.e., ideological) justification was required for their enslavement, hence the story of the curse of Canaan. The slaves of the Arabs were not Canaanites but blacks—so the curse was transferred to them, and blackness added to servitude as part of the hereditary burden. This story, though widespread, was by no means universally accepted. Ibn Khaldūn and some other Arab writers reject it as absurd, and attribute blackness to climatic and geographical factors. The idea, however, that blackness and slavery are somehow associated, as expressed in this story, was derived less from tradition than from reality.

Such ideas have no place in the writings of Muslim jurists, who unanimously reject the enslavement of free Muslims, of whatever race or origin. Nor did the total identification of blackness with slavery, which occurred in

North and South America, ever take place in the Muslim world. There were always white slaves as well as black ones, and free blacks as well as slaves. Nevertheless, the identification of blackness with certain forms of slavery went very far—and in later centuries white slaves grew increasingly rare.

Already in medieval times it became customary to use different words for black and white slaves. White slaves were normally called *mamlūk,* an Arabic word meaning "owned," while black slaves were called *ʿabd.*[10] In time, the word *ʿabd* ceased to be used of any but black slaves and eventually, in many Arabic dialects, simply came to mean a black man, whether slave or free. This transition from a social to an ethnic meaning is thus the reverse of the semantic development of our own word "slave," which began as the designation of an ethnic group and became a social term. In Western Islam—in North Africa and Spain—the word *khādim,* "servant" (dialectal form, *khadem*) is often specialized to mean "black slave," "slave woman," or "concubine."[11]

It is not only in terminology that black and white slaves were distinguished. For one thing, white slaves, especially females, were more expensive;[12] for another, black slaves were far more severely restricted in their social and occupational mobility. In early times black singers were greatly admired, and some of them won fame and fortune—if not for themselves, then for their trainers and owners. Jāḥiẓ, in his essay on singing girls, mentions an Ethiopian slave girl who was worth 120,000 dinars and brought much profit to her master, in the form of gifts and offerings from aspiring and frustrated admirers.[13] Later, the black musicians seem to have been overtaken by whites. The change is ascribed to the great musician Ibrāhīm al-Mawṣilī (742–804), whose son is quoted as saying: "They used not to train beautiful slave girls to sing, but they used only to train yellow and black girls. The first to teach valuable girls to sing was my father." The price of these girls, he adds, was very much higher.[14]

Ibn Buṭlān, in his handbook, suggests a proper ethnic division of labor for both male and female slaves. As guards of persons and property, he recommends Indians and Nubians; as laborers, servants, and eunuchs, Zanj; as soldiers, Turks and Slavs. On female slaves he goes into somewhat greater detail, discussing their racial attributes, of both body and character, and the different functions for which they are best fitted.[15] In the central Islamic lands, black slaves were most commonly used for domestic and menial purposes, often as eunuchs, sometimes also in economic enterprises, as for example in the gold mines of ʿAllāqī in Upper Egypt (where, according to Yaʿqūbī, "the inhabitants, merchants and others, have black slaves who work the mines"),[16] in the salt mines, and in the copper mines of the Sahara, where both male and female slaves were employed.[17] The most famous were the black slave gangs who toiled in the salt flats of Basra. Their task was to remove and stack the nitrous topsoil, so as to clear the undersoil for cultivation, probably of sugar, and at the same time to extract the saltpeter. Consisting principally of slaves imported from East Africa and numbering some tens of thousands, they lived and worked in conditions of extreme misery. They were fed, we are told, on "a few handfuls" of flour, semolina, and dates.

They rose in several successive rebellions, the most important of which lasted fifteen years, from 868 to 883, and for a while offered a serious threat to the Baghdad Caliphate.[18]

Even religious groups with what some would call radical and progressive ideals seem to have accepted the slavery of the black man as natural. Thus, in the eleventh century we are told that the Carmathians established a kind of republic in eastern Arabia, abolished many of the prescriptions regarding persons and property which conventional Islam imposed—and had a force of thirty thousand black slaves to do the rough work.[19]

Jurists occasionally discuss the status of black Muslim slaves. Muslim law unequivocally forbids the enslavement of free Muslims of whatever race, and was usually obeyed in this. There is, however, evidence that the law was not always strictly enforced to protect Muslim captives from black Africa. A *fatwā* (legal ruling) in a collection of such rulings by Spanish and North African authorities, compiled by a fifteenth-century Moroccan jurist, Aḥmad al-Wansharīsī, is instructive. The question to be decided is whether Ethiopian (i.e., black) slaves professing monotheism and observing religious practices could lawfully be bought and sold. The law is clear. An unbeliever may be enslaved, a Muslim may not; but the adoption of Islam by an unbeliever *after* his enslavement does not automatically set him free. Slavery, says the *fatwā,* is a condition arising from current *or previous* unbelief and persists after conversion, the owner of the slave retaining full property rights. If a group is known to have been converted to Islam, then the taking of slaves from this group is forbidden. However, the existence of a doubt as to whether conversion took place before or after enslavement does not invalidate the ownership or sale of the slave. It is significant that the writer of the *fatwā* discusses the question in relation to black slaves, that he is at some pains to insist that Islam does not necessarily involve freedom, and that he gives the benefit of the doubt not to the slave but to the slaveowner.[20] The problem was clearly not academic. Other sources preserve complaints by black Muslim rulers about "holy wars" launched against them to take captives and by jurists—usually black jurists—at the enslavement of free, black Muslims contrary to law.[21]

The question was discussed at some length by an African jurist, Aḥmad Bābā of Timbuktu (1556–1627), in an answer written for a group of Muslims in the oasis of Tuat. This was a major center of the slave trade, and the good men of Tuat, apparently suffering from scruples of conscience, submitted a number of questions on the legality of the enslavement of blacks. In general, Aḥmad Bābā reaffirms the classical Islamic position. Muslims, and also non-Muslims living under Muslim rule and protection, may in no circumstances be enslaved. Idolators captured in a holy war may lawfully be enslaved, and their slave status is not ended by any subsequent conversion to Islam. Aḥmad Bābā draws his interlocutor's attention to the black tribes farther south, who are still heathens and therefore subject to holy war and enslavement. While thus accepting the legality of enslavement, Aḥmad Bābā discusses and dismisses the story that the black races are condemned to slavery because of God's curse on their presumptive ancestor Ham. "Even assuming," he says, "that

Ham was the ancestor of the blacks, God is too merciful to punish millions of people for the sin of a single individual." Slavery arises not from blackness but from unbelief. All unbelievers, black or white, may be enslaved; no Muslim, black or white, may be enslaved.

Aḥmad Bābā's answers, however, make it clear that many Muslim blacks were in fact being illegally enslaved, and he frankly faces the difficulty of distinguishing between lawful and unlawful slaves. Unlike the Moroccan al-Wansharīsī, however, he places the burden of proof not on the slave but on the slavedealer, who must prove his lawful right of ownership over the slave he offers for sale. To the question, "Can one take the word of an enslaved person?"—to which many jurists say no—Aḥmad Bābā replies with a firm and documented yes.[22]

That this ruling was of little practical effect is shown by a later discussion of the illegal enslavement of black Muslims by the nineteenth-century Moroccan historian Aḥmad ibn Khālid al-Nāṣirī (1834–97).[23] Writing within the context of traditional society, he is nevertheless clearly affected by the new anti-slavery ideas current at the time. Al-Nāṣirī recognizes the legality of the institution of slavery in Muslim law but is appalled by its application. He complains in particular of "a manifest and shocking calamity widespread and established since of old in the lands of the Maghrib—the unlimited enslavement of the blacks, and the importation of many droves of them every year, for sale in the town and country markets of the Maghrib, where men traffic in them like beasts, or worse." This abuse is so old and so deep-rooted, says al-Nāṣirī, that "many of the common people believe that the cause of their enslavement in Holy Law is that they are black of color and imported from those parts." This is, of course, untrue, and al-Nāṣirī swears that "by God's life, this is one of the worst and greatest abominations against religion, because the black people are Muslim people, with the same rights and duties as ourselves." While conceding that heathens may be enslaved, al-Nāṣirī argues that by now a majority or at least a substantial minority of the blacks are Muslims and that since the natural condition of man is freedom, they should be given the benefit of the doubt. The evidence of slavetraders is dismissed as interested and unreliable, and the traders themselves are condemned as "men without morals, virtue, or religion."

Al-Nāṣirī then makes a further point against the legality of the slave trade in blacks:

> Some men of integrity and some others have argued that the blacks today, as in the past, raid each other and kidnap each other's children, stealing them in places remote from their homes and dwellings, in the same way that the Bedouin of the Maghrib raid each other and seize and steal each other's mounts and cattle. They are all Muslims but are led to this by lack of religion and the absence of any restraint. How can any man who is scrupulous about his religion allow himself to buy anything of this kind? How can he permit himself to take their women as concubines and thus risk entering on a legally dubious sexual relationship?

Despite such arguments and despite the decrees in favor of emancipation by Aḥmad Bey of Tunis, the enslavement of blacks and their export to the Mediterranean lands and the Middle East continued and was defended by the increasingly flimsy argument that blacks were idolators and therefore that warfare against them was jihad, or holy war, and the captives were legally liable to enslavement. Since, for a conscientious Muslim, only a jihad could supply legally valid slaves, it was necessary to call every slave raid a jihad. One can understand the anger and anguish of a good Muslim like al-Nāṣirī.

White slaves were rarely used for rough labor and filled higher positions in domestic and administrative employment. Both blacks and whites were used as eunuchs, but the blacks soon predominated. The Caliph al-Amīn (reigned 809–13), it is said, collected them in large numbers and formed separate corps of white and black eunuchs, which he called "the locusts" (*jarādiyya*) and the "ravens" (*ghurābiyya*). An Arabic description of the court of the caliph in Baghdad at the beginning of the tenth century speaks of seven thousand black and four thousand white eunuchs.[24] Later, white eunuchs became rare and costly.

The importation of black slaves into the central Islamic lands, which began at the time of the conquest, continued without interruption until the nineteenth century and in some areas into the twentieth. From time to time, Western travelers give us a glimpse of this traffic. Thus Jeremy Bentham, who sailed from Izmir to Istanbul on a Turkish caïque in November 1785, noted in his diary: "Our crew consists of 15 men besides the Captain: we have 24 passengers on the deck, all Turks; besides 18 young Negresses (slaves) under the hatches."[25]

Between white and black slaves—even where the latter were numerous and powerful—there was for a long time one crucial distinction. Whereas white slaves could become generals, provincial governors, sovereigns, and founders of dynasties, this hardly ever happened with black slaves in the central Islamic lands. In Muslim India, a number of soldiers of African slave origin rose to high office, some even becoming rulers.[26] Elsewhere, their opportunities for advancement were very limited. Only one of them ever became the ruler of a Muslim country outside the black zone—the famous Nubian eunuch Abu'l-Misk Kāfūr, "Musky Camphor," who in the tenth century became regent of Egypt (and a very capable one). Historians clearly regarded this as remarkable, and the great Arab poet al-Mutanabbī found in Kāfūr's blackness a worthy object of satirical abuse. In one of his most famous poems, he bitterly attacks the master of Egypt:

> Whenever a wicked slave assassinates his master
> or betrays him, has he to get his training in Egypt?
> There, the eunuch has become a chieftain of the runaway slaves,
> the free man is enslaved, and the slave is obeyed.
>
> . . . .
>
> The slave is no brother to the godly free man,
>   even though he be born in the clothes of the free.

Do not buy a slave without buying a stick with him,
for slaves are filthy and of scant good.
I never thought I should live to see the day when a
dog would do me evil and be praised into the bargain,
nor did I imagine that true men would have ceased to exist,
and that the like of the father of bounty
would still be here,
and that that negro with his pierced camel's lip
would be obeyed by those cowardly hirelings.

. . . . . .

Who ever taught the eunuch negro nobility? his
"white" people, or his royal ancestors?
or his ear bleeding in the hand of the slave-broker?
or his worth, seeing that for two farthings
he would be rejected?
Wretched Kafur is the most deserving of the base
to be excused in regard to every baseness—
and sometimes excusing is a reproach—
and that is because white stallions are incapable
of gentility, so how about black eunuchs?

In another poem he remarks:

More stupid than a slave or his mate is he who makes
the slave his master.

. . . . . .

One who holds you by his word is unlike one who holds
you in his jail—
The morality of the [black] slave is bounded by his
stinking pudenda and his teeth.
He does not keep his engagements of today, nor remember
what he said yesterday.

. . . . . .

Hope for no good from a man over whose head the
slaver's hand has passed,
And, if you are in doubt about his person or
condition, look to his race.
One who is vile in his coat, was usually vile
in his caul.
He who makes his way beyond his merits, still cannot
get away from his root.[27]

The same limitation of opportunity applies to the emancipated slave. The emancipated white slave was free from any kind of restriction; the emancipated black slave was at most times and places rarely able to rise above the lowest levels. In Umayyad times, we still hear of black poets and singers achieving some sort of social standing, even though they complain of discrimination. In later times, the black poet as a figure in Arabic literature disappears and none of any consequence are reported from the mid-eighth century onward. A few religious figures—saints and scholars—are said to have had black ancestry, but these again are exceptional.[28] What is more important is that the black is almost entirely missing from the positions of wealth, power, and privilege. Medieval authors sometimes attribute this want of achievement by black slaves and freedmen to lack of capacity. The modern observer will recognize the effects of lack of opportunity.

9

Slaves in Arms

The military slave, who bears arms and fights for his owner, was a known but not common figure in antiquity. In the late fifth and early fourth centuries B.C., the city of Athens was policed by a corps of armed Scythian slaves, originally numbering some three hundred, who were the property of the city.[1] Some Roman dignitaries had armed slave bodyguards; some owned gladiators, as men in other times might own gamecocks or racehorses, but in general the Greeks and Romans did not approve of the use of slaves in combatant duties.[2] It was not until the medieval Islamic state that we find military slaves in significant numbers, forming a substantial and eventually predominant component in their armies.

The professional slave soldier, so characteristic of later Islamic empires, was not present in the earliest Islamic regimes. There were indeed slaves who fought in the army of the Prophet, but they were there as Muslims and as loyal followers, not as slaves or professionals. Most of them were freed for their services, and according to an early narrative, when the Prophet appeared before the walls of the Ḥijāz town of Ṭā'if, he sent a crier to announce that any slave who came out and joined him would be free.[3] Abū Muslim, the first military leader of the Abbasid revolution which transformed the Islamic state and society in the mid-eighth century, appealed to slaves to come and join him and offered freedom to those who responded. So many, we are told, answered his call, that he gave them a separate camp and formed them into a separate combat unit.[4] During the great expansion of the Arab armies and the accompanying spread of the Islamic faith in the seventh and early eighth centuries, many of the peoples of the conquered countries were captured, enslaved, converted, and liberated, and great numbers of these joined the armies of Islam. Iranians in the East, Berbers in the West, reinforced the Arab armies and contributed significantly to the further advance of Islam, eastward into

Central Asia and beyond, westward across North Africa and into Spain. These were, however, not slaves but freedmen. Though their status was at first inferior to that of freeborn Arabs, it was certainly not servile, and in time the differences in rank, pay, and status between free and freed soldiers disappeared. As so often, the historiographic tradition foreshortens this development and attributes it to a decree of the Caliph ʿUmar, who is said to have ordered his governors to make the privileges and duties of manumitted and converted recruits "among the red people" the same as those of the Arabs. "What is due to these, is due to those; what is due from these, is due from those."[5] The limitation of this concession to the "red people," a term commonly applied by the Arabs to the Iranians and later extended to their Central Asian neighbors, is surely significant. The recruitment of aliens, that is, non-Arabs and often non-Muslims, was by no means restricted to liberated captives, and the distinction between freed subjects, free mercenaries, and bought barbarian slaves is often tenuous.

In recruiting barbarians from the "martial races" beyond the frontiers into their imperial armies, the Arabs were doing what the Romans and the Chinese had done centuries before them. In the scale of this recruitment, however, and the preponderant role acquired by these recruits in the imperial and eventually metropolitan forces, Muslim rulers went far beyond any precedent. As early as 766 a Christian clergyman writing in Syriac spoke of the "locust swarm" of unconverted barbarians—Sindhis, Alans, Khazars, Turks, and others—who served in the caliph's army.[6] In the course of the ninth century, slave armies appeared all over the Islamic empire. Sometimes, as in North Africa and later Egypt, they were recruited by ambitious governors seeking to create autonomous and hereditary principalities and requiring troops who would be loyal to them against their immediate subjects and their imperial suzerains. Sometimes it was the caliphs themselves who recruited such armies. Such, for example, were the palace guards recruited by the Umayyad Caliph al-Ḥakam in Cordova and the Abbasid Caliph al-Muʿtaṣim in Iraq.[7]

This was a new institution in Islam. The patriarchal caliphs, and their successors for more than a hundred years, had no slave praetorian guards, but were protected in their palace by a small force of free Arabs and, under the early Abbasids, freed soldiers and their descendants from Khurāsān. Within a remarkably short time, the slave palace guard became the norm for Muslim rulers, and rapidly developed into a slave army, serving both to maintain the ruler in his palace and his capital and, for a sultan, to uphold his imperial authority in the provinces. In the East, slave soldiers were recruited mainly among the Turkish and to a lesser extent among the Iranian peoples of the Eurasian steppe and of Central and inner Asia; in the West, from the Berbers of North Africa and from the Slavs of Europe. Some soldiers, particularly in Egypt and North Africa, were brought from among the black peoples farther south. As the frontiers of Islam steadily expanded through conversion and annexation, the periphery was pushed farther and farther away, and the enslaved barbarians came from ever-remoter regions in Asia, Africa, and, to a very limited extent, Europe.

Some of these soldiers were captured in wars, raids, and forays. The more usual practice, however, was for them to be purchased, for money, on the Islamic frontiers. It was in this way that Muslims bought and imported the Central Asian Turks who came to constitute the vast majority of eastern Muslim armies. Captured and sold to the Muslims at a very tender age, they were given a careful and elaborate education and training, not only in the military arts but also in the norms of Islamic civilization. From their ranks were drawn the soldiers, then the officers, and finally the commanders of the armies of Islam. From this it was only a step to the ultimate paradox, the slave kings who ruled in Cairo, in Delhi, and in other capitals. Even the Ottomans, though themselves a freeborn imperial dynasty, relied for their infantry on the celebrated slave corps of Janissaries, and most of the sultans were themselves sons of slave mothers.

Various explanations have been offered for the reliance of Muslim sovereigns on slave armies. An obvious merit of the military slave, for the kings or generals who owned him, was his habit of prompt and unquestioning obedience to orders—a quality less likely to be found among freeborn volunteers or even among conscripts, in the relatively few times and places when conscription was known or feasible before the nineteenth century. Perhaps the most convincing explanation of the growth of the slave armies is the eternal need of autocratic rulers for an armed force which would support and maintain their rule yet neither limit it with intermediate powers nor threaten it with the challenge of opposing loyalties. An army constantly renewed by slaves imported from abroad would form no hereditary nobility; an army manned and commanded by aliens could neither claim nor create any loyalties or bases of support among the local population.

Such soldiers, it was assumed, would have no loyalty but to their masters, that is, to the monarchs who bought and employed them. But their loyalty, all too often, was to the regiment and to its commanders, many of whom ultimately themselves became kings. The mamluk sultans and emirs who ruled Egypt, Syria, and western Arabia for two-and-a-half centuries, until the Ottoman conquest in 1517, rigorously excluded their own freeborn and locally born offspring from the apparatus of political and military power, including even the sultanate itself. They nevertheless succeeded in maintaining their system for centuries. In part, the common bond of mamluk regiments was ethnic. Many regiments, and the quarters which they inhabited, were based on ethnic and even tribal groups. But in the main, the bond was social rather than racial. At a certain stage in his career, the mamluk was emancipated, and, on becoming a freeman, himself bought and owned mamluks who, rather than his physical sons, were his true successors. The most powerful bond and loyalty, within the mamluk system, was that owed by the slave to his master, and, after manumission, by the freedman to his patron.

In the military sense, the slave armies were remarkably effective. In the later Middle Ages, it was the mamluks of Egypt who finally defeated and expelled the Crusaders and halted the Mongol advance across the Middle

East, the Ottoman Janissary infantry who conquered Southeastern Europe. It was in accordance with the logic of the system that the mamluk armies of Egypt consisted mainly of slaves imported from the Turkish and Circassian peoples of the Black Sea area, while the Ottoman Janissaries were recruited mainly from the Slavic and Albanian populations of the Balkans.

Ibn Khaldūn, surely the greatest of all Arab historians, writing in the fourteenth century, saw in the coming of the Turks and in the institution of slavery by which they came, the manifestation of God's providential concern for the safety and survival of the Muslim state and people:

> When the [Abbasid] state was drowned in decadence and luxury . . . and overthrown by the heathen Tatars . . . because the people of the faith had become deficient in energy and reluctant to rally in defense . . . then it was God's benevolence that He rescued the faith by reviving its dying breath and restoring the unity of the Muslims in the Egyptian realms. . . . He did this by sending to the Muslims, from among this Turkish nation and its great and numerous tribes, rulers to defend them and utterly loyal helpers, who were brought . . . to the House of Islam under the rule of slavery, which hides in itself a divine blessing. By means of slavery they learn glory and blessing and are exposed to divine providence; cured by slavery, they enter the Muslim religion with the firm resolve of true believers and yet with nomadic virtues unsullied by debased nature, unadulterated by the filth of pleasure, undefiled by ways of civilized living, and with their ardor unbroken by the profusion of luxury. . . . Thus one intake comes after another and generation follows generation, and Islam rejoices in the benefit which it gains through them, and the branches of the kingdom flourish with the freshness of youth.[8]

Most of the military slaves of Islam were white—Turks and Caucasians in the East, Slavs and other Europeans in the West. Black military slaves were, however, not unknown and indeed at certain periods were of importance. Individual black fighting men, both slaves and free, are mentioned as having participated in raiding and warfare in pre-Islamic and early Islamic times. According to the biographies and histories of the Prophet, there were several blacks, both in his army and in the armies of his pagan enemies. One of them, called Waḥshī, an Ethiopian slave, distinguished himself in the battles against the Prophet at Uḥud and at the Ditch; and later, after the Muslim capture of Mecca, he fought for the Muslims in the wars that followed the death of the Prophet.[9] Black soldiers appear occasionally in early Abbasid times,[10] and after the slave rebellion in southern Iraq, in which blacks displayed terrifying military prowess, they were recruited into the infantry corps of the caliphs in Baghdad. Aḥmad b. Ṭūlūn (d. 884), the first independent ruler of Muslim Egypt, relied very heavily on black slaves, probably Nubians, for his armed forces; at his death he is said to have left, among other possessions, twenty-four thousand white mamluks and forty-five thousand blacks.[11] These were organized in separate corps, and accommodated in separate quarters at the military cantonments.[12] When Khumārawayh, the son and successor of

Aḥmad ibn Ṭūlūn, rode in procession, he was followed, according to a chronicler, by a thousand black guards

> wearing black cloaks and black turbans, so that a watcher could fancy them to be a black sea spreading over the face of the earth, because of the blackness of their color and of their garments. With the glitter of their shields, of the chasing on their swords, and of the helmets under their turbans, they made a really splendid sight.[13]

The black troops were the most faithful supporters of the dynasty, and shared its fate. When the Tulunids were overthrown at the beginning of 905, the restoration of caliphal authority was followed by a massacre of the black infantry and the burning of their quarters:

> Then the cavalry turned against the cantonments of the Tulunid blacks, seized as many of them as they could, and took them to Muḥammad ibn Sulaymān [the new governor sent by the caliph]. He was on horseback, amid his escort. He gave orders to slaughter them, and they were slaughtered in his presence like sheep.[14]

A similar fate befell the black infantry in Baghdad in 930, when they were attacked and massacred by the white cavalry, with the help of other troops and of the populace, and their quarters burned.[15] Thereafter, black soldiers virtually disappear from the armies of the eastern caliphate.

In Egypt, the manpower resources of Nubia were too good to neglect, and the traffic down the Nile continued to provide slaves for military as well as other purposes. Black soldiers served the various rulers of medieval Egypt, and under the Fatimid caliphs of Cairo black regiments, known as *ʿAbīd al-Shirāʾ*, "the slaves by purchase," formed an important part of the military establishment. They were particularly prominent in the mid-eleventh century, during the reign of al-Mustanṣir, when for a while the real ruler of Egypt was the caliph's mother, a Sudanese slave woman of remarkable strength of character. There were frequent clashes between black regiments and those of other races and occasional friction with the civil population. One such incident occurred in 1021, when the Caliph al-Ḥākim sent his black troops against the people of Fusṭāṭ (old Cairo), and the white troops joined forces to defend them. A contemporary chronicler of these events describes an orgy of burning, plunder, and rape.[16] In 1062 and again in 1067 the black troops were defeated by their white colleagues in pitched battles and driven out of Cairo to Upper Egypt. Later they returned, and played a role of some importance under the last Fatimid caliphs.

With the fall of the Fatimids, the black troops again paid the price of their loyalty. Among the most faithful supporters of the Fatimid Caliphate, they were also among the last to resist its overthrow by Saladin, ostensibly the caliph's vizier but in fact the new master of Egypt. By the time of the last Fatimid caliph, al-ʿĀḍid, the blacks had achieved a position of power. The black eunuchs wielded great influence in the palace; the black troops formed a major element in the Fatimid army. It was natural that they should resist the vizier's encroachments. In 1169 Saladin learned of a plot by the caliph's chief black eunuch to remove him, allegedly in collusion with the Crusaders in Palestine. Saladin acted swiftly; the offender was seized and decapitated and replaced in his office by a white eunuch. The other black eunuchs of the caliph's palace were also dismissed. The black troops in Cairo were infuriated by this summary execution of one whom they regarded as their spokesman and defender. Moved, according to a chronicler, by "racial solidarity" (*jinsiyya*),[17] they prepared for battle. In two hot August days, an estimated fifty thousand blacks fought against Saladin's army in the area between the two palaces, of the caliph and the vizier.

Two reasons are given for their defeat. One was their betrayal by the Fatimid Caliph al-ʿĀḍid, whose cause they believed they were defending against the usurping vizier:

> Al-ʿĀḍid had gone up to his belvedere tower, to watch the battle between the palaces. It is said that he ordered the men in the palace to shoot arrows and throw stones at [Saladin's] troops, and they did so. Others say that this was not done by his choice. Shams al-Dawla [Saladin's brother] sent naphtha-throwers to burn down al-ʿĀḍid's belvedere. One of them was about to do this when the door of the belvedere tower opened and out came a caliphal aide, who said: "The Commander of the Faithful greets Shams al-Dawla, and says: 'Beware of the [black] slave dogs! Drive them out of the country!' " The blacks were sustained by the belief that al-ʿĀḍid was pleased with what they did. When they heard this, their strength was sapped, their courage waned, and they fled.[18]

The other reason, it is said, was an attack on their homes. During the battle between the palaces, Saladin sent a detachment to the black quarters, with instructions "to burn them down on their possessions and their children." Learning of this, the blacks tried to break off the battle and return to their families but were caught in the streets and destroyed. This encounter is variously known in Arabic annals as "the Battle of the Blacks" and "the Battle of the Slaves."[19] Though the conflict was not primarily racial, it acquired a racial aspect, which is reflected in some of the verses composed in honor of Saladin's victory. Maqrīzī, in a comment on this episode, complains of the power and arrogance of the blacks:

> If they had a grievance against a vizier, they killed him; and they caused much damage by stretching out their hands against the property and families of the people. When their outrages were many and their misdeeds increased, God destroyed them for their sins.[20]

Sporadic resistance by groups of black soldiers continued, but was finally crushed after a few years. While the white units of the Fatimid army were incorporated by Saladin in his own forces, the blacks were not. The black regiments were disbanded, and black fighting men did not reappear in the armies of Egypt for centuries. Under the mamluk sultans, blacks were employed in the army in a menial role, as servants of the knights.[21] There was a clear distinction between these servants, who were black and slaves, and the knights' orderlies and grooms, who were white and free.

Though black slaves no longer served as soldiers in Egypt, they still fought occasionally—as rebels or rioters. In 1260, during the transition from the Ayyubid to the mamluk sultanate, black stableboys and some others seized horses and weapons, and staged a minor insurrection in Cairo. They proclaimed their allegiance to the Fatimids and followed a religious leader who "incited them to rise against the people of the state; he granted them fiefs and wrote them deeds of assignment."

The end was swift: "When they rebelled during the night, the troops rode in, surrounded them, and shackled them; by morning they were crucified outside the Zuwayla gate."[22]

The same desire among the slaves to emulate the forms and trappings of the mamluk state is expressed in a more striking form in an incident in 1446, when some five hundred slaves, tending their masters' horses in the pasturages outside Cairo, took arms and set up a miniature state and court of their own. One of them was called sultan and was installed on a throne in a carpeted pavilion; others were dignified with the titles of the chief officers of the mamluk court, including the vizier, the commander in chief, and even the governors of Damascus and Aleppo. They raided grain caravans and other traffic and were even willing to buy the freedom of a colleague. They succumbed to internal dissensions. Their "sultan" was challenged by another claimant, and in the ensuing struggles the revolt was suppressed. Many of the slaves were recaptured and the rest fled.[23]

Toward the end of the fifteenth century, black slaves were admitted to units using firearms—a socially despised weapon in the mamluk knightly society. When a sultan tried to show some favor to his black arquebusiers, he provoked violent antagonism from the mamluk knights, which he was not able to resist. In 1498 "a great disturbance occurred in Cairo." The sultan (according to the chronicler) had outraged the mamluks by conferring two boons on a black slave called Farajallah, chief of the firearms personnel in the citadel—first, giving him a white Circassian slave girl from the palace as wife, and second, granting him a short-sleeved tunic, a characteristic garment of the mamluks:

> On beholding this spectacle [says the chronicler] the Royal mamluks expressed their disapproval to the sultan, and they put on their . . . armour . . . and armed themselves with their full equipment. A battle broke out between them and the black slaves, who numbered about five hundred. The black slaves ran away and gathered again in the towers of the citadel and fired at the Royal mamluks. The Royal mamluks marched on them, killing Farajallah and about fifty of the black slaves; the rest fled; two Royal mamluks were killed. Then the emirs and the sultan's maternal uncle, the Great Dawādār, met the sultan and told him: "We disapprove of these acts of yours [and if you persist in them, it

would be better for you to] ride by night in the narrow by-streets and go away together with those black slaves to far-off places!" The sultan answered: "I shall desist from this, and these black slaves will be sold to the Turkmans."[24]

In the Islamic West black slave troops were more frequent, and sometimes even included cavalry—something virtually unknown in the East. The first emir of Cordova, ʿAbd al-Raḥmān I, is said to have kept a large personal guard of black troops; and black military slaves were used, especially to maintain order, by his successors. Black units, probably recruited by purchase via Zawīla in Fezzān (now southern Libya), figure in the armies of the rulers of Tunisia between the ninth and eleventh centuries.[25] Black troops became important from the seventeenth century, after the Moroccan military expansion into the Western Sudan. The Moroccan Sultan Mawlāy Ismāʿīl (1672–1727) had an army of black slaves, said to number 250,000. The nucleus of this army was provided by the conscription or compulsory purchase of all male blacks in Morocco; it was supplemented by levies on the slaves and serfs of the Saharan tribes and slave raids into southern Mauritania. These soldiers were mated with black slave girls, to produce the next generation of male soldiers and female servants. The youngsters began training at ten and were mated at fifteen.[26] After the sultan's death in 1727, a period of anarchic internal struggles followed, which some contemporaries describe as a conflict between blacks and whites. The philosopher David Hume, writing at about the same time, saw such a conflict as absurd and comic, and used it to throw ridicule on all sectarian and factional strife:

> The civil wars which arose some few years ago in Morocco between the *Blacks and Whites,* merely on account of their complexion, are founded on a pleasant difference. We laugh at them; but, I believe, were things rightly examined, we afford much more occasion of ridicule to the Moors. For, what are all the wars of religion, which have prevailed in this polite and knowing part of the world? They are certainly more absurd than the Moorish civil wars. The difference of complexion is a sensible and a real difference; but the controversy about an article of faith, which is utterly absurd and unintelligible, is not a difference in sentiment, but in a few phrases and expressions, which one party accepts of without understanding them, and the other refuses in the same manner. . . . Besides, I do not find that the *Whites* in Morocco ever imposed on the Blacks any necessity of altering their complexion . . . nor have the Blacks been more unreasonable in this particular.[27]

In 1757 a new sultan, Sīdī Muḥammad III, came to the throne. He decided to disband the black troops and rely instead on Arabs. With a promise of royal favor, he induced the blacks to come to Larache with their families and worldly possessions. There he had them surrounded by Arab tribesmen, to whom he gave their possessions as booty and the black soldiers, their wives, and their children as slaves. "I make you a gift," he said, "of these *ʿabīd,* of their children, their horses, their weapons, and all they possess. Share them among you."[28]

Blacks were occasionally recruited into the mamluk forces in Egypt at the end of the eighteenth century. "When the supply [of white slaves] proves insufficient," says a contemporary observer, W. G. Browne, "or many have been expended, black slaves from the interior of Africa are substituted, and if found docile, are armed and accoutred like the rest." This is confirmed by Louis Frank, a medical officer with Bonaparte's expedition to Egypt, who wrote an important memoir on the Negro slave trade in Cairo.[29]

In the nineteenth century, black military slaves reappeared in Egypt in considerable numbers; their recruitment was indeed one of the main purposes of the Egyptian advance up the Nile under Muḥammad ʿAlī Pasha (reigned 1805–49) and his successors. Collected by annual *razzias* (raids) from Darfur and Kordofan, they constituted an important part of the Khedivial armies and incidentally furnished the bulk of the Egyptian expeditionary force which Saʿīd Pasha sent to Mexico in 1863, in support of the French.[30] An English traveler writing in 1825 had this to say about black soldiers in the Egyptian army:

> When the negro troops were first brought down to Alexandria, nothing could exceed their insubordination and wild demeanour; but they learned the military evolutions in half the time of the Arabs; and I always observed they went through the manoeuvres with ten times the adroitness of the others. It is the fashion here, as well as in our colonies, to consider the negroes as the last link in the chain of humanity, between the monkey tribe and man in intellect; and I do not suffer the eloquence of the slave driver to convince me that the negro is so stultified as to be unfit for freedom.[31]

Even in Turkey, liberated black slaves were sometimes recruited into the armed forces, often as a means to prevent their reenslavement. Some of these reached officer rank. A British naval report, dated January 25, 1858, speaks of black marines serving with the Turkish navy:

> They are from the class of freed slaves or slaves abandoned by merchants unable to sell them. There are always many such at Tripoli. I believe the government acquainted the Porte with the embarrassment caused by their numbers and irregularities, and this mode of relief was adopted. Those brought by the *Faizi Bari,* about 70 in number, were on their arrival enrolled as a Black company in the marine corps. They are in exactly the same position with respect to pay, quarters, rations, and clothing as the Turkish marines, and will equally receive their discharge at the expiration of the allotted term of service. They are in short on the books of the navy. They have received very kind treatment here, lodged in warm rooms with charcoal burning in them day and night. A negro Mulazim [lieutenant] and some negro tchiaoushes [sergeants], already in the service have been appointed to look after and instruct them. They have drilled in the manual exercise in their warm quarters, and have not been set to do any duty on account of the weather. They should not have been sent here in winter. Those among them unwell on their arrival were sent at once to the naval hospital. Two only have died of the whole number. The men in the barracks are healthy and appear contented. No amount of ingenuity can conjure up any connexion between their condition and the condition of slavery.[32]

While the slave in arms was, with few exceptions, an Islamic innovation, the slave in authority dates back to remote antiquity. Already in Sumerian times, kings appointed slaves to positions of prestige and even power—or, perhaps more accurately, treated certain of their court functionaries as royal slaves. Different words were used to denote such privileged slaves, distinct from those applied to the menial and laboring generality. Under the Abbasid caliphs and under later Muslim dynasties, men of slave origin, usually but not always manumitted, figured prominently in the royal entourage. The system of court slavery reached its final and fullest development in the Ottoman Empire, where virtually all the servants of the state, both civil and military, had the status of *kul,*[33] "slave," of the Gate, that is, of the sultan. The only exceptions were the members of the religious establishment. The Ottoman *kul* was not a slave in terms of Islamic law, and was free from most of the restraints imposed on slaves in such matters as marriage, property, and legal responsibility. He was, however, subject to the arbitrary power of the sultan, who was free to dispose of his assets, his person, and his life in ways not permitted by the law in relation to free- or freedmen. This perception of the status of political officeholders and their relationship to the supreme sovereign power was of course by no means limited to the Ottoman Empire, or indeed to the Islamic world.

10

The Nineteenth Century and After

From the late eighteenth century onward there are numerous accounts, by contemporary, mostly European, observers, of the processes by which African slaves were caught, transported, and sold in the markets of the Middle East and North Africa.[1] A Tunisian traveler who visited Darfur at the beginning of the nineteenth century even offers an otherwise unconcerned story of farms where blacks were raised for sale:

> Certain rich people living in the town have installed these blacks [from the neighboring mountains] on their farms, to have them reproduce, and, as we sell sheep and cattle, so they, every year, sell those of their children that are ready for this. There are some of them who own five or six hundred male and female slaves, and merchants come to them at all times, to buy male and female slaves chosen to be sold.[2]

This new account probably reflects an expansion of the trade, due to events farther north. The establishment of Russian domination in Eastern Europe and the Russian annexation of the Crimea in 1783 had finally ended the profitable trade of the Tatars, who for centuries had reaped an annual harvest of slaves from the villages of the Ukraine and adjoining lands and exported their crop to the slave markets of Istanbul and other Ottoman cities. The once-plentiful supply of white slaves from Central and Western Europe had long since dwindled to a mere trickle; and after the Russian annexation of the Caucasian lands circa 1801–28, the last remaining source of white slaves for the Islamic world was reduced and finally stopped.[3] Deprived of their Georgians and Circassians, the Muslim states turned elsewhere, and a large-scale revival of slaving in black Africa took place. This was furthered by the Egyptian advance up the Nile at the time of Muḥammad ʿAlī Pasha.

The classical routes, developed in medieval times, lay from West Africa (Guinea, from the Berber word *igginaw* [pl. *gnawa*] meaning "black") across the Sahara to Morocco, Algeria, and Tunisia; from the Sudan down the Nile or through the desert to Egypt; and from East Africa across the Red Sea and Indian Ocean to Arabia, Iraq, Iran, and beyond. Other, later routes led from Kano via Agades and Ghadames to Tripoli, and from Waday and Darfur via Borku and Tibesti to Kufra and Cyrenaica.

With the growth of European influence in Egypt and the Maghrib and the involvement of the Ottoman government in the attempt to suppress the traffic in black slaves, those routes and markets which were remote from scrutiny acquired a new importance. One was in the country which is now called Libya. Tripoli and Benghazi became major centers of the slave trade, drawing their supplies from Chad and sometimes as far as Nigeria, and exporting them to the Ottoman provinces in Europe as well as Asia.[4] Often these slaves endured great hardship in the course of the journey from their homes to their destinations. A Turkish letter of November 1849, sent by the reforming Grand Vezir Mustafa Reshid Pasha to the Ottoman governor of Tripoli, refers to the death by thirst of sixteen hundred black slaves, on their way from Bornu to Fezzan in southern Libya: "While our Holy Law permits slavery, it requires that slaves be treated with fatherly care, and those who act in a contrary manner will be condemned by God." The governor was ordered to punish the guilty slavedealers and to ensure that such disasters did not recur. From British consular reports of the late nineteenth century, it is clear that this traffic, and the suffering it entailed, continued.[5] As late as 1912, a Turkish officer serving against the Italians in Tripolitania, noted in his diary:

> A special embassy from the Grand Senussi Sidi Ahmad Sharif is on its way, to bring the Grand Senussi's greetings and gifts: two negresses, ivory, etc. Heavens, what shall I do with the black ladies? He is also sending me his own gun, which he has blessed.[6]

The officer was Enver Bey, later, as Enver Pasha, the Defense Minister of the last Young Turk government in Istanbul. The "Grand Senussi" was the chief of the Sanūsiyya, the dominant Muslim religious order in Libya.

Another important center of the trade was the Ḥijāz, which was exempt from the Ottoman decrees prohibiting or restricting the traffic in African slaves[7] and was not, therefore, subject to restraint or supervision. This gave a new role to the slave market of Mecca. Slaves were imported to the Ḥijāz by sea from East Africa and sent from there to the North and even to Egypt.[8] In a dispatch dated March 17, 1877, the British vice-consul in Damascus, who had been instructed to use his best efforts to prevent this traffic, reported:

> Having brought to the notice of the new Governor General, Zia Pasha, the practice of importing African slaves from the markets of Mecca, with the

> [Pilgrim] Caravan, for sale in Syria, His Excellency informed me that he had already given very strict orders to prevent such abuses.
>
> His Excellency's orders have not, however, met with the success which he stated to me he expected, as slaves were brought as usual.[9]

A third route, by which slaves were exported from the Sudan, both down the Nile to Egypt and across the Red Sea to Arabia, was one of the oldest of all. It was briefly suppressed, thanks to British and Egyptian initiatives in the late seventies and early eighties in the nineteenth century, partially restored with the success of the Mahdist revolt, and suppressed again after the Anglo-Egyptian reconquest in 1896–98.[10]

The main purpose for which blacks were imported was domestic service. A certain number of free blacks also found employment, and in Arabia they could rise to important positions. In Egypt their role was usually humble. At the end of the eighteenth century, W. G. Browne noted that in Cairo "exclusively of negro slaves in every house, there are free blacks from Nubia, who act as porters at the gates of the rich, and sometimes sell *bouza* and eatables."[11] Black slaves for domestic use were very common during the nineteenth century in Egypt, in Turkey, and in the other Ottoman lands; and some survivors can still be met in these countries. The Nubian porter, servant, or hawker remains a familiar figure in Egypt to this day. African women were often kept as concubines, since only the wealthy could afford Circassian or other white slaves. Abyssinians—darker than whites, but lighter than blacks—occupied an intermediate position, as Edward Lane, who was in Egypt between 1833 and 1835, explains:

> The hareem may consist, first, of a wife, or wives (to the number of four); secondly, of female slaves, some of whom, namely, white and (as they are commonly called) Abyssinian (but more properly Galla) slaves, are generally concubines and others (the black slaves) kept merely for servile offices, as cooking, waiting upon the ladies, &c; thirdly, of female free servants, who are, in no case, concubines, or not legitimately so. The male dependents may consist of white and of black slaves, and free servants; but are mostly of the last-mentioned class. Very few of the Egyptians avail themselves of the licence, which their religion allows them, of having four wives; and still smaller is the number of those who have two or more wives, and concubines besides. Even most of those men who have but one wife are content, for the sake of domestic peace, if for no other reason, to remain without a concubine-slave: but some prefer the possession of an Abyssinian slave to the more expensive maintenance of a wife; and keep a black slave-girl, or an Egyptian female servant, to wait upon her, to clean and keep in order the apartments of the hareem, and to cook. . . .
>
> The white female slaves are mostly in the possession of wealthy Turks. The concubine-slaves in the houses of Egyptians of the higher and middle classes are, generally, what are termed "Habasheeyehs," that is, Abyssinians, of a deep brown or bronze complexion. In their features, as well as their complexions, they appear to be an intermediate race between the negroes and white people: but the difference between them and either of the above-mentioned

> races is considerable. They themselves, however, think that they differ so little from the white people that they cannot be persuaded to act as servants, with due obedience, to their master's wives; and the black (or negro) slave-girl feels exactly in the same manner towards the Abyssinian, but is perfectly willing to serve the white ladies. . . . Most of them [the Abyssinians] are handsome. The average price of one of these girls is from ten to fifteen pounds sterling, if moderately handsome; but this is only about half the sum that used to be given for one a few years ago. They are much esteemed by the voluptuaries of Egypt; but are of delicate constitution: many of them die, in this country, from consumption. The price of a white slave-girl is usually from treble to tenfold that of an Abyssinian; and the price of a black girl, about half or two-thirds, or considerably more if well instructed in the art of cookery. The black slaves are generally employed as menials.[12]

A similar distinction between true blacks and Abyssinians was noted by several travelers in Arabia. The same point is made by Arnold Kemball, British assistant resident in the Persian Gulf, in a report on the African slave trade dated July 8, 1842. In the former group,

> the Men are employed in all hard and out door work, the women in cooking, bringing water, etc. and but very rarely as concubines except by the poorer and lower classes.

As to the Abyssinians,

> Slaves of both sexes are at all times much cared for well clothed and well fed. The Males are early sent to school and having learnt to read and write are employed in the performance of house duties . . . and very frequently if intelligent in the most trustworthy situations as supercargos of ships, stewards and superintendents.
>
> The Females are most generally retained as concubines or employed in the lightest duties as attendants in Harems. . . .
>
> Nubian and Hubshee [Abyssinian] Eunuchs are very high priced and only to be seen in the Service of the King, Nobles and very rich Merchants.[13]

Eunuchs were in fact required in considerable numbers, in many countries, for households from the palace downward. They were also employed in the service of mosques. By a custom established in the late Middle Ages which continued into the twentieth century, the custodians of the tomb of the Prophet in Medina were eunuchs, mostly black, recruited by purchase at an early age and groomed for their sacred duties, which gave them an almost priestly status.[14]

In earlier times eunuchs had been recruited from both white and black slaves, and the Ottoman palace establishment, for example, had included separate corps of black and white eunuchs, each with its own chief. From the sixteenth century onward, the white eunuchs in the palace declined both in numbers and in influence. The black eunuchs increased correspondingly, and their chief, known as the *Kızlar Agası,* the "Aga of the Girls," was one of the most powerful figures at the Ottoman court. The corps of eunuchs was virtually the only route by which a black could attain to high office.[15]

Most eunuchs, of course, remained in humble employment.[16] By the nineteenth century they were recruited overwhelmingly from Africa. According to Louis Frank, writing in 1802, between one and two hundred African boys were castrated every year at Abu Tig in Upper Egypt, on the slave caravan route from the Sudan to Cairo. The victims were usually boys between eight and ten years old—never older. A eunuch, he notes, could be sold at double the price of an ordinary Negro, "and it is this increase in price which determines the owners, or rather usurpers, to have some of these wretches mutilated."[17]

Rather more detail is given by the Swiss Arabist J. L. Burckhardt, who traveled extensively in Upper Egypt and the Sudan in 1813 and 1814. He found two places where slaves were mutilated in this way. The less important of the two was at a place west of Darfur, from which a few eunuchs went to Egypt and the remainder were "sent as presents by the Negro sovereigns to the great mosques at Mekka and Medina, by the way of Souakin." The main center was at Zāwiyat al-Dayr, a predominantly Coptic village near Asyut (Siout) in Upper Egypt. Here, says Burckhardt, was

> the great *manufactory* which supplies all European, and the greater part of Asiatic Turkey with these guardians of female virtue. . . . The operators, during my stay in that part of the country, were two Coptic monks, who were said to excel all their predecessors in dexterity, and who had a house in which the victims were received. Their profession is held in contempt even by the vilest Egyptians; but they are protected by the government, to which they pay an annual tax; and the great profits which accrue to the owners of the slaves in consequence of their undergoing this cruel operation, tempts them to consent to an act which many of them in their hearts abhor. The operation itself, however extraordinary it may appear, very seldom proves fatal. I know certainly, that of sixty boys upon whom it was performed in the autumn of 1813, only two died; and every person whom I questioned on the subject in Siout, assured me that even this was above the usual proportion, the deaths being seldom more than two in a hundred. As the greater number undergo the operation immediately after the arrival of the Darfour and Sennaar caravans from Siout, I had no opportunity of witnessing it but it has been described to me by several persons who have often seen it performed. The boys chosen are between the age of eight and twelve years, for at a more advanced age, there is a great risk of its proving fatal.
>
> . . . A youth on whom this operation has been successfully performed is worth one thousand piastres at Siout; he had probably cost his master, a few weeks before, about three hundred; and the Copt is paid from forty-five to sixty for his operation. This enormous profit stifles every sentiment of mercy which the traders might otherwise entertain. About one hundred and fifty eunuchs are made annually. Two years ago, Mohammed Aly Pasha caused two hundred young Darfour slaves to be mutilated, whom he sent as a present to the Grand Signor. The custom of keeping eunuchs has greatly diminished in Egypt, as well as in Syria. In the former country, except in the harems of the

> Pasha and his sons, I do not think that more than three hundred could be found; and they are still more uncommon in Syria. In these countries there is great danger in the display of wealth; and the individual who keeps so many female slaves as to require an eunuch for their guardian, becomes a tempting object to the rapacity of the government. White eunuchs are extremely rare in the Turkish dominions.[18]

Later, castration was forbidden on Egyptian soil, and eunuchs were bought ready-made from the Sudan.

Kemball's indication that African slaves were used for "hard and out door work" as well as the more commonly cited domestic tasks is confirmed in other sources and dates back to early times. Travel accounts—and more particularly consular reports—sent at the time of the British anti-slavery campaign, suggest the wide use of slave labor in agriculture and construction.[19] In nineteenth-century Egypt, African slaves were imported for economic use, chiefly agricultural. Slave gangs were employed in sugar plantations and on irrigation works; the boom in Egyptian cotton during the American Civil War enabled newly prosperous Egyptian farmers to spend "some of their profits in the purchase of slaves to help them in the cultivation of their lands."[20]

Most of the known black slaves were domestic and lived as part of a household. On the evidence of European travelers, they suffered terribly at the hands and under the lash of slavers and slavedealers from capture until final sale but were well treated by their urban masters.

The drying up of the sources of white slaves, while greatly increasing the depredations of the slaveraiders in Africa, also brought some benefit to those black slaves who survived their capture and transportation and reached their destinations. In the absence of white slaves, black slaves were increasingly given tasks and positions which were previously the preserve of whites, and acquitted themselves to the satisfaction of their masters. In the course of the nineteenth century, black slaves—and more frequently black freedmen—are found occupying important positions and often exercising great power. This occurs quite frequently in Arabia, much less frequently in other parts of the Middle East and North Africa.

11

Abolition

In the course of the nineteenth century the revulsion against slavery, which gave rise to a strong abolitionist movement in England, and later in other Western countries, began to affect the Islamic lands. What was involved was not, initially, the abolition of the institution of slavery but its alleviation and in particular the restriction and ultimately the elimination of the slave trade. Islamic law, in contrast to the ancient and colonial systems, accords the slave a certain legal status and assigns obligations as well as rights to the slaveowner. The manumission of slaves, though recommended as a meritorious act, is not required, and the institution of slavery not only is recognized but is elaborately regulated by Sharīʿa law. Perhaps for this very reason the position of the domestic slave in Muslim society was in most respects better than in either classical antiquity or the nineteenth-century Americas.

While, however, the life of the slave in Muslim society was no worse, and in some ways was better, than that of the free poor, the processes of acquisition and transportation often imposed appalling hardships. It was these which drew the main attention of European opponents of slavery, and it was to the elimination of this traffic, particularly in Africa, that their main efforts were directed.

The abolition of slavery itself would hardly have been possible. From a Muslim point of view, to forbid what God permits is almost as great an offense as to permit what God forbids[1]—and slavery was authorized and regulated by the holy law. More specifically, it formed part of the law of personal status, the central core of social usage, which remained intact and effective even when other sections of the holy law, dealing with civil, criminal, and similar matters, were tacitly or even openly modified and replaced by modern codes. It was from conservative religious quarters and notably from the holy cities of Mecca and Medina that the strongest resistance to the proposed reforms came. The emergence of the holy men and the holy places as the last-ditch defenders of slavery against reform is only an apparent paradox. They were upholding an institution sanctified by scripture, law, and tradition and one which in their eyes was necessary to the maintenance of the social structure of Muslim life.

The gradual reduction and eventual elimination of slavery were accomplished in most Muslim countries during the nineteenth and twentieth centuries, with some difference for whites and blacks. Chattel slavery was abolished by law in most of the independent Muslim states of the Middle East at various dates between the two World Wars; in 1962 it was abolished by the newly established republican regime in Yemen, and a few weeks later by royal decree in Saudi Arabia. In Iran, it had formally been outlawed by the constitution of 1906, though some subsequent legislation was needed to give this effect. The last to enact legal abolition appears to have been Mauritania, which took this step in 1980. There are persistent reports that despite these legal measures, slavery, sometimes voluntary, continues in several countries.[2]

The initial impetus for abolition had come from Europe, and for some time progress in this matter was due almost entirely to European urging and action. In the British, French, Dutch, and Russian Empires—in that order—general abolition had been imposed by the imperial authorities. Britain also undertook, by diplomatic pressure supported by naval power, to suppress the slave trade from East Africa to the Middle East and exacted decrees to this end from the sultan of Turkey, the shah of Persia, and the khedive of Egypt, as well as from a number of local rulers in Africa and Arabia.

The first Muslim ruler to order the emancipation of black slaves was the bey of Tunis, who in January 1846 decreed that a deed of enfranchisement should be given to every slave who desired it. Among the reasons for this action, he notes the uncertainty among Muslim jurists concerning the legal basis for "the state of slavery into which the black races have fallen" and, significantly, the need to prevent the black slaves "from seeking the protection of foreign authorities."[3] The abolition of black slavery was completed after the French occupation.

In Turkey, the most important surviving independent Muslim state, the process of emancipation seems to have begun in 1830.[4] In that year a firman was issued, ordering the emancipation of slaves of Christian origin, who had kept to their religion. This was a kind of amnesty for Greek and other Christian subjects of the Porte who had been reduced to slavery as a punishment for participating in the recent rebellions. Those who had become Muslims were excluded from this emancipation and remained the property of their owners.[5]

The overwhelming majority of white slaves, both Christian and Muslim, came from the Caucasian lands. Though the supply was much reduced after the Russian conquest, slaves from these lands continued to arrive in the Ottoman Empire either overland or by ship to the Turkish Black Sea ports. Their movement and subsequent fate were beyond the range of influence or of interference of the Western powers and were an exclusively Ottoman concern. It was thus almost entirely on Ottoman initiative, determined by internal circumstances and pressures, that the Ottoman state undertook, by due process of law, a very substantial improvement in their condition, amounting ultimately to the effective—even if not the legal—abolition of their servile status. Orders against the traffic in white slaves from Georgia and Circassia were issued in 1854 and 1855 and were in general put into effect.[6]

In 1847 the British were able to win some concessions from the Ottoman government about black slaves; and in 1857 they obtained a major Ottoman firman, prohibiting the traffic in black slaves throughout the empire, with the exception of the Ḥijāz.[7]

The reasons for this exception are of some interest. By early 1855, reports were reaching the Ḥijāz of current and impending Ottoman measures against the slave trade. The alarm caused by the limitation of the supply of white slaves from the Caucasus and the increasingly severe restriction of the importation of black slaves from Africa was heightened by news of an order from the governor of Suez, acting on instruction from the capital, that slaves brought from the Ḥijāz to Egypt should be sent back. On April 1, 1855, a group of prominent merchants in Jedda addressed a letter to the leading members of the ulema as well as to the sharif of Mecca expressing their concern. They referred with disapproval to the steps which had already been taken and quoted a report that a general ban on the slave trade would soon be imposed throughout the empire, together with other pernicious and Christian-inspired changes such as the emancipation of women and the toleration of religiously mixed marriages. This ban, with the whole program of reform of which it was alleged to be a part, was condemned by the writers of the letter as anti-Islamic, the more so since all the black slaves imported from Africa embraced the Muslim religion.

The letter caused some excitement in Mecca and may indeed have been instigated by its ruler, the Sharīf ʿAbd al-Muṭṭalib. It provided an occasion for him to consult with the chief of the ulema of Mecca, Shaykh Jamāl. According to an Ottoman source, the sharīf told the shaykh that the Crimean War, then in progress, would mean the doom of the Ottoman Empire whichever way it ended. In any case, the Turks had become apostates from Islam, and this was an opportunity to rid the holy cities of their domination. The suppression of the slave trade, he is quoted as saying, would be a good pretext.

The crisis came a few months later when the governor of the Ḥijāz sent an order to the district governor of Mecca prohibiting the trade in slaves. The district governor was instructed to read the order aloud at the Sharīʿa court of Mecca in the presence of the ulema and the sharifs. This took place on October 30, 1855, and the audience declared their readiness to obey.

This was the moment for which the sharīf had been waiting. On his instructions, Shaykh Jamāl issued a *fatwā* denouncing the ban on the slave trade as contrary to the holy law of Islam. Because of this anti-Islamic act, he said, together with such other anti-Islamic actions as allowing women to initiate divorce proceedings and to move around unveiled, the Turks had become apostates and heathens. It was lawful to kill them without incurring criminal penalties or bloodwit, and to enslave their children.

> The Turks have become renegades. It is obligatory to make war against them and against those who follow them. Those who are with us are for heaven and those who are with them are for hell. Their blood is lawful and their goods are licit.[8]

The *fatwā* produced the desired effect. The Ottoman authorities in the holy cities were attacked by local leaders and populace, and the qadi—an Ottoman appointee—was also compelled to sign a declaration condemning the ban on the slave trade. Ottoman soldiers were set upon all over Mecca as were also some foreign protected persons. A holy war was proclaimed against the Ottomans, and the revolt began.

By June of the following year, the revolt had been completely crushed. The sultan's government had, however, noted the warning, and took steps to forestall a secession of the Ottoman south. In the ban on the trade in black slaves promulgated in 1857, the province of the Ḥijāz was exempted. The Sharif ʿAbd al-Muṭṭalib was in due course reappointed, and his continued presence in the Ḥijāz encouraged the slavetraders to ignore the anti-slaving laws and to shift their trade to that area.

The actual enforcement of the ban of 1857 was no easy matter, and despite the efforts of both the Ottoman authorities and the British navy, the traffic continued. It now tended to concentrate in two main areas. One of these was the Red Sea, where the exemption of the Ḥijāz from the Ottoman ban on the slave trade gave the slavetraders a secure base which they lacked elsewhere; the other was Libya, which, after the establishment of British rule in Egypt and French rule in Tunisia and Algeria, was the only part of Ottoman Africa not subject to foreign control. During the third quarter of the nineteenth century, a substantial proportion of the export of slaves from black Africa to the Ottoman lands passed through the ports of Tripoli and later Benghazi. Here, too, great efforts were made to stop the trade in blacks, and when slaves were detected they were promptly freed. This created another problem, since the freed slaves were in urgent need of food and shelter and also of protection against their former owners, seeking to reenslave them. The care of freed slaves was a continuing concern of the Ottoman authorities, who took measures of various kinds to meet these needs. On several occasions, the government of Istanbul sent orders to Benghazi instructing Turkish officials there to transfer freed black slaves to Istanbul or Izmir, where the men were to be drafted into the army or navy and the women placed as domestic servants.

The other major center was Arabia. Thanks to the exemption from the ban on the slave trade, the flow of slaves from Africa into Arabia and through the Gulf into Iran continued for a long time. Apart from commercial channels, the supply was augmented through the practice by which a wealthy pilgrim brought a retinue of slaves from his own country and sold them one by one—as a kind of traveler's check[9]—to pay the expenses of the pilgrimage. In time the Red Sea trade dwindled as a result of the wars in the Sudan and in Ethiopia. The extension of British, French, and Italian control around the coasts of the Horn of Africa deprived the slavetraders of their main ports of embarkation. The British occupation of Egypt in 1882 and later the Anglo-Egyptian control of the Sudan and the consequent suppression of the slaveraiders further hampered the traffic by cutting off one of the main sources of supply. In spite of the reconquest of the Sudan and all the efforts by Turkish, Egyptian, British, French, and Italian authorities, the traffic continued into modern times. From the 1890s onward, however, the slave trade, though it remained active, was of necessity clandestine.

By the end of the nineteenth century, white slavery had, apart from the Arabian peninsula, virtually disappeared, and black slavery had been reduced to a mere fraction of its former dimensions. The capture, sale, and transportation of blacks from Africa to Arabia and Iran continued, however, albeit on a much reduced scale, at least until the mid-twentieth century.[10]

British efforts to end the slave trade in Arabia and elsewhere were by no means universally approved. They were, of course, resented and resisted by those immediately affected, the slaveraiders and slavedealers. They were also criticized by other, less-interested parties. The famous Dutch orientalist Snouck Hurgronje, who visited Mecca in 1885, complained of the "undeserved applause" given to British measures against the slave trade, and to the "fantasies" which inspired them. In their place, he offered what he called a "sober reality." According to Snouck,

> public opinion in Europe has been misled concerning Muslim slavery by a confusion between American and Oriental conditions. . . . As things are now, for most of the slaves their abduction was a blessing. . . . They themselves are convinced, that it was slavery that first made human beings of them. Concubines, specifically Abyssinians, are for various reasons more highly esteemed by the Meccans than their free wives; the practice is, by both religion and custom, recognized as fully legal. . . . Their bond with their owner is firmer than the easily dissolvable Muslim marriage. All in all, since I know the situation, the anti-slavery campaign is, for me, in the highest degree repugnant.[11]

Snouck quotes with approval from some earlier travelers who defend the enslavement of blacks in Arabia and condemn British efforts to free them, sometimes on frankly racist grounds. One such was the Englishman J. F. Keane, who visited Arabia in 1881. Using arguments familiar from other places and times, he observes that

> the Negro is to be found here [in Arabia] in his proper place, an easily-managed, useful worker. The Negroes are the porters, water-carriers, and performers of most of the real labour in Meccah. Happy, healthy, well-fed, well-clothed (as such things go in Meccah), they are slaves, proud of their masters, in a country where a slave is "honoured only after his master." Slavery in the East has an elevating influence over thousands of human beings, and but for it hundreds of thousands of souls must pass their existence in this world as wild savages, little better than animals; it, at least, makes *men* of them, *useful men* too, sometimes

> even *superior men*. Could the Arab slave-trade be carried on with safety, it might be executed more humanely; and it would, philanthropically speaking, do good to many of the human race. . . . While every settled town under Turkish or native rule in all wide Arabia has a slave market to be stocked, our greatest efforts can but increase the demand and raise the markets. Witness: a strong male adult might be bought for $40.00 four years ago in Meccah, and the same will now fetch $60.00. Were our cruisers doubled, the weekly landing of slaves among the creeks and reefs along the coast of the Hejaz could not be prevented. . . . That there are evils in Arab slavery I do not pretend to deny, though not affecting the Negro, once a slave. The exacting slave-driver is a character wholly unknown in the East, and the slave is protected from the caprice of any cruel master in that he is transferable and of money value. The man who would abuse or injure his slave would maim and willfully deteriorate the value of his horse. Whatever the Arab may not know, he most assuredly knows what is to his own immediate interest better than that. And the Negro himself . . . may through this medium be raised from a savage, existing only for the moment . . . to a profitable member of society, a strong tractable worker, the position Nature seems to have made him to occupy.[12]

Similar views were expressed by an Austrian, Ludwig Stross, who visited Arabia in 1886. Stross begins by agreeing that slavery "as such" is indefensible:

> That whole Negro villages are burned, all the men killed, and their women and children are taken on months-long terrible marches finally to be offered as merchandise in markets and distant lands, must appear to us as an injustice that cries to heaven.

Nevertheless, he continues "it is at the very least dubious" whether it is a good work to insist on freeing the black slave when he has already been taken from his home. In Stross's view, slavery is so deep-rooted, and the slave trade so extensive in Africa and the Arab lands, that to uproot it is impossible and merely to free those blacks who are already enslaved and on their way to their destination does more harm than good.

> The liberated Negroes will not work even for money. For them freedom means their native idleness. They form a proletariat, than which nothing worse can be found.
>
> The theory of human rights and self-determination certainly sounds very fine, but in such cases can hardly find its proper application.
>
> I would rather compare the Negroes with children, who must be made to do their stint.
>
> As long as the Negroes stay in their homelands, no one can object if they idle away their lives in their own way. But in fact they have been brought, by force of circumstances, into other lands and other conditions. Since one cannot prevent their coming, however unwillingly, one should also not prevent their being made to work.[13]

Like almost all the other European travelers, Stross condemns the horrors of the abduction and transportation of the slaves, which he describes in some detail; but he insists that once a slave

> has arrived and is in firm hands, he is usually well cared for. The conditions of slavery in the Orient have nothing in common with those which arose earlier in North America and Brazil. The slave is, for the Mohammedan, a member of the family and is almost without exception well treated. Mistreatments are rare and are usually richly deserved. . . . As regards work, as a rule only very reasonable demands are made of the slaves; and one may safely assume that a Negro would have to work very much harder in order to earn his living as a free man. . . . Often liberated slaves are the heirs of their masters and continue their businesses. In Jedda and Mecca I know many liberated slaves who are respected merchants.
>
> It will thus be seen that slavery in the Orient, though it has many shadowy sides, has nothing to do with the sort of conditions described for lovers of sentimental reading in *Uncle Tom's Cabin.*

Most observers, however, were less willing to be convinced by the apologetics of slavery; and in time virtually all civilized governments, including that of the Ottoman Empire, joined in the effort to suppress the slave trade.

An obvious question, since so many blacks entered the central lands over so long a period, is why they have left so little trace.[14] There is nothing in the Arab, Persian, and Turkish lands that resembles the great black and mulatto populations of North and South America. One reason is obviously the high proportion of eunuchs among black males entering the Islamic lands. Another is the high death rate and low birth rate among black slaves in North Africa and the Middle East. In about 1810, Louis Frank observed in Tunisia that most black children died in infancy, and that infinitesimally few reached the age of manhood.[15] A British observer in Egypt, some thirty years later, found conditions even worse:

> The mortality among the slaves in Egypt is frightful,—when the epidemical plague visits the country, they are swept away in immense multitudes, and they are the earliest victims of almost every other domineering disease. I have heard it estimated that five or six years are sufficient to carry off a generation of slaves, at the end of which time the whole has to be replenished. This is one of the causes of their low market-value. When they marry, their descendants seldom live; in fact, the laws of nature seem to repel the establishment of hereditary slavery.[16]

Concubinage at higher, and intermarriage at lower, social levels seem to have taken place but must have been on a rather limited scale and, probably for social more than biological reasons, produced little effect. Even now, members of the comparatively small number of recognizably black families in the Middle East tend on the whole to marry among their own kind.[17]

12

Equality and Marriage

The voice of Islamic piety on miscegenation is clear and unequivocal—there are no superior and inferior races and therefore no bar to racial intermarriage. In practice, however, this pious doctrine is frequently disregarded or even overruled. Marriage is regulated by the holy law of Islam and is indeed the only important issue on which questions of race and color become the concern of the law. This concern arises under the legal doctrine of *Kafā'a,* which might be roughly translated as equality of birth and social status in marriage. The purpose of *Kafā'a* was to ensure that a man should be at least the social equal of the woman he marries. It does not forbid unequal marriages and is thus in no sense a Muslim equivalent of the Nuremberg laws of Nazi Germany or the apartheid laws of South Africa. Its aim is to protect the honor of respectable families, by enabling them, if they wish, to stop unsuitable marriages. The principle of *Kafā'a* may be invoked by the father or other legal guardian of a woman in order to prevent her from contracting a marriage without his permission or to annul it if contracted without permission or with permission fraudulently obtained, provided there is no child or pregnancy. The rule operates to restrain a woman from marrying a man who is below her and thus disgracing her family. For a man to marry a woman below him does not matter—the woman is, in the view of the jurists, in the inferior situation anyway, and no immediate social injury can therefore result.

The notion of *Kafā'a* has its antecedents in pre-Islamic Arabia, where tribal custom required a measure of social compatibility between husband and wife. Though not sanctioned by the Qur'ān and indeed in a sense contrary to the spirit of the Qur'ān, it survived into Islamic times and became part of the holy law of Islam. There were, however, from the beginning, differences between the juristic schools, more specifically between what might be called the more lax and more rigorous approaches. For one group, with its origins among the jurists of Medina, the notion of *Kafā'a* was basically religious and was intended to save a devout woman from being forcibly married to a dissolute man. This remained the dominant view in the Mālikī school of jurisprudence; their founder, Mālik ibn Anas, is quoted as strongly denouncing the idea that a *mawlā* woman is inferior to an Arab woman and proclaiming that "all the people of Islam are equal [*akfā'*] to one another, in accordance with God's revelations." But for another group, deriving from the school of Kufa and perhaps influenced by the social hierarchies of pre-Islamic Iran, *Kafā'a* was determined by a number of matters—not only piety and character but also wealth and profession and three other factors which have direct bearing on the question of race and status: freedom, Islam, and descent.[1]

Freedom refers to the question of whether the prospective bridegroom is free, freed, or slave and involves not only his personal status but that of his immediate forbears. A freedman is not as good as the son of a freedman, and he in turn not as good as the grandson of a freedman. This principle is pursued up to three generations, after which all Muslims are deemed equally free. The same is true of Islam. Non-Muslims are of course excluded. But that is not all. A convert is not as good as the son of a convert; the son of a convert is not as good as the grandson of a convert. Here too the rule is limited to three generations, after which all are equal in their Islam.

Descent is another matter. Partly this is a social issue—the distinction between "good" (i.e., well-connected or well-descended) families and others; partly, however, it may also be concerned with ethnic origins. Most jurists make a distinction between Arab and non-Arab. Some maintain that a non-Arab man is not the equal of an Arab woman in any circumstances and that even the manumitted slave of a non-Arab owner is not the equal of the manumitted slave girl of an Arab owner. Generally speaking, the jurists do not bother to distinguish between the various kinds of non-Arabs, though some make the general observation that the non-Arabs are ranked among themselves just as are the Arabs.

The restriction of intermarriage is a grievance frequently mentioned by Muslim critics, especially by Shiʿite opponents of the Sunni order. A limitation on marriages between Muslims and non-Muslims was accepted without question. Muslim men might marry Christian or Jewish women; Christian or Jewish men were forbidden to marry Muslim women under pain of death. The logic of this distinction is that in any religiously mixed marriage Islam must prevail, and the male is the dominant partner (the jurists were often unworldly). The rules regarding *Kafā'a* introduced distinctions even between Muslims—and these were challenged as contrary to the true spirit of Islam. A Shiʿite tract enumerating the misdeeds of the first three caliphs, seen by the Shīʿa as usurpers, illustrates the point vividly. Among other crimes, the Caliph ʿUmar is accused of having introduced ethnic impediments to marriage, and of discriminating not only between Arabs and non-Arabs but also between the noble Arab tribe of Quraysh and the other Arabs.

> When this man seized power over the people he said that the Arabs may not marry women of Quraysh but Quraysh may marry women from the rest of the Arabs and the non-Arabs. The Persians and other *mawālī*[2] may not marry women of the Arabs, but the Arabs may marry any of them. In this way he put the rest of the Arabs in the same relationship to Quraysh as are the Jews and Christians in relation to the Muslims, since the Muslims may marry Christian and Jewish women, but they may not marry Muslim women.[3]

In this, as in some other respects, the Shiʿite polemicist is attributing to ʿUmar the results of a long process of development. But the doctrine of *Kafā'a* was still invoked among Muslims, and the distinction on the one hand between Arab and non-Arab Muslims and on the other between the tribe and family of the Prophet and the rest of the Arabs remained a factor of importance.

Occasionally writers on the subject make reference to the question of color. Sometimes they express the pious view and assert that a man of true piety, "even a black," is acceptable. In this connection they quote a story about Bilāl, the Ethiopian muezzin of the Prophet, who wished to marry an Arab girl. Her family refused, and the Prophet (according to tradition) then sent a personal message to the family asking them to give their daughter to Bilāl. The story is probably not authentic, since it deals with a prejudice which does not seem to have existed in the Prophet's lifetime. It is one of many such tales invented for the purpose of proving the egalitarian point. The same point is made in a story included in a tenth-century compilation.[4] According to this tale, a man came to the Prophet and asked: "Do my blackness and the ugliness of my face bar me from entering paradise?" To which the Prophet answered no. The man then complained that although he had become a believing and loyal Muslim, "I have already asked everyone, present and absent, for the hand of one of their daughters in marriage, and they have all rejected me because of my black complexion and ugly face. Now in my tribe I am noble, but in my case the dark complexion of my mother's family has predominated." The Prophet then sent him to see a certain man of the tribe of Thaqīf, a recent adherent to Islam, and the father of "a freeborn daughter who was very beautiful and very wise." "Go then," said the Prophet, "knock gently on his door, give him greeting, and when you are inside say 'the Prophet has given me your daughter as wife.' " When the man of black complexion reached the door, knocked, and gave his greeting, they heard the voice of a stranger and opened the door; but when they saw how black and ugly he was, they shrank back. "The Prophet has given me your daughter as my wife," he said; but they drove him away in a nasty way. The girl's father went to see the Prophet and, when confronted with this rejection of the Prophet's will, excused himself: "I thought that this man must be lying in what he said. If he was telling the truth, my daughter is his, and I seek refuge in Allah from the wrath of Allah." The marriage was agreed, and the bride price was set at four hundred pieces of silver. When the suitor was about to go to his family to raise the money, the Prophet offered to raise it from three prominent

Muslims. But as the suitor with his money was on his way to complete the transaction, he heard the call of the muezzin and, looking heavenward, decided to spend the money "in the service of God," that is, in the jihad. With the bride-money he bought a horse and weapons and rode out to do battle for the faith. In due course, he was killed and, dying, was tended by the Prophet himself, who saw him go to paradise, to be greeted by the houris. His body was brought to his prospective bride, and the bearers told her: "Allah has already married him to a better maid than any of yours." The story is obviously a moral tale, designed to make a point against racist prejudice—though, it may be noted, the man is Arab and noble on his father's side, and, since he dies a hero's death, the marriage does not in fact take place. Similar evasions are familiar in Western popular entertainment.

The condemnation of racial discrimination in marriage predominates in religious and legal discussions of the question. There are, however, other dicta, even traditions, which state the exact opposite and thus come closer to certain popular attitudes and practices. According to one undoubtedly spurious tradition, the Prophet said: "Be careful in choosing mates for your offspring, and beware of marrying the Zanjī, for he is a distorted creature."[5] Another similar tradition quotes the Prophet as forbidding intermarriage with blacks with the words: "Do not bring black into your pedigree."[6] The same idea is expressed in a verse cited by Masʿūdī: "Do not intermarry with the sons of Ham, for they are the distorted among God's creatures, apart from Ibn Akwaʿ."[7]

Ibn Ḥabīb, a ninth-century Andalusian jurist, goes even further:

> A black woman may be repudiated if there is no blackness in her family; likewise a scald-head, because such things are covered by kinship.[8]

Ibn Ḥabīb's meaning is clear. Blackness, like skin diseases, runs in families. A Muslim bridegroom, it will be recalled, may not see his bride unveiled until after marriage. If he finds her black or scabby, he may repudiate her—unless he has taken a bride from a family known to have black or scabby members, in which case he has no grounds for complaint.

There is ample evidence that marriages of black men with white women were frowned upon. In earlier times it seems to have been virtually impossible for a black to marry an Arab woman. Later it became theoretically possible but was in fact usually excluded by the rule of *Kafāʾa,* the general principle of which was, in the form adopted by the jurists, "Marry like with like." The black poet Nuṣayb had a son who sought to marry an Arab girl of the tribe of which he was a freedman. Nuṣayb's personal standing secured the acceptance of the girl's uncle and guardian, but he himself objected. He had his son beaten for aspiring to a marriage which he regarded as improper and advised the girl's guardian to find her a true Arab husband. Ironically, Nuṣayb's own daughters, dark-skinned like himself, remained unmarried. "My color has rubbed off on to them," he is quoted as saying, "and they are left on my hands. I don't want blacks for them, and whites don't want them." Their fate became proverbial for old maids with choosy fathers.[9]

For a white male to mate with a black woman was in general considered acceptable—with Nubians and other Nilotics much more than with the Zanj. Ethiopian women were, indeed, highly esteemed. Such mating usually took the form of concubinage—a legally and socially acceptable practice—rather than marriage. Some authors disapprove even of this, because of the harm it brought to a family's honor. Thus the Syrian author Abu'l-ʿAlā' (d. 1057) remarked in a letter:

> We often see a man of mark who has in his house women of high degree setting above them a girl in a striped gown purchased for a few coins and so we may see a man whose grandfather on the father's side is a fair-haired descendant of ʿAlī while his maternal grandfather is a black idolator.[10]

In early Islamic and pre-Islamic times the Arabs looked down on the sons of slave mothers, regarding them as inferior to the sons of freeborn Arab mothers.[11] The stigma was attached to the status, not the race, of the mother and affected the sons of white as well as black concubines. Before long, however, a distinctive color prejudice appeared; and the association of blackness with slavery and whiteness with freedom and nobility became common.

Even princes were affected. ʿAbd al-Rahman ibn Umm Ḥakam, a nephew of the Caliph Muʿāwiya and his governor in Kufa, had to endure mockery because of his dark skin and his Ethiopian ancestresses.[12] An episode in the biography of the Abbasid prince Ibrāhīm ibn al-Mahdī (779–839) is even more striking. His father was the caliph, his mother a high-born Persian lady from Daylam who was enslaved after the defeat of her father and the conquest of her country; but he was of swarthy color, so much so that some sources—mistakenly, it would seem—say that his mother was black. Because of this dark skin and large body, says his Arabic biographer, he was known as *al-Tinnīn*—the dragon. After an unsuccessful bid for power, he was pardoned and summoned before his nephew, the Caliph al-Ma'mūn. A curious and instructive dialogue followed, which is reported on the authority of Ibrāhīm himself. The caliph greeted the dark-complexioned and unsuccessful pretender with a taunt: "Are you then the black caliph?" To this Ibrāhīm returned a soft answer, reminding al-Ma'mūn that he had pardoned him and quoting the verse of the black slave poet Suḥaym, "Though I am black of color my character is white." The caliph responded more kindly. Addressing Ibrāhīm as uncle, he indicated that his remark was meant in jest and capped his quotation with another, from an unnamed poet:

> Blackness does not degrade a man of quality,
> nor one of gallantry, refinement and wit.
> Though blackness has a share of you
> my share is the whiteness of your character.[13]

Ibrāhīm was a prince and a scholar, and his mother, though a concubine, was born a Persian lady or princess. Others were less fortunate; and many stories are told of people with an African mother or grandmother and with a dark complexion, who were subject to insult and humiliation on this account.[14] A vivid example occurs in a satire ascribed, probably falsely, to Ḥassān ibn Thābit:

> Your father is your father and you are his son
> Miserable little son and miserable father!
> Your mother is a short-necked black woman
> With fingers like dung-beetles.[15]

Whiteness was seen as a mark of superior birth. Thus the eleventh-century Tunisian poet Ibn Rashīq, in an ode in praise of the city of Qayrawān, boasts of the nobility of its inhabitants:

> How many nobles and gentlemen [*sayyid*] were in it,
> with white faces and proud right arms.[16]

In time, this perception of society was sufficiently well established to provide a poetic metaphor for natural phenomena, as when the thirteenth-century Andalusian poet Ibn Sahl celebrated the advent of spring.

> Spring has come, with his whites and his blacks
> Two classes, his lords and his slaves
> The branches his army of spears, and above
> The leaves his unfurled flags.[17]

To the present day, in North Africa, a man with Negroid features, even of the highest social status, is sometimes described as *ould khadem,* "the son of a slave woman."[18]

Similar attitudes seem to have persisted among the Bedouin, though much less among the townspeople, in the Middle East. The local literary and documentary sources rarely discuss such matters; but Western visitors—at first travelers, later ethnologists and anthropologists—agree on the general picture. In the cities, notably in Arabia, cohabitation with black concubines was common and acceptable, and even marriage not unusual. As elsewhere, Ethiopians and Nubians were preferred for the bed. John Lewis Burckhardt, who visited Arabia in 1814, noted the frequency of African racial traits among the people of the Ḥijāz:

> The colour of the Mekkawy and Djiddawy is a yellowish sickly brown, lighter or darker according to the origin of the mother, who is very often an Abyssinian slave. . . . There are few families at Mekka, in moderate circumstances, that do not keep slaves. . . . The male and female servants are Negroes, or *noubas,* usually brought from Sowakin; the concubines are always Abyssinian slaves. No wealthy Mekkawy prefers domestic peace to the gratification of his passion; they all keep mistresses in common with their lawful wives; but if a slave gives birth to a child, the master generally marries her, or if he fails to do so, is censored by the community. The keeping of Abyssinian concubines is still more prevalent at Djidda. Many Mekkawys have no other than Abyssinian wives, finding the Arabians more expensive, and less disposed to yield to the will of the husband. The same practice is adopted by many foreigners, who

> reside in the Hedjaz for a short time. Upon their arrival, they buy a female companion, with the design of selling her at their departure; but sometimes their stay is protracted; the slave bears a child; they marry her, and become stationary in the town. This, indeed, is general in the East, and nowhere more so than at Mekka. The mixture of Abyssinian blood has, no doubt, given to the Mekkawys that yellow tinge of the skin which distinguishes them from the natives of the desert.
>
> The Mekkawys make no distinction whatever between sons born of Abyssinian slaves and those of free Arabian women.[19]

The absence of social barriers against persons of part-African origin, and even against freed slaves of pure African descent, is confirmed by most other travelers.[20]

Among the Bedouin, marriages with blacks were considered shameful, and even the use of black concubines, according to some accounts, was disapproved.[21] Even where miscegenation was socially tolerated, it seems to have been a one-way street. In the words of a leading authority on the topic:

> Whereas for example, the Qaramanli sultans of Tripoli married off their daughters to European slaves to avoid dynastic rivalries, it would have been unthinkable for an Arab or a Berber, a Turk or a Persian, to consent to his daughter marrying a black African, slave or freed. Marriages the other way around, between a black slavegirl and an Arab man, could and did take place.[22]

In Arabia even a pariah tribe like Hutaym disdains miscegenation. "Arabs of noble race," according to an observer, ". . . do not intermarry with Hutaym. . . . Hutaym in turn are not supposed to intermarry with negroes."[23]

Marriage was one thing, concubinage another. Like many North American slaveowners and still more South American ones, Muslim men who owned women slaves were accustomed to mate with them. But the two situations were very different. In the West, concubinage was condemned by law, religion, and society. It was usually furtive, and its offspring, without recognition or legitimacy, merged into the general slave population. In Islam, concubinage was sanctioned by the law and indeed by the Qur'ān itself. A man could, if he chose, recognize his offspring by his slave woman as legitimate, thereby conferring a formal legal status on both mother and child. In theory, this recognition was optional, and in the early period was often withheld. By the high Middle Ages it became normal and was unremarkable in a society where the sovereigns themselves were almost invariably the children of slave concubines. White-skinned women were usually preferred for the bed, and the occasional assertion, by an author, of the sexual attractions of the dark-skinned usually presents an appearance of bravado or paradox. A major change occurred in the nineteenth century, when, because of the consolidation of the power of both Eastern and Western Europe, white slaves, both female and male, became rare and expensive, and blacks of both sexes were able to rise from their previous subordination to higher status and functions.[24]

13

Image and Stereotype

The literature and folklore of the Middle East reveal a sadly normal range of traditional and stereotypical accusations against people seen as alien and, more especially, inferior. The most frequent are those commonly directed against slaves and hence against the races from which slaves are drawn—that they are stupid; that they are vicious, untruthful, and dishonest; that they are dirty in their personal habits and emit an evil smell. The black's physical appearance is described as ugly, distorted, or monstrous.[1] The point is made in an anecdote about an Arab poet known as al-Sayyid al-Ḥimyarī—the South Arabian Ḥimyarite Sayyid (723–89):

> The Sayyid was my neighbor, and he was very dark. He used to carouse with the young men of the camp, one of whom was as dark as he was, with a thick nose and lips, and a Negroid [*muzannaj*] appearance. The Sayyid had the foulest smelling armpits of anybody. They were jesting together one day, and the Sayyid said to him: "You are a Zanjī in your nose and your lips!" whereat the youth replied to the Sayyid: "And you are a Zanjī in your color and armpits!"[2]

Ibn Buṭlān notes of the Zanj women that

> their bad qualities are many, and the blacker they are the uglier their faces and the more pointed their teeth. They are of little use and may cause harm and are dominated by their evil disposition and destructiveness. . . . Dancing and rhythm are instinctive and ingrained in them. Since their utterance is uncouth, they are compensated with song and dance. . . . They have the cleanest teeth of all people because they have much saliva, and they have much saliva because they have bad digestions. They can endure hard work . . . but there is no pleasure to be got from them, because of the smell of their armpits and the coarseness of their bodies.[3]

The Egyptian writer al-Abshīhī (1388–1446), in a chapter on slaves, tells a bloodcurdling story of the wickedness of a black slave, and concludes:

> Is there anything more vile than black slaves, of less good and more evil than they? As for the mulatto, if you show kindness to one of them all your life and in every way, he will not be grateful; and it will be as if you had done nothing for him. The better you treat him, the more insolent he will be; the worse you treat him, the more humble and submissive. I have tried this many times, and how well the poet says:
>
> If you honor the honorable you possess him
> If you honor the ignoble, he will be insolent.
>
> It is said that when the [black] slave is sated, he fornicates, when he is hungry, he steals. My grandfather on my mother's side used to say: The worst use of money is bringing up slaves, and mulattoes are even worse and wickeder than Zanj, for the mulatto does not know his father, while the Zanjī often knows both parents. It is said of the mulatto that he is like a mule, because he is a mongrel. . . . Do not trust a mulatto, for there is rarely any good in him.[4]

At the turn of the eighteenth century, the Ottoman erotic poet Fazıl Bey (ca. 1757–1810) wrote a "Book of Women," describing the attractions and other qualities of girls of about forty different races and regions, and a similar book on beautiful boys. Fazıl was a Palestinian Arab, the grandson of the famous Shaykh Dāhir Āl-ʿUmar. Born in Safad, he was brought up in Istanbul and wrote in Turkish. He speaks well of the Ethiopians of both sexes but has little good to say of those whom he calls "the blacks." Though they may have good qualities inside, their darkness makes them unattractive, and their faculties are correspondingly dull. The black boy, says Fazıl "is not meet to kiss and embrace, unless the lover's eye is blind," while the black girl "is not worthy of the bed but is right for the kitchen." It is foolish, thinks Fazıl, to make love to blacks when whites are available, and it is unwise to raise up those whose proper place is as servants.[5]

Despite this and many other similar descriptions, physical rejection, of the type professed by some Western racists, seems to have been rare. Masʿūdī notes a few examples, as oddities:

> Ṭāwūs the Yemenite, the disciple of ʿAbdallah ibn ʿAbbās, would never eat meat butchered by a Zanjī because, he said, the Zanjī was a distorted creature. I have heard that the Caliph al-Rāḍī would accept nothing from the hand of a black man, because he was a distorted slave. I do not know whether he was adopting the principles of Ṭāwūs in this or following any particular opinion or doctrine.[6]

Another accusation, which also sometimes appears as praise, is that the black is frivolous and lighthearted—that is, in other terms, cheerful and of happy disposition. Other positive stereotypes show the black as brave, generous, musical, and with a strong feeling of rhythm. Thus Ibn Buṭlān remarks that "if a Zanjī were to fall from heaven to earth he would beat time as he goes down."[7]

One of the commonest positive stereotypes of the black is that of simple piety. There are many anecdotes of a well-known religious type in which the black appears as the simple pious man contrasted with the clever but wicked.[8] And here again one cannot help feeling that this is an example of the *trajectio ad absurdum.* The point that the narrator seeks to make is the superiority of simple piety over clever wickedness, and the black is chosen as the ultimate example of simplicity.

A close parallel with the more familiar type of prejudice current in our society may be found in the sexual stereotype attributed to the black. A common theme is his immense potency and unbridled sexuality. A fairly restrained example of this, in the framework story of *The Thousand and One Nights,* has already been quoted. Others, sometimes in more extreme forms, occur in folklore, in the literature of light entertainment, in tales of the strange and marvelous, and in books on the art of love. The superbly endowed and sexually inexhaustible black slave appears in some of these writings, sometimes as the seducer or ravisher of his owner's wives and daughters, sometimes as the victim, willing or unwilling, of sexual aggression by voracious and frustrated white ladies.[9]

The stereotypes of sexuality refer not only to the black male. In his defense of the blacks, Jāḥiẓ quotes some verses which he ascribes to the Arab poet Farazdaq (d. ca. 730), "the greatest connoisseur of women"—

> How many a tender daughter of the Zanj
> walks about with a hotly burning oven
> as broad as a drinking-bowl.[10]

There is a good deal of Arabic poetry which shows the same kind of prurient interest in the Negress as one finds in European anti-Semitic writings about the Jewess. The interrelated European themes of *la belle juive* and *l'affreuse juive* have close parallels in the simultaneous interest shown by Arab poets in the repulsive ugliness and incandescent sexuality which they ascribe to the black woman.[11] That there are resemblances between these stereotypes of blacks and those common in our own society will be obvious.

There is, however, one aspect of this which deserves deeper exploration: the emotional content attached to the concepts of blackness and whiteness—the idea that black is somehow connected with sin, evil, deviltry and damnation, while white has the opposite associations. Thus in the Qur'ān itself (III: 102), we find reference to

> the day when some faces will become white and some faces will become black. As for those whose faces have become black—will you disbelieve after having believed? Then taste the punishment for the unbelief which you have been showing. But as for those whose faces have become white—in the mercy of Allah will they be, therein to abide.

It is obvious that no reference to black and white races is intended in this passage,[12] which makes use of the common Arabic idiom—shared with many other languages, even including those of black Africa—associating whiteness with joy and goodness, blackness with suffering and evil. Similar associations underlie a good deal of Muslim legend, folklore, literature, proverb, and even language.

The portrayal of blacks in Islamic literature begins at an early date, and soon falls into a few stereotyped categories. They appear—usually though not always as slaves—in the stories of the Prophet and his Companions; as demons and monsters in Persian mythology; as the remote and exotic inhabitants of the land of the Zanj and other places, as for example the cannibal islands of South and Southeast Asia. They figure in the mythical adventures of Alexander, in Arabic called Iskandar. The romance of Alexander was a popular theme of Muslim writers, in both verse and prose. In the Persian legend, Alexander is the son of the mythical Dārāb, and the half-brother of King Darius, from whom he claimed his heritage. In one episode of the romance, the hero Iskandar goes to Egypt, which he delivers from the menace of the Zanj. In the course of his struggle against them, Iskandar invades the land of Zanj, engages and defeats their army, and takes a number of captives. The adventures in Africa are attributed to both Iskandar and his father, Dārāb.[13] Similar adventures are ascribed, in medieval popular romances in Arabic, to such figures as the legendary Yemenite hero Sayf ibn Dhī Yazan, who conquers and converts a variety of pagan Africans.[14]

Most commonly, however, the black portrayed in literature is none of these but is a familiar household figure, as slave or servant or attendant. The black slave or attendant is often part of the background depicted in narrative or belles-lettres.

Occasionally—though infrequently—he plays a more prominent role in the story. This may be either negative or positive. Where negative, his crimes are usually lechery, greed, and ingratitude; where positive, he is the prototype of simple piety and loyalty, which achieve their ultimate reward from God. Paradoxically, this reward may take the form of his turning white.

The portrayal of blacks in Islamic art falls into much the same categories as in narrative literature—not surprisingly, since much of the pictorial art came into being as book illustrations. There is little sculpture, and that only in the earliest period, before the Islamic ban on images had fully taken effect. Probably the earliest portrayals of Africans in the Islamic world are some figures in statuary and carved plaster reliefs, in the Umayyad palace at Khirbat al-Mafjar, in the Jordanian desert. This palace and its ornamentation, dating probably from the early eighth century, still show marked pre-Islamic influences, notably in the use of such carved figures. Some of these have recognizable African features. They may be intended to portray domestic slaves, or more probably some kind of entertainers. Thereafter, under Islamic influence, sculpture virtually disappeared. Painting, however, survived and flourished, at first almost entirely in the form of interior decoration in buildings, then extending to tiles, stucco, and pottery. It achieved its main development in the art of the book, which from the late twelfth century onward became by far the principal form of painting in Islamic lands. Among the Arabs, Persians, and Turks, as well as among the remoter peoples absorbed into the world of Islam, the art of the book reached a high degree of perfection, and illustrated manuscripts—later supplemented by separate miniatures—give us a vivid and varied insight into the life of the Muslim cities.

Among the mixed population of these cities, blacks formed a significant element; and not surprisingly they figure from time to time in book illustration and other paintings. Their portrayal falls into certain well-recognized and easily definable categories, some of them with obvious parallels in the Christian art of medieval Europe.

One such category is sacred history—the lives of the Prophet Muḥammad and of his Companions, offering obvious analogies to Christian portrayals of the birth and life of Jesus. The ban on the portrayal of human figures, which long inhibited the development of Muslim pictorial art, applied with particular force to the sacred biography, and books dealing with the lives of the Prophet and his Companions remained bare of any illustrations. By the sixteenth century, however, Ottoman artists began to turn their attention to this hitherto forbidden subject. The Topkapı Treasury in Istanbul contains a magnificent example. Prepared by order of Sultan Murad III, and dated 1594–95, the text consists of a fourteenth-century Turkish translation of a much earlier Arabic work on the life of the Prophet and includes many illustrations by an unknown artist. Among the many personalities who figure in the biography of the Prophet, two are identified as black and depicted accordingly. One of them is the emperor of Ethiopia, in Arabic called al-Najāshī (Negus), who gave shelter to some of Muḥammad's Companions when they fled from Mecca to escape the persecution of the reigning pagan oligarchy. This episode was a favorite theme of the defenders of the Ethiopians against their detractors. Another figure of almost demiurgic importance is the famous Bilāl, the first muezzin and a Companion of the Prophet. Some minor black figures, apparently slaves, also appear in these pictures.

In another common stereotype, the black appears as a kind of monster or bogeyman. These figure prominently in Iranian mythology, and are consequently depicted from time to time in the great Persian epics. Some particularly magnificent examples may be seen in the illustrations to the *Shāhnāma* of Firdawsī, prepared for the shah of Iran in the city of Tabrīz in 1537. In one of the two pictures reproduced here, the Persian hero Hūshang is shown killing the Great Black Devil; in another, a different hero, Isfandiyār, similarly disposes of a black sorceress. The demonology of Iran is not monochromatic. The Great White Devil of Māzandarān is no less disagreeable than his black colleagues.

An important group of illustrations depict the black as an exotic figure in a strange and distant land. The best-known examples of these are the illustrations found in manuscripts of the different Arabic, Persian, and Turkish versions of the romance of Alexander. In one picture, illustrating a manuscript of the book of Alexander by the Persian poet Niẓāmī, and painted in Qazvīn toward the end of the sixteenth century, Alexander (Iskandar) is seen fighting the blacks.

Most of the traditional themes of Persian letters and art were adopted in Muslim India, where they helped to inspire the rich art of the Mughal period. A manuscript, *Dārābnāma,* with illustrations by various artists, made at the Mughal court between 1580 and 1585, depicts several phases of the war against the Zanj. In one of the three pictures reproduced here, two other persons watch Dārāb fighting the blacks, while the body of another figure is seen floating in the water. In another, Dārāb is seen going into battle against the blacks; and in a third, by the same artist, he has defeated them and is receiving their homage.

The sexual theme occurs far less frequently in Islamic art than in Islamic letters, and the literary portrayal of both the black male and the black female as creatures of immense sexual appetites and powers is rarely paralleled in the pictorial arts. A few examples do, however, occur in the Mughal art of India. In one of them, also an illustration to the same manuscript of the *Dārābnāma,* Homay, the mother of Dārāb, is murdered by a black groom. According to the story, he had a secret passion for her and murdered her one night when he came to her and she refused to submit to him. A later Mughal manuscript, completed in India in 1629, illustrates a story by the Persian poet Saʿdī, and depicts an old man who upbraids a black and a girl for flirting. Much more dramatic than either of these is a Persian manuscript of the famous *Maṯnavī* of Rūmī, completed in Tabrīz in about 1530, illustrating an episode in the poem in which a woman discovers her maidservant copulating with an ass and tries, with disastrous results, to do the same.

The overwhelming majority of blacks who appear in Islamic paintings are, however, none of these things—neither sacred figures nor monsters, neither exotic nor erotic. They are quite simply slaves and servants. They appear in countless pictures of court life, domestic life, and various outdoor scenes; in illustrations of narrative literature and other forms of belles-lettres; and—in Ottoman times—in the sumptuous albums portraying celebrations of special occasions at the Ottoman court. In these pictures the black appears with fair frequency. When he does so, he is almost invariably carrying a tray, pushing a broom, leading a horse, wielding a spade, pulling an oar or a rope, or discharging some other subordinate or menial task. Blacks appear as servants and attendants, as masons and gardeners, as grooms and huntsmen, or as boatmen. Mostly they are male, though female figures occasionally appear. Some of the finest examples of thirteenth-century descriptive art occur in illustrations of the Arabic literary works known as *maqāmāt,* a kind of poetic prose narrative. In one of them, dated 1237 and probably completed in Mesopotamia, the artist vividly portrays a slave market in the Yemen, in which black slaves imported from Africa are bought and sold. In another similar manuscript, completed a few years earlier in Syria, a black slave is shown bringing food. In numerous Persian, Indian, and Turkish miniatures of the fifteenth and sixteenth centuries, blacks variously appear as grooms, huntsmen, and servants of various kinds.

In Ottoman times the chief black eunuch of the court, sometimes known as the Aga of the Gate of Felicity, or more informally as the Aga of the Girls, was a major personage at the Ottoman court. His dignity and position are vividly portrayed by court artists. From the late sixteenth century we have a number of magnificent albums depicting various aspects of the life of the Ottoman court, and several of these portray the black eunuchs and other functionaries. A manuscript dated 1597 shows an Ottoman prince and grand vizier with black attendants, the heir apparent with black eunuchs, and, in a particularly interesting picture, the funeral of the sultan's mother, Nurbanu (born Cecilia Venier-Baffo, of Venice), with black eunuchs in attendance. A much later volume, illustrated by the great painter Levni in about 1720–32, depicts in great detail the ceremonies and celebrations at the circumcision of a young prince. In one picture, we see princes, pages, and black eunuchs at an evening party by the Golden Horn; in another, the chief black eunuch conducts the young prince to the circumcision ceremony.[15]

One of the greatest of Persian painters, the famous Behzād, who flourished in the late fifteenth and early sixteenth centuries, seems to have used a black figure as a kind of signature. In many of his paintings such a figure appears, usually in a very minor capacity. This mannerism was picked up by some of his disciples and successors, and became characteristic of the school of Herāt, which he founded. Clearly, the primary role of the black as menial was by this time so well understood that he could acquire a secondary role as a symbol.

14

Myth and Reality

In reviewing the evidence of prejudice and discrimination in the Middle Eastern past, I have tried to correct the false picture drawn by the myth makers, a picture of idyllic freedom from such evils. But in correcting an error, one should not fall into the opposing error. At no time did the peoples of the Middle East ever practice the kind of racial oppression which exists in South Africa at the present time or which existed until recently in the United States. My purpose is not to set up a moral competition—to compare castration and apartheid as offenses against humanity or to argue the relative wickedness of Eastern and Western practices; it is rather to refute the claims of both exclusive virtue and exclusive vice and to point to certain common failings of our common humanity. The correction of error—even of emotionally satisfying and politically useful error—is a legitimate, indeed a necessary task of the historian.

This raises another, and an important, question. If, as the evidence overwhelmingly demonstrates, the conventional picture of a society totally free from racial prejudice and discrimination is false, how then did it come to be? The sources of this Western-made myth may be found in European and American, rather than Middle Eastern, history. The American Civil War brought the issue of slavery sharply before European opinion, the more so since it coincided with a renewed and determined British effort, by both diplomatic and naval action, to induce Muslim rulers in Turkey, Arabia, and elsewhere to ban, and indeed suppress, the slave trade. Comparisons were inevitable, and the obvious contrasts led some European observers to defend Muslim slavery, or at least to praise Muslim racial attitudes.

The defenses took a variety of forms. One of the first to make the comparison was the Austrian scholar-diplomat Alfred von Kremer, in a book published in 1863. Kremer abhors slavery and describes the abduction and transportation of the African slaves in blood-chilling terms. He notes, however, as did many previous travelers, that the slave, once he reached his destination, was relatively well treated. More significantly, he acquits the Muslims of race prejudice:

> The color prejudice that is maintained in so crude a form by the free sons of America, not only against genuine Africans but even against their descendants in the fourth and fifth degrees, is not known in the Orient. Here a person is not considered inferior because he is of a darker complexion. This can easily be explained from the nature of slavery in the Orient, where the slave is not separated by an insurmountable barrier from the family of his master, where the slave does not belong to a caste that is despised and barely considered human, but where in contrast, between master and slave, there is the most intimate and manifold relationship. In the Orient there can hardly be a Muhammedan family that is without slave blood.[1]

Snouck Hurgronje draws a similar distinction between Muslim and American attitudes, and complains that the Americans have given slavery a bad name. European public opinion, he says, has been misled by a confusion between the two types of black slavery and warns his reader that if he goes into an Arabian slave market with European ideas, "perhaps even with recollections of a reading of *Uncle Tom's Cabin* in his head," he will get a very negative impression. But, he goes on, the first impression is false, and unfortunately most travelers to the Orient bring back "little but their false first impressions."[2]

Kremer's assertion of the total absence of race prejudice or discrimination in Islamic society was surely exaggerated, and even Snouck Hurgronje, in his defense of black slavery in Arabia, written twenty years later and with the advantage of a visit to the holy cities, uses a more cautious formulation. But the contrast between Islamic and American conditions was real, and the exaggeration a natural consequence of European revulsion from American attitudes and practices. In the horrors of the abduction of Africans from their homes, for delivery to Islamic and American purchasers, there was little to choose, and indeed the same intermediaries may have served in both cases. Nor was there much difference in the dangers and hardships of the journey, until the human merchandise reached its ultimate destination, across ocean or desert. It was in the treatment accorded to the slaves by their new masters, and the place assigned to them in the societies to which they had come, that the main contrast was to be seen. Some European observers, particularly from the conservative and monarchical societies, derived ironic amusement from the spectacle of slavery in free America; others were shocked and horrified. Even the European colonial empires had long since outlawed slavery, first at home and then in their overseas possessions, where it had in any case never reached the American level of racial discrimination and oppression.

Travelers who compared Islamic with American slavery mostly overlooked the fact that they were comparing two different types of slave employment, domestic and economic. The slaves whom Western travelers in the East encountered and described were those employed in households, and their lot and degree of acceptance were certainly far better than those of domestic slaves in the Americas. But there were also slave workers in the Middle East, for example, in southern Iraq, where, according to British consular reports, agricultural labor in the pestilential climate was largely assigned to black slaves imported by sea.[3] Later in the century, the sudden wealth accruing to Egypt from the export of cotton during the American Civil War enabled Egyptian farmers to grow rich and also to import black slaves to cultivate their fields.[4] These were rarely seen or described by Western travelers. There were also some black laborers in the cities. Thus even Snouck Hurgronje noted that "shining pitchblack negro slaves" were used in Mecca for "the hardest work of building, quarrying, etc." and believed that "their allotted work . . . is generally not too heavy for them, though most natives of Arabia would be incapable of such bodily efforts in the open air."[5]

In fact, the limits of toleration accorded to persons of African or part-African origin varied considerably from time to time and from place to place. In Arabia, where Islamic sentiments were strongest, African slaves and freedmen could occupy positions of power and authority, though they were far less likely to reach such positions than their white colleagues. It was only after the virtual disappearance of the white slave that the black slave was commonly able to attain such heights. Children of Arab fathers and black—usually Ethiopian—concubines suffered no significant disability in the holy cities, where they were able to rise to the social level of their free Arab fathers. If their fathers were sharīfs, they, too, were, or could be, sharīfs. The swarthy son of a free Arab father and an African mother, by virtue of his father's status, could marry a white woman. But few, if any, Arab families were willing to give their daughters in marriage to a genuine African man.

The myth of Islamic racial innocence was a Western creation and served a Western purpose. Not for the first time, a mythologized and idealized Islam provided a stick with which to chastise Western failings. In the eighteenth century, the philosophers of the Enlightenment had praised Islam for its lack of dogmas and mysteries, its freedom from priests and Inquisitors and other persecutors—recognizing real qualities but exaggerating them as a polemical weapon against the Christian churches and clergy. In the early nineteenth century, West European Jews, newly and still imperfectly emancipated, appealed to a legendary golden age in Muslim Spain, of complete tolerance and acceptance in symbiotic harmony.[6] This, too, had some foundation in reality but was greatly overstated to serve at once as a reproach and an encouragement to their somewhat dilatory Christian emancipators.

In the same way, the myth of total racial harmony in the Islamic world appears to have arisen as a reproach to the practices of white men in the Americas and in Southern Africa, beside which indeed even Islamic realities shone in contrast. This idea won particular favor in the nineteenth century among Christian missionaries in Africa, who sought some explanation of the failure of their missions as contrasted with the success of Islam, despite every advantage of power, wealth, and (as they saw it) truth. The explanation which some missionaries found was in the difference between the second-class status accorded to black Christians by white rulers and the immediate equality received by black converts to Islam. There may indeed be a great deal of truth in this, but it overlooks two important points—first, that the Muslim preachers were themselves black and represented the far limit of Islamic expansion into Africa, and second, that even so, there were shades of difference, perhaps invisible to the outsider but vitally important to the people themselves.

It is significant that one of the most influential proponents of the myth was Edward W. Blyden, a black West Indian who was educated in Liberia under missionary auspices but was convinced by his African experiences that Islam was better suited than Christianity to black African needs. His writings, with their stress on Christian guilt and on a somewhat romanticized Muslim tolerance, were widely read.[7] Writers of this school usually make the illogical assumption that the reprobation of prejudice in a society proves its absence. In fact, of course, it reveals its presence. Anti-Semitism is a criminal offense in Germany and Russia, but not in England or America.

That the myth has survived and been taken up enthusiastically in our time is due, I think, to another factor, to what might be called nostalgia for the white man's burden. The white man's burden in Kipling's sense—the Westerner's responsibility for the peoples over whom he ruled—has long since been cast off and seized by others. But there are those who still insist on maintaining it—this time as a burden not of power but of guilt, an insistence on responsibility for the world and its ills that is as arrogant and as unjustified as the claims of our imperial predecessors.

Notes

Preface

1. For a rare example of a fair and honest approach to a delicate and sensitive topic, see Samir M. Zoghby, "Blacks and Arabs: Past and present," *Current Bibliography on African Affairs* 3, no. 5 (May 1970), pp. 5–22.

Chapter 1

1. See below, p. 151.

2. On pre-classical antiquity, see Isaac Mendelsohn, *Slavery in the Ancient Near East* (New York, 1949); G. R. Driver and John C. Miles, *The Babylonian Laws,* vol. 1 (Oxford, 1952), pp. 478–90; Muhammad A. Dandamaev, *Slavery in Babylonia, from Nabopolassar to Alexander the Great (626–331* B.C.*),* trans. Victoria A. Powell (De Kalb, IL, 1984). There is a vast literature on slavery in the Greek and Roman worlds. For some modern studies, citing earlier work, see William L. Westermann, *The Slave Systems of Greek and Roman Antiquity* (Philadelphia, 1955); Keith Hopkins, *Conquerors and Slaves: Sociological Studies in Roman History,* vol. 1 (Cambridge, 1978); K. R. Bradley, *Slaves and Masters in the Roman Empire: A Study in Social Control* (New York and Oxford, 1987); M. I. Finley, ed., *Slavery in Classical Antiquity* (Cambridge and New York, 1968); idem, ed., *Classical Slavery* (London, 1987); idem, *Ancient Slavery and Modern Ideology* (New York, 1980); Zvi Yavetz, *Slaves and Slavery in Ancient Rome* (New Brunswick, NJ, and Oxford, 1988). The question whether Greek and Roman societies were based on a slave system of production has given rise to vigorous, often heated, and still continuing controversy. It need not detain us here. On slavery in general, including a thoughtful comparative study of ancient and Middle Eastern slavery, see David Brion Davis, *The Problem of Slavery in Western Cultures* (Ithaca, NY, 1966); idem, *Slavery and Human Progress* (New York and Oxford, 1984).

3. On slavery in Roman law, see W. W. Buckland, *The Roman Law on Slavery* (Cambridge, 1908); Olis Robleda, *Il diritto degli schiavi nell'antica Roma* (Rome, 1976).

4. E.g., Deut 15:15. The Passover prayers and rituals, celebrating the Exodus, are an annual reminder to Jews that they are the descendants of slaves who won freedom. On slavery among Jews, in law and practice, see E. E. Urbach, "The laws regarding slavery as a source for the social history of the period of the second Temple, the Mishnah and Talmud," in *Papers of the Institute of Jewish Studies,* ed. J. G. Weiss, vol. 1 (Jerusalem and London, 1964), pp. 1–94; Simha Assaf, *Be-ohalē Yaʿaqōv* (Jerusalem, 1943), pp. 223–56; Salo W. Baron, *A Social and Religious History of the Jews,* 2nd ed., vol. 4 (New York, 1957), pp. 187–96. For the Talmudic laws regarding slavery, see *Giṭṭin* 8a–9a, 11b–15a, 37b–45a, 46b–47a (*The Babylonian Talmud, Seder Nashim,* ed. I. Epstein, *Giṭṭin,* trans. Maurice Simon, vol. 4 [London, 1936], pp. 27–31, 39–55, 155–98, 206–7) and *Yebamot,* passim. See, further, Westermann, *Slave Systems,* pp. 124–26.

5. As, for example, in Maimonides, *Mishneh Torah, Hilkhōt ʿAvadim* 9:8.

6. It is interpreted in this sense by Maimonides, who quotes this verse, along with other texts, in an eloquent plea for the humane treatment of the Canaanite, i.e., the non-Jewish slave (ibid). Recommendations for the good treatment of Jewish slaves sometimes appear extreme: "[The slave] must be [equal to] thee in food and drink, that thou shouldst not eat white bread and he black bread, thou drink old wine and he new wine, thou sleep on a feather bed and he on straw. Hence it was said, Whoever buys a Hebrew slave is like buying a master for himself" (*Qiddūshīn,* 20a [*Babylonian Talmud, Ḳiddushin,* trans. H. Freedman, vol. 4, p. 92]).

7. Gal 3:28; cf. similar statements in 1 Cor 12:13 and Col 3:11, "Where there is neither Greek nor Jew, circumcision nor uncircumcision, Barbarian nor Scythian, bond nor free, but Christ is all, and in all."

8. E.g., Luke 12:37–38, 17:7–9, 19:13–22, 20:10–12; Mark 12:2–5, etc. By using "servant" to render the Greek *doulos,* "slave," the English (and other European) translators of the Bible sub-edited slavery out of Christianity. For the Hebrew *ʿebhed* in the Old Testament, the English translators use "slave," "bondsman," and sometimes "servant." The Vulgate, correctly, translates both *doulos* and *ʿebhed* as *servus.*

9. For other acceptances of slavery, see 1 Cor 7:21–23 and Col 3:21; G. E. M. de Ste. Croix, "Early Christian attitudes to property and slavery," in *Church, Society, and Politics,* ed. Derek Baker (Oxford, 1975), pp. 15–16; Westermann, *Slave Systems,* pp. 128–29, 149–62.

10. Piero A. Milani, *La schiavitù nel pensiero politico dai Greci al basso medio evo* (Milan, 1972), pp. 147ff., 161ff., and, on the Roman Stoics, pp. 204ff.; Westermann, *Slave Systems,* pp. 109–17.

11. Philo Judaeus, *Quod omnis probus,* 79; cf. Josephus, *Antiquities of the Jews,* 18, 21: "Essenes . . . do not own slaves. . . . They believe it contributes to injustice"; Davis, *Problem of Slavery,* pp. 81–82; Westermann, *Slave Systems,* p. 117. For other examples, see Robert Schlaifer, "Greek theories of slavery from Homer to Aristotle," *Harvard Studies in Classical Philology* 10, no. 7 (1936), pp. 127–29 (reprinted in Finley, *Slavery,* pp. 199–201); Milani, *La schiavitù,* pp. 145ff.

12. Aristotle, *Politics* 1254b20.

13. Milani, *La schiavitù,* pp. 68ff.; Pierre Vidal-Naquet, "Réflexions sur l'historiographie grecque de l'esclavage," in *Travail et esclavage en Grèce ancienne,* by Jean-Pierre Vernant and Pierre Vidal-Naquet (Paris, 1985).

14. Significantly, even in the Middle Ages, Jewish legal texts dealing with slavery

refer to the non-Jewish slave as a Canaanite, e.g., Maimonides, *Mishneh Torah,* section on slaves. On the curse of Ham, see below, chap. 8, n. 9, pp. 123–25.

15. See W. Montgomery Watt, *Muhammad at Medina* (Oxford, 1965), pp. 293–96, 344. On the Banū Qurayẓa, of whom the men were beheaded and the women and children sold into slavery, see *Encyclopedia of Islam,* 2d ed.—hereafter *EI*[2]—s.v. "Ḳurayẓa" (by W. Montgomery Watt) and sources cited there.

16. Slavery in the Islamic world still awaits a comprehensive study. In the meantime, the best short accounts are those of R. Brunschvig, s.v. "ʿAbd" in *EI*[2], and of Hans Müller, "Sklaven" in *Handbuch der Orientalistik,* ed. B. Spuler, pt. 1, *Der Nahe und der Mittlere Osten,* vol. 6, *Geschichte der Islamischen Länder,* sec. 6, *Wirtschaftsgeschichte des Vorderen Orients in Islamischer Zeit,* pt. 1 (Leiden and Cologne, 1977), pp. 54–83; also, by the same author, a brief general introduction to the subject, "Zur Erforschung des islamischen Sklavenwesens," in *Zeitschrift der Deutschen Morgenländischen Gesellschaft,* suppl. 1, vol. 2, *Deutsche Orientalistentag, Würzburg 1968* (Wiesbaden, 1969), pp. 611–22. A selection of translated documents relating to slavery will be found in Bernard Lewis, *Islam from the Prophet Muhammad to the Capture of Constantinople,* vol. 2, *Religion and Society* (New York, 1974), pp. 236–56. See also A. Mez, *Die Renaissance des Islams* (Heidelberg, 1922), pp. 152ff. (*The Renaissance of Islam,* trans. S. Khuda-Bukhsh and D. S. Margoliouth [London, 1937], pp. 156 ff.); Franz Rosenthal, *The Muslim Concept of Freedom Prior to the Nineteenth Century* (Leiden, 1960), pp. 29–34; D. I. Nadiradze, "Vopros o rabstve v khalifate VII–VIII vekov," *Narodi Azii i Afriki* 5 (1968), pp. 75–85; I. P. Petrushevsky, *Islam in Iran,* trans. Hubert Evans (Albany, NY, 1985), pp. 154–59; idem, "K istorii rabstva v khalifate VII–X vekov," *Narodi Azii i Afriki* 3 (1971), pp. 60–71; Walid ʿArafat, "The attitude of Islam to slavery," *Islamic Quarterly* 10 (1966), pp. 12–18. The laws concerning slavery are treated in most, though not all, standard works on Islamic law, usually not as a separate heading but as part of the discussion of the various topics of personal, commercial, and criminal law. For useful presentations, see David Santillana, *Istituzioni di diritto musulmano malichita, con riguardo anche al sistema sciafiita,* vol. 1 (Rome, 1926), pp. 111–26, where the major Arabic treatises are cited; Th. W. Juynboll, *Handbuch des islamischen Gesetzes nach der Lehre der Schafiʿitischen Schule* (Leiden and Leipzig, 1910), pp. 202–8. An earlier German dissertation deals specifically with the laws on slavery: Kurt E. Weckwarth, *Der Sklave im Muhammedanischen Recht* (Berlin, 1909), mainly on the basis of translated Ottoman evidence and without reference to Arabic sources. A new study, which comes to hand as this book goes to press, is Murray Gordon, *Slavery in the Arab World* (New York, 1989). While devoting some attention to earlier history, it is mainly concerned with modern and recent times.

17. Santillana, *Istituzioni,* vol. 1, p. 111, citing Mālik ibn Anas: "Every Muslim is the equal of every other Muslim" (*Al-Mudawwana al-Kubrā,* vol. 4 [Cairo, 1323/1905], pp. 13–14; *Muwatta'*, vol. 3 [Cairo, 1310/1892–93], pp. 57, 262).

18. For example in Ibn Saʿd's account of the Prophet's address to the Muslims at the "Farewell Pilgrimage" (*Kitāb al-Tabaqāt al-Kabīr,* ed. E. Sachau, vol. 2 [Leiden, 1925], p. 133). For *ḥadīth*s on slavery, see A. J. Wensinck et al., *Concordance et indices de la tradition musulmane,* 8 vols. (Leiden, 1933–88), s.vv. *ʿAbd, Ghulām,* etc. Among the Greeks and Romans it was a common practice to address an adult male slave as "boy" (Greek, *pais;* Latin, *puer*). There are many examples of this in papyri from Egypt and in other sources, including the Greek Testament and the Latin Vulgate translation. This has often been compared with the use of "boy" by colonial and American slaveowners, and it was generally assumed that this appellation served the same purpose of degrading and diminishing the adult slave. An Islamic tradition may

suggest another explanation. According to a frequently cited *ḥadīth,* the Prophet told the Muslims not to address a slave or slave woman as "my slave" or "my slave woman," but rather as "my young man" or "my young woman." The Arabic terms are *fatā* and *fatāt.* In the context in which it is cited, the purpose of this instruction is very clearly not to diminish, but rather to elevate, the status of the slave, by treating him or her as a member of the owner's family. For another version, with numerous other traditions and dicta urging kind treatment for slaves, see ʿAbd al-Wahhāb al-Shaʿrānī, *Kitāb Kashf al-Ghumma,* vol. 2 (Cairo, 1370/1950), p. 154. Some jurists, especially among the Shīʿa, maintain that only Muslim slaves should be liberated; the majority of Sunni authorities approved the manumission of all the "People of the Book," i.e., Christians and Jews (Petrushevsky, *Islam in Iran,* p. 158).

19. Santillana, *Istituzioni,* vol. 1.

20. Mendelsohn, *Slavery,* p. 5; Westermann, *Slave Systems,* pp. 6, 30, 70, 84–86. Free children could also be enslaved by kidnapping or by legal adoption.

21. On Muslim and Christian laws concerning prisoners of war, see Erwin Gräf, "Religiöse und rechtliche Vorstellungen über Kriegsgefangene in Islam und Christentum," *Die Welt des Islam,* n.s., 8, no. 3 (1963), pp. 89–139. On exchanges of prisoners with Byzantium, see Petrushevsky, "K istorii rabstva," p. 64. On the large numbers of slaves acquired during the conquests, see ibid., pp. 62ff., relying especially on Christian (Syriac, Armenian, etc.) historians, who understandably give more attention to the taking and disposal of slaves from among their co-religionists than do the Muslim historians.

22. For examples of such deeds of manumission, from both medieval and Ottoman times, see A. Grohmann, *Arabic Papyri in the Egyptian Library,* vol. 1 (Cairo, 1934), pp. 61–64; idem, "Arabische Papyri aus den Staatlichen Museen zu Berlin," *Der Islam* 22 (1935), pp. 19–30; K. Jahn, *Türkische Freilassungerklärungen des 18 Jahrhunderts (1702–76)* (Naples, 1963). On Ottoman usage, see further Alan Fisher, "Studies in Ottoman slavery and slave trade, II: Manumission," *Journal of Turkish Studies* 4 (1980), pp. 49–56.

23. See *Encyclopedia of Islam,* 1st ed.—hereafter *EI*[1]—s.v. "Umm Walad" (by J. Schacht).

24. See S. D. Goitein, *A Mediterranean Society: The Jewish Communities of the Arab World as Portrayed in the Documents of the Cairo Geniza* (Berkeley and Los Angeles, 1967–88), vol. 3, pp. 147–48; vol. 5, pp. 311, 321–22, 486–87. According to a ruling by a ninth-century rabbi in Iraq, "If a Jew is caught in fornication with his slave girl, she is taken from him and sold and the money distributed among the poor, and he is flogged, his head is shaven, and he is shunned for thirty days" (Rabbi Natronay, cited in Assaf, *Be-ohalē Yaʿaqōv,* p. 230). Among Christians, committed by their faith to monogamy, the ban on concubinage was categorical, and enforced by the threat of excommunication (see, e.g., Mez, *The Renaissance,* p. 156). There are nevertheless reports of cohabitation with slave women by delinquent members of both communities.

25. On the redemption of captives, see Eliezer Bashan, *Sheviya u Pedūt ba-ḥevra ha-yehūdīt be-artsōt ha-yam ha-tīkhōn* (Jerusalem, 1980). In the devastation of Polish Jewry by the Cossacks and their Tatar allies in 1648, those who fell into Tatar hands were enslaved and sent to Turkey, and most were redeemed. Those who fell into Cossack hands were killed.

26. Baron, *Social and Religious History,* vol. 4, pp. 156, 187–96; Assaf, *Be-ohalē Yaʿaqōv,* pp. 224ff.

27. For an example, see Assaf, *Be-ohalē Yaʿaqōv,* pp. 243–44.

28. Such, for example, were Johann Schiltberger (1396–1402), Georgius de Hun-

garia (1475–80), Gian Maria Angiolello (1470–?1483), Bartholomeus Georgievitz (ca. 1548), and Albert Bobowski (ca. 1667). Some Europeans were even taken to Mecca, as slaves of Muslim pilgrims. Such, for example, were the German Johann Wilden (1604) and the Englishman Joseph Pitts (1680). For bibliographical details of those and other works, see Carl Göllner, *Turcica: Die europäischen Türkendrücke des XVI Jahrhunderts* (Bucharest and Berlin, 1961, 1968); Shirley Howard Weber, *Voyages and Travels in Greece, the Near East, and Adjacent Regions Made Previous to the Year 1801* (Princeton, NJ, 1953) s.vv. Among numerous accounts by Europeans who had been slaves in North Africa, particular interest attaches to the memoirs of Maria ter Meetelen, one of the few female slaves to have written a book about her adventures. Originally published in Dutch in 1748, the book was translated into French by F. H. Bousquet and G. W. Bousquet-Mirandelle, *L'Annotation ponctuelle de la description de voyage étonnante et de la captivité remarquable et triste durant douze ans de moi Maria ter Meetelen et de l'heureuse délivrance d'icelle, et mon joyeux retour dans ma chère patrie, le tout décrit selon la vérité et mon expérience personnelle.* Institut des Hautes-Études Marocaines, Notes et Documents, vol. 17 (Paris, 1956). Among several modern accounts written from within the harem, see Melek Hanum (Mme. Kibrizli-Mehemet Pasha), *Thirty Years in the Harem,* 2 vols (Berlin, 1872); Princess Musbah Haidar, *Arabesque,* 2nd ed. (London, 1968).

29. For numerous examples, see Petrushevsky, "K istorii rabstva," pp. 62ff.

30. Text in al-Maqrīzī, *Kitāb . . . al-Khiṭaṭ,* vol. 1 (Būlāq, 1270/1854), pp. 199–200 (= ibid., ed. G. Wiet, vol. 3 [Cairo, 1922–], pp. 290–92). English translation in Yusuf Fadl Hasan, *The Arabs and the Sudan from the Seventh to the Early Sixteenth Century* (Edinburgh, 1967), pp. 22–24. For critical historical discussions of the pact, see Martin Hinds and Hamdi Sakkout, "A letter from the governor of Egypt to the king of Nubia and Muqurra concerning Egyptian-Nubian relations in 141/758," in *Studia Arabica et Islamica: Festschrift for Ihsan ʿAbbas on His Sixtieth Birthday* (Beirut, 1981), pp. 209–30; V. Christides, "Sudanese at the time of the Arab conquest of Egypt," *Byzantinische Zeitschrift* 75 (1982), pp. 6–13. For a contemporary document, complaining that among other breaches of the pact, the Nubians are sheltering runaways and are not sending the Muslims young and healthy slaves but "that in which there is no good—the one-eyed, or the lame, or the weak old man, or the young boy," see J. Martin Plumley, "An eighth-century Arabic letter to the King of Nubia," *Journal of Egyptian Archeology* 61 (1975), pp. 241–45.

31. See B. I. Beshir, "New light on Nubian Fatimid relations," *Arabica* 22 (1975), pp. 15–24, where a number of Arabic sources are cited and examined. See, further, Ugo Monneret de Villard, *Storia della Nubia Cristiana* (Rome, 1938), pp. 71–83. The imposition of a levy of slaves, as part of a tax or tribute, is still recorded in early-nineteenth-century Egypt and even later in tropical Africa. See Gabriel Baer, "Slavery in nineteenth century Egypt," *Journal of African History* 8 (1967), p. 420; Gustav Nachtigal, *Sahara and Sudan,* trans. Allan G. B. Fisher and Humphrey J. Fisher, 4 vols. (London, 1971–87), index (*Sahara und Sudan. Ergebnisse sechsjähriger Reisen in Afrika,* 3 vols. [Berlin-Leipzig, 1879–89; reprinted Graz, 1967]).

32. For examples, see Ṭabarī, *Ta'rīkh al-rusul wa'l-mulūk,* ed. M. J. de Goeje et al., vol. 2 (Leiden, 1879–1901), pp. 1238, 1245–46; Balādhurī, *Futūḥ al-Buldān,* ed. M. J. de Goeje (Leiden, 1863), p. 421 (in English, *The Origin of the Islamic State,* trans. Philip K. Hitti and Francis Murgotten, 2 vols. [New York, 1916–24]), *Ta'rīkh-i Sīstān,* ed. Bahār (Tehran, 1314/1935), p. 82. According to this text, the rulers of the eastern Iranian region of Sīstān, in surrendering to the Arabs in 650 A.D., agreed to pay to the caliph an annual tribute of one million silver dirhams, plus one thousand slave

girls (*waṣīfat*), "each with a golden cup in her hand." The later Arabic historian Ibn al-Athīr (*Kāmil,* ed. C. J. Tornberg, vol. 3 [Leiden, 1883], p. 50) doubles the numbers to two million dirhams and two thousand slaves (*waṣīf*). Cf. C. E. Bosworth, *Sistān under the Arabs, from the Islamic Conquest to the Rise of the Saffarids (30–250/651–864)* (Rome, 1968), p. 17; Yaʿqūbī, *Ta'rīkh,* ed. T. Houtsma, vol. 2 (Leiden, 1889), pp. 344ff. Another way of ensuring a supply of slaves is indicated in a passage in Balādhurī, *Futūḥ,* p. 225 (cf. Hitti, pp. 353–54) according to which ʿAmr ibn al-ʿĀṣ told a group of Luwāṭa Berbers: "You will sell your wives and children to pay poll-tax for yourselves." See, further, Petrushevsky, "K istorii rabstva," pp. 65–66.

33. See David Ayalon, "The plague and its effects on the Mamluk Army," *Journal of the Royal Asiatic Society* (1946), pp. 67–73; Michael W. Dols, *The Black Death in the Middle East* (Princeton, NJ, 1977), pp. 178f., 185ff. For a nineteenth-century description, see above, p. 84.

34. On eunuchs in the Islamic world, see *EI*², s.v. "Khaṣī" (by Ch. Pellat [classical], A. K. S. Lambton [Iran], and C. Orhonlu [Ottoman]); David Ayalon, "On the eunuchs in Islam," *Jerusalem Studies in Arabic and Islam* 1 (1979), pp. 67–124; idem, "The eunuchs in the Mamluk sultanate," in *Studies in Memory of Gaston Wiet,* ed. M. Ayalon (Jerusalem, 1977), pp. 267–95. On the nineteenth and twentieth centuries, see Ehud R. Toledano, "The Imperial eunuchs of Istanbul: From Africa to the heart of Islam," *Middle Eastern Studies* 20 (1984), pp. 379–90; Gordon, *Slavery,* pp. 91–98. On eunuchs in antiquity, see Hopkins, *Conquerors and Slaves,* pp. 172–96.

35. On slavery and the slave trade in Europe, including Muslim Spain, see the numerous studies of Charles Verlinden, especially *L'Esclavage dans l'Europe médiévale,* 2 vols. (Bruges, 1955). On the slave trade from black Africa to the Islamic world, see UNESCO, *The African Slave Trade from the Fifteenth to the Nineteenth Century: Reports and Papers of the Meeting of Experts Organized by UNESCO at Port-au-Prince, Haiti, 31 January to 4 February 1978* (Paris, 1979), esp. the contributions by Mbaye Guaye, Ibrahima Baba Kake, Bethwell A. Ogot, Herbert Gerbeau, and the bibliography assembled by Y. A. Talib. On African slaves exported to India, see J. J. L. Duyvendak, *China's Discovery of Africa* (London, 1949), pp. 13–24; Joseph E. Harris, *The African Presence in Asia: Consequences of the East African Slave Trade* (Evanston, IL, 1971).

36. On the Saqāliba, see Ayalon, "On the eunuchs," pp. 92–124.

37. See Alan Fisher, "Chattel slavery in the Ottoman Empire," *Slavery and Abolition* 1 (1980), pp. 25–45; idem, "The sale of slaves in the Ottoman empire: Market and state taxes on slave sales," *Boğazici Üniversitesi Dergisi* 6 (1978), pp. 149–71; idem, "Muscovy and the Black Sea slave trade," *Canadian-American Slavic Studies* 6 (1972), pp. 575–94; idem, "Studies in Ottoman slavery, II: Manumission," *Journal of Turkish Studies* 4 (1980), pp. 49–56; Halil Inalcik, "Servile labor in the Ottoman Empire," in *Mutual Effects of Islamic and Judeo-Christian Worlds: The East European Pattern,* ed. Abraham Ascher, Tibor Halasi-Dun, and Bela K. Kiraly (New York, 1980), pp. 23–52; Halil Sahillioğlu, "Slaves in the social and economic life of Bursa in the late 15th and early 16th centuries," *Turcica* 17 (1985), pp. 43–112; Ibrahim Metin Kunt, "Kulların Kulları," *Boğaziçi Üniversitesi Dergisi, Hümaniter Bilimler* 3 (1975), pp. 27–42 (on slaves owned by the sultan's slaves). For an earlier study, see Cornelius Gurlitt, "Die Sklaverei bei den Türken im 16 Jahrhundert nach europäischen Berichten," in *Beiträge zur Kenntnis des Orients,* ed. Hugo Grothe, vol. 10, *Jahrbuch des Deutschen Vorderasienkomites* (Halle, 1913), pp. 84–102. For a contemporary comment on slavery in sixteenth-century Turkey, see *The Turkish Letters of Ogier Ghiselin de Busbecq, Imperial Ambassador at Constantinople, 1554–1562,* trans. Edward Seymour Forster (Oxford, 1917), pp. 100–102.

38. On the *devşirme,* see *EI*², s.v. (by V. L. Ménage), where further sources and studies are cited. Paul Wittek ("Devshirme and Sharīʿa," *Bulletin of the School of Oriental and African Studies* 17 [1955], pp. 271–78) argued that the Ottomans were following a Shāfiʿī rule of law, according to which the status of *dhimmī* was available only to those who had become Christians *before* the advent of Islam. Greeks were considered as such, and therefore exempt from enslavement. Balkan Christians, converted later, were enslavable. One weakness of this argument is the lack of evidence that it was ever adduced by the Ottomans themselves. See, further, Claude Cahen, "Notes sur l'esclavage musulman et le devshirme ottoman, à propos de travaux récents," *Journal of Economic and Social History of the Orient* 13 (1970), pp. 211–18.

39. On galley slaves in Turkey, see Michel Fontenay, "Chiourmes Turques au XVIIᵉ siècle," in *Le genti del mare Mediterraneo,* ed. Rosalba Ragosta (Naples, 1981), pp. 877, 903.

40. See Alan Fisher, *The Crimean Tatars* (Stanford, 1978), pp. 15–16, 26–29, 42; idem, *The Russian Annexation of the Crimea, 1772–1783* (Cambridge, 1970), pp. 19–21.

41. C. N. Pischon, "Das Sklavenwesen in der Türkei. Eine Skizze, entworfen im Jahre 1858," *Zeitschrift der Deutschen Morgenländischen Gesellschaft* 14 (1860), p. 248.

42. For some brief descriptions of the slave markets of Cairo by European visitors from the fifteenth to the nineteenth century, see A. Raymond and G. Wiet, *Les Marchés du Caire: Traduction annotée du texte de Maqrīzī* (Cairo, 1979), pp. 223–29. For detailed descriptions of the slave markets in Cairo and Istanbul, see Louis Frank, *Mémoire sur le commerce des Nègres au Kaire* (Paris, 1802), pp. 32–35; Charles White, *Three Years in Constantinople,* vol. 2 (London, 1845), pp. 281–83. See, further, Ehud R. Toledano, *The Ottoman Slave Trade and Its Suppression* (Princeton, NJ, 1982), pp. 48–54.

43. See Goitein, *Mediterranean Society,* vol. 1, pp. 130ff.; E. Ashtor, *Histoire des prix et des salaires dans l'Orient médiéval* (Paris, 1969), pp. 57ff., 208ff., 360ff., 499ff.; Mez, *The Renaissance,* p. 156.

44. Pischon, "Das Sklavenwesen," p. 254.

45. Oluf Eigilssen, *En Kort Beretning om de Tyrkiske Sørøveres onde Medfart og Omgang* (Copenhagen, 1641), p. 34. This is a Danish version from the Icelandic original.

46. See Mohamed Talbi, "Law and economy in Ifriqiya (Tunisia) in the third Islamic century: Agriculture and the role of slaves in the country's economy," in *The Islamic Middle East 700–1900: Studies in Economic and Social History,* ed. A. L. Udovitch (Princeton, NJ, 1981), pp. 209–49; also in French in idem, *Études d'Histoire Ifriqiyenne et de civilisation musulmane médiévale* (Tunis, 1982), pp. 185–229; Talbi, *L'Emirat Aghlabide* (Paris, 1966), passim; Inalcik, "Servile Labor in the Ottoman Empire," pp. 25–52, esp. 30ff.; *EI*² s.v. "Filāḥa," 4 (by H. Inalcik); idem, "Rice cultivation and the çeltükci reʿāyā system in the Ottoman Empire," *Turcica* 1 (1982), pp. 69–141.

47. See *EI*² suppl., s.v. "Bighāʾ."

Chapter 2

1. When I joined the British Army in 1940, one of the items on the form which I had to complete was "race." This was the first time I had seen the word "race" in an official document, and, given the circumstances at the time, I was at a loss what to write. Nowadays, asked the same question, I would unhesitatingly write "white" or "Cauca-

sian." It would not have occurred to me to do so then. For me at that time, white was a color, not a race; Caucasian—except among anthropologists—meant natives of the region of the Caucasus Mountains. The only people who were currently using the term "race" in official documents were our enemies, and I was sure that the British Army did not want to know whether I was or was not Aryan. I therefore sought the guidance of the sergeant, who explained to me that as far as the British Army was concerned, there are four and only four races—English, Scottish, Welsh, and Irish. Even a black recruit—and there were some already—was obliged to choose one of these four. The choice was of course entirely voluntary. You put down what you felt yourself to be.

2. When I called my first article on this topic—published in England in 1970—"Race and Colour in Islam," these two words, at that time and in that place, meant different things. Today, such a title would be tautologous.

3. According to Sabatino Moscati, *Historical Art in the Ancient Near East* (Rome, 1963), pp. 48–50:

> The characterization of peoples is very clearly defined in constant schemata in the art of the ancient Near East. Egyptian examples are well known: Asiatics with full heads of hair bound with ribbons, and pointed beards; Libyans with long curls along their ears; beardless Hittites with broad, protruding noses; Negros [*sic*] with flat noses and thick, kinky hair; the "Peoples from the Sea" with feathered head coverings, etc. And Mesopotamian examples, albeit little studied, are also noteworthy: for example, in Neo-Assyrian reliefs, the Hebrews deported from Lachish are depicted with straight, protruding noses, kinky hair joining rounded, tightly curled beards, and wearing long, unbelted tunics; Arabs in short belted skirts are represented with smooth straight hair contrasting with their curled beards; and Persians, with broad, ornate bands on their hair, the thin nose that forms a single line with the forehead, the short flat beard and the elegant armour.

4. Juvenal, *Satires* III, 62; Ammianus Marcellinus, *History* XIV, 4. Glen W. Bowersock (*Rome and Arabia* [Cambridge, 1983], p. 124, n. 4) has dismissed as absurd the notion that "the Roman Empire knew cultural but not racial prejudice." The examples of prejudice which he quotes, directed against Syrians, Arabs, and Jews, can only be defined as racial if one defines Syrians, Arabs, and Jews as races.

5. The "Southern boundary, made in the year 8, under the Majesty of the King of Upper and Lower Egypt, Khekure (Sesostris III) who is given life forever and ever; in order to prevent that any Negro should cross it, by water or by land, with a ship, (or) any herds of the Negroes, except a Negro, who shall come to do trading in Iken, or with a commission. Every good thing shall be done with them, but without allowing a ship of the Negroes to pass by Heh, going downstream, for ever" (J. H. Breasted, ed., *Ancient Records of Egypt,* vol. 1 [Chicago, 1906–07], pp. 293, 652).

6. In the Roman Empire, the number of Ethiopian and other dark-skinned slaves, even in Egypt, was small (William L. Westermann, *The Slave Systems of Greek and Roman Antiquity* [Philadelphia, 1955], p. 97).

7. Thus Cicero, in *De provinciis consularibus,* speaks of the Syrians and the Jews as "nations born for slavery." This occurs in a letter in which he is commiserating with certain tax farmers who had been handed over as slaves to the Syrians and the Jews.

8. A. J. Toynbee, *A Study of History,* vol. 1 (London 1939), p. 266. For the historical record of Muslim racial attitudes, the reader must look elsewhere. The problem of relations between Arab and non-Arab Muslims in early Islamic society was first examined, with a wealth of documentation, in Ignaz Goldziher's classic *Muhammedanische Studien,* vol. 1 (Halle, 1888) (*Muslim Studies,* vol. 1 [London, 1967]); that

of color in K. Vollers, "Über Rassenfarben in der arabischen Literatur," in *Centenario della nascita di Michele Amari,* vol. 1 (Palermo, 1910), pp. 84–95. Briefer and more general accounts are given in R. Levy, *The Social Structure of Islam* (Cambridge, 1957) (rev. ed. of *Sociology of Islam* [London, 1931–33]), chap. 1; G. E. von Grunebaum, *Medieval Islam,* 2d ed. (Chicago, 1953), p. 199ff. (The German version, *Der Islam im Mittelalter* [Zurich-Stuttgart, 1963], pp. 256ff., has fuller documentation.)

The place of the black in Arab-Islamic society was extensively studied in an excellent German doctoral thesis by G. Rotter (*Die Stellung des Negers in der islamisch-arabischen Gesellschaft bis zum XVI Jahrhundert* [Bonn, 1967]) and, in a brief but illuminating survey, by J. O. Hunwick, "Black Africans in the Islamic world: An understudied dimension of the Black Diaspora," *Tarikh* 5, no. 4 (1978), pp. 20–40. Mention may be made of three studies in Arabic: an article by ʿAwn al-Sharīf Qāsim, on the blacks in Arabic life and literature, "Al-Sūdān fī ḥayāt al-ʿArab wa-adabihim," *Bulletin of Sudanese Studies* (Khartoum) 1 (1968), pp. 76–92, and two books by ʿAbduh Badawī, *Al-Sūd wa 'l-Ḥaḍāra al-ʿArabiyya* (Cairo, 1976) on the blacks and Arab civilization and *Al-Shuʿarāʾ al-Sūd wa-khaṣāʾiṣuhum fi'l-Shiʿr al-ʿArabī* (Cairo, 1973) on black poets in Arabic literature. For a pioneer study on some racial attitudes in classical Persian literature, see Minoo Southgate, "The negative images of blacks in some medieval Iranian writings," *Iranian Studies* 17, no. 1 (1984), pp. 3–36. Some Turkish images of blacks have been studied in two articles by Pertev Naili Boratav: "The Negro in Turkish folklore," *Journal of American Folklore* 64 (1951), pp. 83–88, and "Les Noirs dans le folklore turc et le folklore des Noirs de Turquie," *Journal de la Société des Africanistes* 28 (1958), pp. 7–23. For two studies dealing specifically with North Africa, see Leon Carl Brown, "Color in Northern Africa," *Daedalus* 96 (1967), pp. 464–82, and Lucette Valensi, "Esclaves chrétiens et esclaves noirs à Tunis au XVIIIe siècle," *Annales* 6 (1967), pp. 1267–88. For translations of relevant texts, see B. Lewis, *Islam from the Prophet Muhammad to the Capture of Constantinople,* vol. 2, *Religion and Society* (New York, 1974), esp. chaps. 5–12; Graham W. Irwin, *Africans Abroad* (New York, 1977), pp. 57–119. A number of relevant articles dealing with aspects of the problem may be found in J. R. Willis, ed., *Slaves and Slavery in Muslim Africa,* vol. 1, *Islam and the Ideology of Slavery,* and vol. 2, *The Service Estate* (London, 1985), and in UNESCO, *African Slave Trade* (Paris, 1979).

9. *The Thousand and One Nights,* trans. E. W. Lane, rev. ed., vol. 1 (London, 1859), pp. 4–5. I have preferred Lane's sometimes rather coy translation to that of Sir Richard Burton, who not only preserves but also greatly augments the indecencies of the original. His is the more serious misrepresentation.

10. 467th and 468th nights, R. F. Burton, *The Book of the Thousand Nights and a Night,* vol. 4 (London, 1894), pp. 212–14. This story is omitted by Lane. The theme of whiteness as a reward is a common one. Cf. Rotter, *Stellung des Negers,* pp. 179–80. Another rather humorous story in the *Thousand and One Nights* tells of a Yemenite who arrived in Baghdad with six slave women, one black, one white, one fat, one thin, one yellow, one brown (Burton, *Thousand Nights and a Night,* vol. 3 [London, 1894], pp. 360–81.) In a kind of literary competition organized by their owner, the slave girls are divided into three pairs, and each girl is invited to sing the praises of her own qualities and decry those of her paired opponent in poetry and prose. The fat and the thin discuss the merits and defects of fatness and thinness; the others deal with color—black against white, and yellow against brown. The narrator adopts a position of apparent neutrality, but the narrative reveals a number of underlying assumptions. For an excellent analysis, see André Miquel, *Sept contes des mille et une nuits, ou il n'y a pas de contes innocents* (Paris, 1981), pp. 165–89.

Chapter 3

1. This would appear to be the original meaning of the Arabic *shuʿūb wa-qabāʾil.* According to some later commentators, the terms *shuʿūb* and *qabāʾil* denote, respectively, non-Arab and Arab groupings.

2. Ignaz Goldziher, *Muhammedanische Studien,* vol. 1 (Halle, 1888), pp. 103–4, 268–69 (*Muslim Studies,* vol. 1 [London, 1967], pp. 99–100, 243–44); cf. G. E. von Grunebaum, "The nature of Arab unity before Islam," *Arabica* 10 (1963), p. 10. On the interesting question of the classical Arabic terms for colors, see W. Fischer, *Farb- und Formbezeichnungen in der Sprache der altarabischen Dichtung* (Wiesbaden, 1965); Guy and Jacky Ducatez, "Formation des dénominations de couleur et de luminosité en arabe classique et pré-classique: Essai de périodisation selon une approche linguistique et anthropologique," *Peuples Mediterranéens* 10 (1980), pp. 139–72.

3. Sometimes the Greeks and other Europeans are called yellow (*aṣfar*). It is not clear, however, whether this word denotes racial color or has some other significance. See *EI*[2], s.v. "Aṣfar" (by I. Goldziher). On the use of red for the Greeks, see Frithiof Rundgren, "Sillaġdun = al-aḥāmira = al-Rūm nebst einigen Bemerkungen zu Ibn al-Sīrāfīs Sarḥ abyāt Iṣlāḥ al-manṭiq," in *Donum natalicium H. S. Nyberg Oblatum,* ed. Erik Gren, Bernhard Lewin, Helmer Ringgren, and Stig Wikander (Upsala, 1954), pp. 135–43.

4. The expedition is referred to in the Qurʿān, chapter CV.

5. Abu'l-Faraj al-Iṣfahānī, *Kitāb al-Aghānī,* vol. 2 (Būlāq, 1285/1868–69), p. 149. See also R. A. Nicholson, *A Literary History of the Arabs* (Cambridge, 1938), p. 155.

6. W. Ahlwardt, ed., *The Divans of the Six Ancient Arabic Poets* (London, 1870), p. 32, line 9. See *EI*[2], s.v. "ʿAntara" (by R. Blachère).

7. ʿAntara, *Dīwān* (Cairo, 1329/1911), p. 196.

8. Ibid.

9. Ibn Qutayba, *Kitāb al-Shiʿr wa'l-Shuʿarāʾ,* ed. M. J. de Goeje (Leiden, 1904), p. 146.

10. See above, pp. 18 and 54.

11. These are listed by Muḥammad ibn Ḥabīb, *Kitāb al-Muḥabbar,* ed. Ilse Lichtenstadter (Haydarabad, 1361/1942), pp. 306–9.

12. *EI*[2], s.v. (by W. Arafat), where sources are cited.

13. An interesting example of present-day usage of color terms may be seen in the Republic of the Sudan. The term *Sūdān* in Arabic means "blacks," and is a shortened form of the medieval *Bilād al-Sūdān,* "land of the blacks," used loosely of black Africa as a whole. In the modern Sudan the northerners, Arabic-speaking, Muslim, and light-brown, are known as "reds"; while the southerners, deep black, speaking a variety of Nilotic languages and professing either Christianity or traditional African religions, are known as "blues."

14. Ibn ʿAbd al-Ḥakam, *Futūḥ Miṣr,* ed. C. C. Torrey (New Haven, CT, 1922), p. 66; cf. G. Rotter, *Die Stellung des Negers* (Bonn, 1967), p. 92. This passage is now available in an English translation by Daniel Pipes ("Black soldiers in early Muslim armies," *International Journal of African Historical Studies* 13 [1980], pp. 90–91). ʿUbāda's concluding remark means no more than that his command includes a large number of men of swarthy or dark complexion. Pipes's inference, that ʿUbāda commanded a separate unit of a thousand Africans, is not supported by any other evidence in the rich Arabic historiography dealing with this period.

Chapter 4

1. These and other poets are discussed, with specimens of their verse, in the great literary anthology, Abu'l-Faraj al-Iṣfahānī (897–967), *Kitāb al-Aghānī,* 20 vols. (Būlāq, 1285/1868–69); ibid (Cairo, 1345/1927–)—hereafter *Aghānī* (1868) and *Aghānī* (1927). For studies in Arabic on the black poets, see ʿAbduh Badawī, *Al-Shuʿarāʾ al-Sūd wa-khaṣāʾiṣuhum fiʾl-shiʿr al ʿarabī* (Cairo, 1973); Muḥammad Bāqir Firʿawn, "*Aghribat al-ʿArab,*" *Al-Mawrid* 2 (1973), pp. 11–13. According to Badawī, "This name [the crows of the Arabs] was applied to those [Arabic] poets to whom blackness was transmitted by their slave mothers, and whom at the same time their Arab fathers did not recognize, or recognized only under constraint from them." The reason for this reluctance, according to Badawī, was their color, since "the Arabs despised the black color as much as they loved the white color; they described everything that they admired, material or moral, as white. A theme in both eulogy and boasting was the whiteness of a man, just as one of the signs of beauty in a woman was also whiteness. It was also a proof of her nobility. In the same way, a man could be eulogized as 'the son of a white woman.' Similarly, they would boast that they had taken white women as captives" (*Al-Shuʿarāʾ,* p. 1). For general accounts, see R. Blachère, *Histoire de la littérature arabe* (Paris, 1952); Fuat Sezgin, *Geschichte des arabischen Schrifttums,* vol. 2 (Leiden, 1975).

2. *Dīwān,* ed. Maymanī (Cairo, 1369/1950), p. 26. On Suḥaym, often referred to by Arabic authors as "the slave of the Banu'l-Ḥasḥās," see *Aghānī* (1868), vol. 20, pp. 2–9; Blachère, *Histoire de la litterature arabe,* pp. 318–19; and the German translations of his poems by O. Rescher, *Beiträge zur arabische Poesie,* ser. 6, pt. 2 (Istanbul, 1956–58), pp. 30–50. He was killed and burned by his owners because of his attentions to their women.

3. Suḥaym, *Dīwān,* p. 55; cf. F. Rosenthal, *The Muslim Concept of Freedom* (Leiden, 1960), p. 91.

4. Suḥaym, *Dīwān,* p. 69.

5. For a detailed study, see U. Rizzitano, "Abū Miḥǵan Nuṣayb b. Rabāḥ," *Revista degli studi orientali* 20 (1943), pp. 421–71; idem, "Alcuni frammenti poetici di . . . Nuṣayb," *Rivista degli studi orientali* 22 (1945), pp. 23–35. Nuṣayb's full name is significant. Unlike freemen, slaves are usually known by a single name, without patronymic and without tribal, regional, or other cognomen. Nuṣayb's patronymic, ibn Rabāḥ, "son of Rabāḥ," is the same as that of Bilāl, the first black Muslim and a Companion of the Prophet, and is surely a conscious evocation, as is that of Sunayḥ ibn Rabāḥ, an earlier black poet. In the same way, converts to Islam were usually called ibn ʿAbdallah or equivalent, adopting the Prophet's patronymic, and not their physical, infidel father's name. Cf. the similar use of ben Abraham, "son of Abraham," by converts to Judaism.

6. The translation of this line is slightly paraphrased. The poet is playing on the two associated meanings of the root *ẓ-l-m,* the one conveying the idea of darkness or blackness, the other of oppression or wrongdoing.

7. *Aghānī* (1868), vol. 1, pp. 140–41; *Aghānī* (1927), vol. 1, pp. 352–54; Rizzitano, "Abū Miḥǵan Nuṣayb," pp. 453, 456, and frags. 3, 34.

8. An untranslatable play on words. *Sabṭ,* used of hair, means "straight" or "lank," as contrasted with curly or frizzy. Used of the hand, it means "openhanded, generous."

9. For the story and poem, see Jāḥiẓ, "Fakhr al-Sūdān," in *Rasāʾil,* ed. ʿAbd al-Salām Muḥammad Hārūn, vol. 1 (Cairo, 1965), pp. 182–85; German translation in

O. Rescher, *Orientalische Miszellen,* vol. 2 (Istanbul, 1926), pp. 149–51. Jāḥiẓ relates a similar story, with an appropriate exchange of insults, concerning Jarīr and Sunayḥ ibn Rabāḥ. See, further, Badawī, *Al-Shu'arā',* pp. 123–25; J. O. Hunwick, "Black Africans in the Islamic world," *Tarikh* 5, no. 4 (1978), pp. 35–36.

10. *Aghānī* (1868), vol. 20, p. 25; Badawī, *Al-Shu'arā'*, p. 158.

11. Mohammed Ben Cheneb, *Abû Dolâma, poète bouffon de la cour des premiers califes abbassides* (Algiers, 1922), pp. 35, 136.

12. *Aghānī* (1868), vol. 1, p. 130; *Aghānī* (1927), vol. 1, p. 325; Rizzitano, "Abū Miḥǵan Nuṣayb," p. 431.

13. *Aghānī* (1868), vol. 1, p. 136; *Aghānī* (1927), vol. 1, p. 341; Rizzitano, "Abū Miḥǵan Nuṣayb," p. 439; G. Rotter, *Die Stellung des Negers* (Bonn, 1967), pp. 89–90.

14. *Aghānī* (1868), vol. 5, p. 137; *Aghānī* (1927), vol. 6, p. 10.

15. *Aghānī* (1868), vol. 3, p. 87; *Aghānī* (1927), vol. 3, pp. 282–83; R. Levy, *The Social Structure of Islam* (Cambridge, 1957), pp. 62–63; Rotter, *Die Stellung des Negers,* pp. 80–90. On the musician Ibn Misjaḥ, see H. G. Farmer, *A History of Arabian Music* (London, 1929), pp. 77–78, and *EI*², s.v. "Ibn Misdjaḥ" (by J. W. Fück). Part of the text is translated in Graham W. Irwin, ed., *Africans Abroad* (New York, 1977), pp. 58–59.

16. One of the most notable among them was Dhu'l-Nūn al-Miṣrī, born in Upper Egypt in about 796 A.D. He is known as al-Miṣri, the Egyptian, because of his Egyptian birth; but his parents were Nubian, and his father is said to have been a freed slave. Dhu'l-Nūn traveled and studied extensively and at one time was arrested and imprisoned in Baghdad but was released by the order of the caliph. He returned to Egypt, where he died in 861 A.D. He is known as "the head of the Sufis" and is regarded as a founder of the Sufi school of Islamic mysticism. Some books on magic and alchemy are attributed to him but are probably not authentic. A number of his prayers and some of his poems are preserved by other writers; and it is on these and on his disciples that we must rely, in the main, for knowledge of his mystical doctrines. He is said to have been the first to formulate the characteristic Sufi doctrine of the ecstatic states, the stations on the mystic way toward Gnosis, the true knowledge of God. Interestingly, he is credited with having named music as a means to this end: "Music is a divine influence which stirs the heart to see God; those who listen to it spiritually strain to God, and those who listen to it sensually fall into unbelief" (cited in R. A. Nicholson, *The Mystics of Islam* [London, 1914], p. 65). Like other Sufis, Dhu'l-Nūn preached the merits of penitence, renunciation, self-discipline, and sincerity and saw in affliction and solitude aids toward spiritual progress. He was among the first to use the language of passionate love in his religious poems, thus helping to establish what became a major feature of the Sufi tradition not only in Arabic but also—indeed, more—in Persian, Turkish, and other Islamic languages.

17. On Jāḥiẓ, see C. Pellat, *Le Milieu basrien et la formation de Ǵâhiz* (Paris, 1953); idem, *The Life and Works of Jāḥiẓ* (London, 1969); *EI*² s.v. "Djāḥiẓ" (by C. Pellat).

18. First edited by G. van Vloten, in Jāḥiẓ, *Tria opuscula, auctore al-Djahiz* (Leiden, 1903), pp. 58–85; reedited by 'Abd al-Salām Muḥammad Hārūn, in Jāḥiẓ, *Rasā'il al-Jāḥiẓ,* vol. 1 (Cairo, 1385/1965), pp. 173–226; German translation by Rescher, *Orientalische Miszellen,* vol. 2, pp. 146–86; cf. Pellat, *Life and Works of Jāḥiẓ,* pp. 195–98; abridged English translation in B. Lewis, *Islam from the Prophet Muhammad to the Capture of Constantinople,* vol. 2, *Religion and Society* (New York, 1974), pp. 210–16. The word *Zanj* refers strictly to the natives of East Africa—south of Ethiopia—and thence more generally to Bantu-speaking Africans. See above, p. 50.

19. Jāḥiẓ, *Kitāb al-Bukhalā'* (Damascus, 1357/1938), p. 253; French translation by C. Pellat, *Le Livre des avares* (Paris, 1951), p. 232.

20. Jāḥiẓ, *Kitāb al-Ḥayawān,* vol. 2 (Cairo, 1356/1938), p. 314; cf. Rotter, *Die Stellung des Negers,* p. 100.

21. Jāḥiẓ, *Al-Bayān wa'l-tabyīn,* vol. 3 (Cairo, 1380/1960), pp. 12–13.

22. Cf. Rotter, *Die Stellung des Negers,* pp. 98ff.

23. Al-Ṣāhib ibn ʿAbbād, *Al-Tadhkira fi 'l-Uṣūl al-Khamsa,* in Muḥammad Āl Yāsīn, ed., *Nafā'is al-Makhṭūṭāt,* 2d ser. (Baghdad, 1373/1954), p. 91.

24. Translated by E. van Donzel in his article "Ibn al-Jawzi on Ethiopians in Baghdad," in *The Islamic World from Classical to Modern Times,* ed. C. E. Bosworth, Charles Issawi, Roger Savory, and A. L. Udovitch (Princeton, NJ, 1989), p. 113.

25. On this literature, see Rotter, *Die Stellung des Negers,* pp. 10–20; Akbar Muhammad, "The image of Africans in Arabic literature: Some unpublished manuscripts," in *Slaves and Slavery in Modern Africa,* ed. J. R. Willis, vol. 2 (London, 1985), pp. 47–74. The examples cited are Jamāl al-Dīn Abu' l-Faraj ibn al-Jawzī (d. 1208), *Tanwīr al-Ghabash fi faḍl al-Sūdān wa'l-Ḥabash,* New Haven, Yale University Library, Landberg 197; Jalāl al-Dīn al-Suyūṭī (d. 1505), *Rafʿ Sha'n al-Ḥubshān,* London, British Museum, Or. 4634; Muḥammad al-Nuʿmān ibn Muḥammad ibn ʿArrāq (sixteenth century), *Kitāb Kanz al-Zinād al-Wārī fī Dhikr Abnā' al-Sarārī,* Leiden, University library, De Goeje no. MMDLXI; Muḥammad ibn ʿAbd al-Bāqī al-Bukhārī al-Makkī (sixteenth century), *Al-Ṭirāz al-Manqūsh fi Maḥāsin al-Ḥubūsh,* Baghdad, *Waqf* collection, no. 3031. None of these works has yet been printed. The first three chapters of the *Ṭirāz* have been published in German translation (M. Weisweiler, *Buntes Prachtgewand* [Hanover, 1924]). The Turkish text cited (*Rāfiʿ al-Ghubūsh fi Faḍa'il al-Ḥubūsh,* Ms. Fatih 4360) was written by one ʿAlī ibn ʿAbd al-Ra'ūf al-Ḥabashī (d. 1623–24) (see *Istanbul Kütüpaneleri Tarih-Coğrafya yazmaları kataloğları, i, Turkçe tarih yazmaları,* pt. 3 [Istanbul, 1945], p. 321).

26. *Aghānī* (1868), vol. 1, p. 32; *Aghānī* (1927), vol. 1, p. 65; cf. Ignaz Goldziher, *Muhammedanische Studien,* vol. 1 (Halle, 1888), p. 270 (*Muslim Studies,* vol. 1 [London, 1967], p. 245).

27. "Ka'l-Zanjī in jāʿa saraqa wa'in shabiʿa zanā" (Maydānī, *Amthāl alʿArab,* vol. 2, *Arabum proverbia,* ed. G. Freytag [Bonn, 1839], p. 404). The *ḥadīth* as cited also allows the Ethiopians two good qualities—skill at providing food and fortitude in adversity. The proverb makes no such allowance.

28. Hava Lazarus-Yafeh, *Some Religious Aspects of Islam* (Leiden, 1981), p. 30, citing Al-Bukhārī, *Ṣaḥīḥ,* ed. L. Krehl (Leiden, 1862–68), vol. 1, bk. 25, pp. 403ff. (*Bāb Hadm al-Kaʿba*).

29. Cf. Goldziher, *Muhammedanische Studien,* vol. 1, p. 269 (*Muslim Studies,* vol. 1, p. 344); K. Vollers, "Über Rassenfarben in der arabischen Literatur," in *Centenario della nascita di Michele Amari,* vol. 1 (Palermo, 1910), p. 87.

30. A. J. Wensinck, ed., *Concordance et indices de la tradition musulmane,* vol. 1 (Leiden, 1936–69), p. 327, where further references are given. See, e.g., Muttaqī, *Kanz al-ʿUmmāl,* vol. 3 (Haydarabad, 1313/1895–96), p. 197, where this and similar traditions are cited, and Ṭabari, *Ta'rīkh,* ed. M. J. de Goeje, vol. 1 (Leiden, 1879), pp. 2861–62. Cf. S. D. Goitein, *Studies in Islamic History and Institutions* (Leiden, 1966), pp. 203–4; G. E. von Grunebaum, *Medieval Islam,* 2d ed. (Chicago, 1953) p. 209; Rotter, *Die Stellung des Negers,* pp. 94–95. For some modern examples from Morocco, see Lawrence Rosen, *Bargaining for Reality: The Constitution of Social Relations in a Muslim Community* (Chicago, 1984), p. 178: "Even a woman can understand the Qur'ān. . . . Even a black man can be learned."

31. ʿAbd al-Wahhāb al-Shaʿrānī, *Kitāb Kashf al-Ghumma,* vol. 2 (Cairo, 1370/1950), p. 154.

32. Ibn Māja, *Sunan,* vol. 1 (Cairo, 1372/1952), p. 597 (*Nikāḥ* 6); cf. Rotter, *Die Stellung des Negers,* p. 132.

33. Muḥammad ibn Sa'd, *Kitāb al-Ṭabaqāt al-Kabīr,* ed. E. Sachau et al., vol. 4, pt. 1 (Leiden, 1904–40), p. 134, cited in A. S. Tritton, *Muslim Theology* (London, 1947), p. 13.

34. A reference to Qur'ān, XLIX:13. See above, p. 31. A similar sentiment—but without racial implications—is found in the Mishnaic ruling that a learned bastard ranks above an ignorant high priest. (*Horayoth* 13a; *The Babylonian Talmud, Seder Nashim,* ed. I. Epstein, trans. Israel W. Slotki, vol. 4 [London, 1935], p. 99).

35. Ibn Ḥazm, *Jamharat Ansāb al-'Arab,* ed. E. Lévi-Provencal (Cairo, 1948), p. 1. The same author, in a treatise on morals, admonishes his reader with a no doubt imaginary example: "Even if you were king of all the Muslims you should know that the king of the Sudan, a wretched black man with bare genitals, and ignorant, has a wider kingdom than yours" (*Kitāb al-Akhlāq wa'l-siyar,* ed. and trans. [into French] Nada Tomiche [Beirut, 1961], Arabic text p. 67, trans. p. 86, cited in G. von Grunebaum, *Der Islam in Mittelalter* [Zurich-Stuttgart, 1963], pp. 536–37). Ibn Ḥazm didn't care for Jews either. His anti-Jewish tract was analyzed by E. García Gomez, "Polémica religiosa entre Ibn Ḥazm y Ibn al-Nagrīla," *Al-Andalus* 4 (1936), pp. 1–28, and, with other similar material, by M. Perlmann, "Eleventh-century Andalusian authors on the Jews of Granada," *Proceedings of the American Academy for Jewish Research* 18 (1949), pp. 269ff., esp. 280–84. The Arabic text was published in Cairo in 1380/1960, in a critical edition by Dr. Iḥsān 'Abbās (*Al-Radd 'alā Ibn Naghrila al-Yahūdī wa-rasā'il ukhrā*). Ibn Ḥazm's case against the Jews is basically religious, but with recognizable racial overtones.

36. Rotter, *Die Stellung des Negers,* p. 103; Goldziher, *Muhammedanische Studien,* vol. 1, p. 74 (*Muslim Studies,* vol. 1, p. 75).

37. For examples, see Rotter, *Die Stellung des Negers,* p. 181.

38. Abu'l-'Alā' al-Ma'arrī, *Risālat al-ghufrān* (Cairo, 1321/1903), p. 73; cf. Rotter, *Die Stellung des Negers,* p. 180. In one of his letters (*The Letters of Abu'l-'Alā' of Ma'arrat al-Nu'mān,* in *Anecdota Oxoniensia,* ed. and trans. D. S. Margoliouth [Oxford, 1898], text p. 61, trans. p. 67) Abu'l-'Alā' remarks that "names do not prove any real superiority in their subjects; many a hideous ill-smelling black is called Camphor or Amber; many an ugly creature has the name 'New Moon' or 'Full Moon.' " In another letter, the same author, writing to a friend, sends greetings to his black slave (*ghulām*), "who, though his skin be black, is more highly esteemed by us than an untrustworthy white" (text p. 41, trans. p. 50).

39. Ibn Hishām, *Sīrat Rasūl Allāh,* ed. F. Wüstenfeld (Göttingen, 1858–59), p. 266; English translation by A. Guillaume, *The Life of Muhammad* (London, 1955), pp. 183–84; Ibn Sa'd, *Kitāb al-Tabaqāt,* vol. 1, pt. 2, pp. 120ff.; English translation by S. Moinul Haq and H. K. Ghazanfar, vol. 1 (Karachi, 1967), pp. 484ff.; Vollers, "Über Rassenfarben," pp. 90–91.

Chapter 5

1. B. Lewis, *Islam from the Prophet Muhammad to the Capture of Constantinople,* vol. 2, *Religion and Society* (New York, 1974), p. 211.

2. See above, pp. 42 and 65.

3. Ibn 'Abd Rabbihi, *Al-'Iqd al-farīd,* vol. 3 (Cairo, 1372/1953), pp. 326–27. Translations in Lewis, *Islam,* vol. 2, pp. 201–6. A Qurashī is a member of Quraysh,

the Meccan Arab tribe to which the Prophet belonged. The *kunya* was a name formed with *Abū* ("father of"). Its use, in early Islamic times, was a prerogative of Arabs.

4. Maslama's father was the Caliph ʿAbd al-Malik; his mother was a slave girl. On his career and exclusion, see *EI*[1], s.v. (by H. Lammens); Francesco Gabrieli, "L'Eroe Omayyade Maslamah ibn ʿAbd al-Malik," *Rendiconti della classe di scienze morali, storiche e filologiche* (Accademia Nazionale dei Lincei), ser. 8, vol. 5/1–2 (1950), pp. 22–39.

5. For a critical survey of recent theories and literature on the Abbasid revolution, see R. Stephen Humphreys, *Islamic History: A Framework for Inquiry* (Minneapolis, 1988), pp. 99–119.

6. ʿAlāʾ al-Dīn ʿAlī ibn Husām al-Dīn al-Muttaqī, *Kanz al-ʿUmmāl,* vol. 6 (Haydarabad, 1312/1894–98), pp. 214–15.

7. See Bernard Lewis, *Islam in History* (London, 1973), pp. 247–48.

8. Cf. the comments of Ibn al-Muqaffaʿ, *"Conseiller" de calife,* ed. and trans. Charles Pellat (Paris, 1976), pp. 37–39.

9. ʿAbduh Badawī, *Al-Shuʿarāʾ al-Sūd wa-khaṣāʾiṣuhum fiʾl-shiʿr al-ʿarabī* (Cairo, 1973), p. 21.

10. H. Lammens, *Le Berceau de l'Islam,* vol. 1 (Rome, 1914), pp. 298ff.

11. Ibn Ḥabīb, *Kitāb al-Muḥabbar,* ed. Ilse Lichtenstädter (Haydarabad, 1361/1942), p. 306.

12. On Shiʿite abuse of ʿUmar as al-Adlam—the swarthy or dusky—see I. Goldziher, "Spottnamen der ersten Chalifen bei den Shiʿiten," *Wiener Zeitschrift für Kunde des Morgenlandes* 15 (1901), pp. 301, 308.

13. See above, pp. 10ff.

14. See above, p. 17.

15. See Frank M. Snowden, *Blacks in Antiquity: Ethiopians in the Greco-Roman Experience* (Cambridge, MA, 1970); idem, *Before Color Prejudice: The Ancient View of Blacks* (Cambridge, MA, 1983). There was, however, already in antiquity, an export trade in "better quality" slaves from East Africa to Egypt and, "rarely," to the East. This is attested by a Greek geographical text of the first century A.D. (Lionel Casson, ed. and trans., *The Periplus Maris Erythraei* [Princeton, NJ, 1989], pp. 55, 59, etc.).

16. See above, p. 25.

17. Al-Balādhurī, *Ansāb al-Ashrāf,* ed. Muḥammad Ḥamīdullāh, vol. 1 (Cairo, 1959), p. 505.

18. Tabarī, *Taʾrīkh,* ed. M. J. de Goeje, vol. 1 (Leiden, 1879), p. 3177; cf. G. Rotter, *Die Stellung der Negers* (Bonn, 1967), p. 53, n. 2.

19. Jahshiyārī, *Kitāb al-Wuzarāʾ wa ʾl-Kuttāb* (Cairo, 1938), p. 81; German translation by J. Latz, *Das Buch der Wezire und Staatssekretär . . .* (Walldorf-Hessen, 1958), p. 129.

20. Buzurg ibn Shahriyār, *Kitāb ʿAjāʾib al-Hind,* ed. P. A. van der Lith (Leiden, 1883–86), pp. 50–60; French translation in *Mémorial Jean Sauvaget,* vol. 1 (Damascus, 1954), pp. 221–27; English translation in Lewis, *Islam,* vol. 2, pp. 82–87. Similar sentiments were expressed by black slaves in nineteenth-century Arabia; see C. M. Doughty, *Travels in Arabia Deserta,* 3d ed., vol. 1 (London, 1923), pp. 554–55.

Chapter 6

1. For a discussion of Arabic terms for the alien or outsider, see Bernard Lewis, *The Political Language of Islam* (Chicago, 1988), p. 118, n. 5.

2. The fullest critical account of Arab tribal rivalries and of "the war between the tribes" that convulsed the Umayyad Caliphate is still that of Julius Wellhausen, *The Arab Kingdom and Its Fall* (Calcutta, 1927).

3. On the *Mawālī,* see above, pp. 37ff.

4. On the Shuʿūbiyya, see *EI*[1], s.v. (by D. B. MacDonald); Ignaz Goldziher, *Muhammedanische Studien,* vol. 1 (Halle, 1888), pp. 147–216 (*Muslim Studies* [London, 1976], pp. 173–38); H. A. R. Gibb, "The social significance of the Shuʿubiyya," in his *Studies on the Civilization of Islam* (London, 1962), pp. 62–73; above, p. 32. ʿAbd al-ʿAzīz al-Dūrī (*Al-Judhūr al-ta'rīkhiyya li'l-Shuʿūbiyya* [Beirut, 1962]) discusses the medieval Shuʿūbiyya in the light of recent and current Arab experience.

5. On the Shūʿubiyya in Spain, see Ignaz Goldziher, "Šuʿūbijja unter den Muhammedanern in Spanien," *Nachrichten über Angelegenheiten der D.M.G.* 53 (1899), pp. 601–20.

6. According to a probably late *ḥadīth,* the Prophet said: "O people! The Lord is one Lord; the father is one father; the religion is one religion. Arabic is neither father nor mother to any of you, but is a language. Whoever speaks Arabic is an Arab" (Bernard Lewis, *Islam from the Prophet Muhammad to the Capture of Constantinople,* vol. 2, *Religion and Society* [New York, 1974], p. 196). This is a far cry from the meticulous distinctions of the age of the conquests.

7. A term commonly used by Qur'ān commentators and other Muslim scholars for these narratives of Jewish and Christian origin is *Isrā'īliyyāt* (see *EI*[2], s.v. [by G. Vajda]). In later times the word acquired somewhat negative connotations, and came to be used in the sense of superstitious fables.

8. See, for example, Masʿūdī, *Murūj al-dhahab,* ed. Charles Pellat (Beirut, 1965–), vol. 1, pp. 44–45, vol. 2, pp. 244, 266, 276, vol. 4, p. 126; Yaʿqūbī, *Ta'rīkh,* ed. T. L. Houtsma, vol. 1 (Leiden, 1883), pp. 12–13; Muḥammad b. ʿAbdallah al-Kisā'ī, *Vita prophetarum,* ed. I. Eisenberg (Leiden, 1923), pp. 98–102; Ṭabarī, *Ta'rīkh,* ed. M. J. Goeje, vol. 1 (Leiden, 1879), pp. 187–216 (English translation by William M. Brinner, *The History of Tabari,* vol. 2, *Prophets and Patriarchs* [New York, 1987]); Ibn Saʿd, *Ṭabaqāt,* ed. E. Mittwoch (Leiden, 1905), vol. 1, pt. 1, pp. 10–20; al-Thaʿlabī, *ʿArā'is al-Majālis* (Cairo, 1374/1954), pp. 54–61; Ibn Qutayba, *Al-Maʿārif,* ed. Tharwat ʿUkāsha, 2d ed. (Cairo, 1969), pp. 23–28; Ibn Hishām, *Kitāb al-Tījān fi Mulūk Ḥimyar* (Haydarabad, 1347/1928–29), pp. 24–40.

9. As, for example, in the universal chronicle of Rashīd al-Dīn. On some of the mythological genealogies, ser Bahaeddin Ögel, *Türk Mitolojisi* (Ankara, 1971), pp. 73, 145ff., 373ff., 382ff.

10. On the Curse of Ham, see chap. 8, n. 9, pp. 123–25.

11. The Arabic text of this translation is lost, and the book is known only from a retranslation into Muslim Persian made in the thirteenth century. The Persian text was first edited by James Darmesteter in *Journal Asiatique* in 1894; reedited with important additional material by Mujtaba Minovi, *Nāme-i Tansar be Gushnasp* (Tehran, 1932); and translated into English by Mary Boyce, *The Letter of Tansar* (Rome, 1968). A retranslation from Persian into Arabic, with valuable annotation, was made by Yaḥyā al-Khashshāb, *Kitāb Tansar* (Cairo, 1954).

12. Minovi, *Nāme-i Tansar,* p. 41; Boyce, *Letter of Tansar,* p. 64. In Minovi's annotations to this passage (pp. 64–66), he remarks that while the ancient Persians respected the Byzantines, Indians, and Turks, they despised the Arabs as barbarians who ate lizards and drank camel's milk. Curiously, he documents this only with quotations from Arabic authors, who tell the story in order to rebut Persian accusations.

13. Ibn al-Faqīh al-Hamadānī, *Mukhtaṣar Kitāb al-Buldān,* ed. M. J. de Goeje,

vol. 5, *Bibliotheca geographorum arabicorum* (Leiden, 1885), p. 162. Avicenna, in a mnemonic medical poem, has these lines on human colors:

> Do not draw inferences from the color of the skin if
> it is conditioned by the country.
> Among the Zanj heat has transformed their bodies until
> blackness covers their skins
> While the Slavs have become so pale that their skins
> are soft and white.
> If you define the seven climates you will know their
> various temperaments.
> The fourth climate is balanced and temperate and their
> color depends on temperament.
> (*Poème de la medicine,* ed. and trans. Henri Jahier and Abdelkader Noureddine [Paris, 1956], p. 15)

14. Ibn Qutayba, *Al-Maʿārif,* ed. Tharwat ʿUkāsha, 2d ed. (Cairo 1969), p. 26.

15. Jāḥīẓ, *Kitāb al-Ḥayawān,* vol. 2 (Cairo, 1356/1938), p. 314.

16. Jāḥiẓ's essay on the Turks was first edited by G. van Vloten in Jāḥiẓ, *Tria opuscula, auctore al-Djaḥiẓ* (Leiden, 1903) and reedited by ʿAbd al-Salām Muḥammad Hārūn in Jāḥiẓ, *Rasāʾil al-Jāḥiẓ,* vol. 1 (Cairo, 1385/1965). An English translation was published by C. T. Harley Walker, in *Journal of the Royal Asiatic Society* (1915), pp. 631–97. For discussions, see Francesco Gabrieli, "La *Risāla* di al-Ġahiz sui Turchi," *Rivista degli studi orientali* 32 (1957), pp. 477–83; Ramazan Şeşen, *Hilafet Ordusunun Menkıbeleri ve Türklerin Faziletleri* (including a Turkish translation) (Ankara, 1967). On the essay in defense of the blacks, see above, pp. 31–32.

17. See Susanne Enderwitz, *Gesellschaftliche Rang und ethnische Legitimation: Der arabischer Schriftsteller Abū ʿUṯmān al-Ġāḥiẓ (gest 868) über die Afrikaner, Perser und Araber in der islamischen Gesellschaft* (Freiburg, 1979).

18. Notably Abū Ḥayyān al-Tawḥīdī, *Kitāb al-Imtāʿ waʾl-Muʾānasa,* ed. Aḥmad Amīn and Aḥmad al-Zayn, vol. 1 (Cairo, 1939), pp. 70–93, 211–13; abridged translation in Marc Bergé, "Mérites respectifs des nations," *Arabica* 19 (1972), pp. 165–73, and in Joel L. Kraemer, *Philosophy in the Renaissance of Islam: Abū Sulaymān al-Sijistānī and His Circle* (Leiden, 1986), pp. 147–48, where the essay is situated in the intellectual context of the time.

19. Cf. the remarks of Ibn Sīnā, above, p. 55.

20. "Manāqib al-Turk," in Jāḥiẓ, *Rasāʾil,* ed. ʿAbd al-Salām Hārūn, vol. 1 (Cairo, 1965), pp. 66ff.; cf. Kraemer, *Philosophy,* p. 146.

21. Cited by Abū Ḥayyān al-Ṭawḥīdī, *Al-Muqābasāt,* ed. Ḥasan al-Sandūbī (Cairo, 1929), p. 260; translation in Kraemer, *Philosophy,* p. 146, where other such dicta are cited.

22. The evolution of Arab attitudes toward the Turks—first their slaves and then their masters—was examined in two important studies by Ulrich W. Haarman: "Ideology and history, identity and alterity: The Arab image of the Turk from the ʿAbbasids to modern Egypt," *International Journal of Middle Eastern Studies* 20 (1988), pp. 175–96, and "Rather the injustice of Turks than the righteousness of the Arabs—changing ʿUlamāʾ attitudes towards Mamluk rule in the late fifteenth century," *Studia Islamica* 68 (1988), pp. 61–77.

23. Ibn Khaldūn, *Muqaddima,* ed. Etienne Quatremère, vol. 1 (Paris, 1858), p. 155; translations in Ibn Khaldūn, *The Muqaddimah,* trans. F. Rosenthal (New York, 1956), p. 174, and in C. Issawi, *An Arab Philosophy of History* (London, 1950), p. 46.

24. Ṣāʿid al-Andalusī, *Ṭabaqāt al-Umam,* ed. L. Cheikho (Beirut, 1912), p. 9;

idem. (Cairo, n.d.), pp. 11–12; trans. (into French) R. Blachère (Paris, 1935), pp. 37–38. Similar statements about the northern and southern peoples are to be found in earlier authors, notably Masʿūdī.

25. For a critical survey of this literature, see Hans Müller, *Die Kunst des Sklavenkaufs nach arabischen, persischen und türkischen Ratgebern vom 10, bis zum 18. Jahrhundert* (Freiburg, 1980). For brief examples in English, see Kai-Kā'ūs ibn Iskandar, *Qābūsnāma,* ed. R. Levy, E. J. W. Gibb Memorial series, n.s., vol. 18 (London, 1951), pp. 62–67; English translation by R. Levy, *A Mirror for Princes* (London, 1951), pp. 99–108; Naṣīr al-Dīn Ṭūsī, *Akhlāq-i Nāṣirī;* English translation by G. M. Wickens, *The Nasirean Ethics* (London, 1964), p. 184. The first of these dates from 1082 A.D.; the second from 1235 A.D.

26. On Ibn Buṭlān, see Müller, *Kunst des Sklavenkaufs,* pp. 45–80; and translated excerpts in Lewis, *Islam,* vol. 2, pp. 243–51.

27. Kınalızade Alaettin Ali Çelebi, *Ahlâk-i Alâiye,* vol. 2 (Būlāq, 1248/1832–33), pp. 52–65 (cf. Müller, *Kunst der Slavenkaufs,* pp. 181–87); Gelibolulu Mustafa Ali, *Kunh al-Ahbar,* vol. 5 (Istanbul, 1869) pp. 9–14; idem, *Meva'iddü'n-Nefa'is fi kavaidi'l-mecalis* (Istanbul, 1956), pp. 152–53; Bernard Lewis, *The Muslim Discovery of Europe,* rev. ed. (New York, 1988), pp. 154–55; Alan Fisher, "Chattel slavery in the Ottoman Empire," *Slavery and Abolition* 1 (1980), pp. 40–41.

Chapter 7

1. See Bernard Lewis, *The Muslim Discovery of Europe,* rev. ed. (New York, 1988).

2. See André Miquel, *La Géographie humaine du monde musulman jusqu'au milieu du 11e siècle,* vol. 2, *Géographie arabe et representation du monde: La terre et l'étranger* (Paris, 1975), pp. 127–202 ("L'Afrique noire"); Tadeusz Lewicki, *Arabic External Sources for the History of Africa to the South of the Sahara* (London, 1974); Yusuf Fadl Hasan, *The Arabs and the Sudan, from the Seventh to the Early Sixteenth Century* (Edinburgh, 1967); Osman Sīd Ahmad Ismaʿil al-Beʿily, " 'Al-Sudan' and 'Bilad al-Sudan' in early and medieval Arabic writing," *Bulletin of the Cairo University—Khartoum* 2 (1972); Giovanni Vantini, "Greek and Arab geographers on Nubia (ca. 550 B.C.–1500 A.D.)," in *Graeco-Arabica: First International Congress on Greek and Arabic Studies,* ed. V. Christides and M. Papathomopoulos, vol. 3 (Athens, 1984), pp. 21–50. Kizobo O'Bweng, "Les Négro-Africains dans les relations Arabo-Byzantines (Ve–Xe)," in *Graeco-Arabica,* vol. 3, pp. 85–94. Selected translations in Bernard Lewis, *Islam from the Prophet Muhammad to the Capture of Constantinople,* vol. 2, *Religion and Society* (New York, 1974), pp. 106–20. The best-known Arabic sources on medieval black Africa have been conveniently collected by two Russian scholars, L. E. Kubbel and V. V. Matveev, and reedited with Russian translation and notes: *Arabskiye istočniki VIII–X vekov po etnografii i istorii Afriki yužneye Sakhari* (Moscow-Leningrad, 1960); V. V. Matveev and L. E. Kubbel, *Arabskiye istočniki X–XII vekov po etnografii i istorii Afriki yužneye Sakhari* (Moscow-Leningrad, 1965)—hereafter Kubbel and Matveev, *Arabskiye istočniki* (1960), and Matveev and Kubbel, *Arabskiye istočniki* (1965). For an English translation of these and other sources, see N. Levtzion and J. F. P. Hopkins, eds., *Corpus of Early Arabic Sources for West African History,* trans. J. F. P. Hopkins (Cambridge, 1981). For translations into French, see Joseph M. Cuoq, *Recueil des sources arabes concernant l'Afrique occidentale du VIIIe au XVIe siècle (Bilād al-Sūdān)* (Paris, 1975). On East Africa, see M.

Devic, *Les Pays des Zendjs . . . d'après les ecrivains arabes* (Paris, 1883); F. Storbeck, "Die Berichte der arabischen Geographen des Mittelalters über Ostafrika," *Mitteilungen des Seminars für Orientalische Sprachen zu Berlin* 17, no. 2 (1914), pp. 97–169; in general, John Wansbrough, "Africa and the Arab geographers," in *Languages and History in Africa,* ed. D. Dalby (London, 1970), pp. 89–101.

3. According to a story related by two tenth-century Arab geographers, in almost identical language, "in the outer reaches of the land of the Zanj there are cool highlands in which live white Zanj" (Abū Isḥāq Ibrāhīm ibn Muḥammad al-Iṣṭakhrī, *Kitāb Masālik al-Mamālik,* ed. M. J. de Goeje [Leiden, 1870], p. 36; Ibn Ḥawqal, *Kitāb Ṣūrat al-Arḍ,* ed. J. H. Kramers, vol. 1 [Leiden, 1938–39], p. 59).

4. Yaʿqūbī, *Kitāb al-Buldān,* ed. M. J. de Goeje, 2d ed., *Bibliotheca geographorum arabicorum,* vol. 7 (Leiden, 1892), p. 345; French translation by G. Wiet, *Les Pays* (Cairo, 1937), p. 205; Kubbel and Matveev, *Arabskiye istočniki* (1960), p. 43; Levtzion and Hopkins, *Corpus,* pp. 302–3.

5. Maqdisī, *Kitāb al-Bad' wa'l-ta'rīkh,* ed. and trans. (into French) Clément Huart (Paris, 1903), text 4, pp. 69–70, trans. p. 65; Matveev and Kubbel, *Arabskiye istočniki* (1965), p. 14.

6. Idrīsī, *Opus geographicum,* ed. A. Bombaci, U. Rizzitano, R. Rubinacci, and L. Veccia Vaglieri, vol. 1 (Naples and Rome, 1970), pp. 61, 18. The earlier edition of the passage on the Zanj, by Youssouf Kamal, *Monumenta Cartographica Africae et Aegypti,* vol. 3, pt. 4 (Leiden, 1934), p. 831 (Matveev and Kubbel, *Arabskiye istočniki* [1965], p. 258) is defective. The passage on Takrūr occurs in Idrīsī, *al-Maghrib wa-arḍ al-Sūdān,* ed. and trans. R. Dozy and M. J. de Goeje (Leiden, 1964), p. 4 (Matveev and Kubbel, *Arabskiye istočniki* [1965], p. 236). The reference to dates is paralleled in an Arabic proverb: "Blacks are caught with dates." Freytag, I/2, pl. 651, n. 176. An external confirmation of this practice is provided by a twelfth-century Chinese author, who, apparently speaking of the people of an East African island, observes that "their bodies are black as lacquer and they have frizzled hair. They are enticed by (offers of) food and then captured and sold as slaves to the Arabic countries, where they fetch a very high price. . . . thousands of them are sold as foreign slaves" (Chou Ch'u-fei, cited in J. J. L. Duyvendak, *China's Discovery of Africa* [London, 1949], pp. 22–23).

7. Ibn Baṭṭūṭa, *Voyages* (*Tuḥfat al-nuẓẓār*), ed. and trans. C. Defrémery and B. R. Sanguinetti, vol. 4 (1854; reprint, Paris, 1969), pp. 441–45; English translation in Ibn Baṭṭūṭa, *Travels in Asia and Africa, 1325–1354,* trans. H. A. R. Gibb (London, 1929), pp. 336–37.

8. Ibn Khurradādhbih, *Al-Masālik wa'l-mamālik,* ed. M. J. de Goeje, *Bibliotheca geographorum arabicorum,* vol. 6 (Leiden, 1889), pp. 60–61, 170; Kubbel and Matveev, *Arabskiye istočniki* (1960), pp. 32–33.

9. Ibn Qutayba, *Al-Maʿārif,* ed. Tharwat ʿUkāsha, 2d ed. (Cairo, 1969), p. 26 (Kubbel and Matveev, *Arabskiye istočniki* [1960], p. 21); Ibn Qutayba, *ʿUyūn al-Akhbār,* ed. Aḥmad Zakī al-ʿAdwī, vol. 2 (Cairo, 1343–49/1925–30), p. 67. On the filing of the teeth by African slaves in the eighteenth century, see W. G. Browne, *Travels in Africa, Egypt, and Syria from the year 1792 to 1798,* 2d ed. (London, 1806), p. 396.

10. Masʿūdī, *Murūj al-dhahab,* ed. Charles Pellat (Beirut, 1965–), vol. 1, p. 91; translated by Charles Pellat, *Les Prairies d'or,* vol. 1 (Paris, 1962), p. 69.

11. Maqdisī, *Kitāb al-Bad',* vol. 4, pp. 69–70.

12. *Ḥudūd al-ʿĀlam,* ed. M. Sotoodeh (Tehran, 1340/1962), pp. 195–200; English translation by V. Minorsky (London, 1937), pp. 163–66.

13. See above, pp. 32ff.

14. Ṭūsī, *Taṣawwurāt,* ed. W. Ivanow (Leiden, 1950), pp. 52–53; cf. Ivanow's translation, pp. 57–58.

15. In the translation of F. Rosenthal, Ibn Khaldūn, *The Muqaddimah,* vol. 1 (New York, 1958), p. 301 (hereafter simply Rosenthal). For another English translation, see C. Issawi, *An Arab Philosophy of History* (London, 1950), p. 98. The original of this passage may be found in Ibn Khaldūn, *Muqaddima,* ed. Etienne Quatremère, vol. 1 (Paris, 1858), p. 269; ibid. (Beirut, 1901), p. 148; ibid., ed. Naṣr al-Ḥūrīnī (Būlāq, 1274/1857), pp. 124–25 (hereafter simply Quatremère, Beirut, and Būlāq). French translations by M. de Slane, *Les Prolegomènes d'Ibn Khaldoun,* vol. 1, (1862; reprint, Paris, 1934), p. 309 ("Il est vrai que la plupart des nègres s'habituent facilement à la servitude; mais cette disposition résulte, ainsi que nous l'avons dit ailleurs, d'une infériorité d'organisation qui les rapproche des animaux bruts"); and by Vincent Monteil, *Discours sur l'histoire universelle (Al-Muqaddima),* vol. 1 (Beirut, 1967), p. 294 ("C'est ainsi que les nations nègres sont, en général, soumises à l'esclavage, parce que les Noirs sont une humanité inférieure (*naqṣ al-insāniyya*), plus prôche des animaux stupides"). For parallel passages see Rosenthal, vol. 1, pp. 118ff., 168ff. In another passage in his *Muqaddima* (Quatremère, vol. 1, pp. 95–96; Rosenthal, vol. 1, pp. 118–19; Levtzion and Hopkins, *Corpus,* pp. 319–20), Ibn Khaldūn, after describing the known peoples of black West Africa, observes that "beyond them to the south there is no civilization in the proper sense. There are only humans who are closer to dumb animals than to rational beings. They live in thickets and caves, and eat herbs and unprepared grain. They frequently eat each other. They cannot be considered human beings" (Rosenthal, vol. 1, pp. 118–19). In his historical work, the *Kitāb al-ʿIbar* (Cairo, 1867), vol. 5, pp. 433ff. (translation in Levtzion and Hopkins, *Corpus,* pp. 322ff.), Ibn Khaldūn gives a lengthy account of the West African peoples and kingdoms. In another passage, Ibn Khaldūn makes a more general observation about the inhabitants of the zones that are "far from temperate." Speaking of the blacks, he says: "Their foodstuffs are *durra* and herbs, their clothing is the leaves of trees, which they sew together to cover themselves, or animal skins. Most of them go naked. The fruits and seasonings of their countries are strange and inclined to be intemperate. In their business dealings, they do not use the two noble metals, but copper, iron, or skins, upon which they set a value for the purpose of business dealings. Their qualities of character, moreover, are close to those of dumb animals. It has even been reported that most of the Negroes of the first zone dwell in caves and thickets, eat herbs, live in savage isolation, and do not congregate, and eat each other. The same applies to the Slavs" (Quatremère, vol. 1, pp. 149–50; Rosenthal, vol. 1, p. 168); Issawi, *Arab Philosophy of History,* p. 44.

16. For an edited, translated, and annotated example of late medieval Egyptian scholarship on black Africa, see Dierk Lange, "Un Texte de Maqrīzī sur 'les races des Sudan,' " *Annales Islamologiques* 15 (1979), pp. 187–209.

17. Al-Qalqashandī, *Ṣubḥ al-Aʿshā,* vol. 8 (Cairo, 1313–19/1895–1901), pp. 116–17. A full translation may be found in Levtzion and Hopkins, *Corpus,* pp. 347ff.

Chapter 8

1. ʿAbd al-Wahhāb al-Shaʿrānī (*Kitāb Kashf al-Ghumma,* vol. 2 [Cairo 1370/1950], p. 216), rejects the idea outright. On the enslavement of Arabs, see Ibn Hishām, *Kitāb al-Sīra,* ed. F. Wüstenfeld, vol. 2 (Göttingen, 1859), pp. 877ff.; English

translation by A. Guillaume, *The Life of Muhammad* (Oxford, 1955), pp. 592ff.; Majid Khadduri, *War and Peace in the Law of Islam* (Baltimore, 1955), pp. 130–32. For a description, ascribed to ʿUmar, of the Bedouin as "the root of the Arabs and the stuff of Islam," see Abū Yūsuf, *Kitāb al-Kharāj* (Būlāq, 1302/1885), p. 8; English translation by A. Ben Shemesh, *Taxation in Islam,* vol. 3 (London, 1969), p. 47. On Arab privileges, see above, pp. 37ff. and 86ff.

2. Aristotle, *Politics* 1254b20, 1255a1ff., 1255a8, 1278b23.

3. Joel L. Kraemer, "The Jihād of the Falāsifa," *Jerusalem Studies in Arabic and Islam* 10 (1987), p. 313, where further sources are cited.

4. Al-Fārābī, *Fuṣūl Muntazaʿa,* ed. F. M. Najjar (Beirut, 1971), pp. 76–77.

5. Abu'l-Ḥasan Muḥammad al-ʿĀmirī (d. 992), *Al-Saʿāda wa'l-Isʿād,* ed. Mojtaba Minovi (Wiesbaden, 1957–58), p. 188, cf. p. 363. On Muslim use of Aristotle's *Politics,* see, further, S. Pines, "Aristotle's *Politics* in Arabic philosophy," *Israel Oriental Studies* 5 (1975), pp. 150–66; Franz Rosenthal, *The Muslim Concept of Freedom* (Leiden, 1960), pp. 31–32; and, on natural slavery, S. M. Stern, *Aristotle on the World State* (Oxford, 1968), pp. 30ff.

6. Aristotle, *Politics* 1285a20.

7. Cited in E. I. J. Rosenthal, *Political Thought in Medieval Islam* (Cambridge, 1958), pp. 154–55.

8. Kirmānī, *Rāḥatu'l-ʿaql* [*sic*], ed. M. Kamil Hussein and M. Mustafa Hilmy, (Cairo, 1953), p. 241.

9. In the biblical version, as noted, the curse falls only on Canaan, and consists only of servitude. With the exception of one passage, neither the Babylonian nor the Jerusalem Talmud departs from this biblical version. This exception is a curious story in both Talmuds (*Sanhedrin,* 108b; *The Babylonian Talmud: Seder Nashim,* ed. I. Epstein, trans. Jacob Shachter and H. Freeman [London, 1935], p. 745) and in a few midrashim which tells of how three creatures transgressed in the Ark: the dog, the raven, and Noah's son Ham. All three were smitten in punishment. Ham's punishment, in the Babylonian Talmud, was that *laqa beʿoro,* (lit., "he was smitten in his skin"). In the Jerusalem Talmud, Ham is *mefuḥam* (lit. "charred," cf. *peḥam,* "charcoal"). Later commentators, including the Soncino translator, assume this to refer to blackness, perhaps under the influence of medieval versions of the story. There is, however, nothing in the text to indicate that the hereditary curse had been extended from servitude to blackness or that it was transferred from Canaan, who was white, to Kush, who was black. Neither Kush nor racial blackness is mentioned, nor is there anything to show that blackness as such was seen as a punishment, appropriate to the term "smitten." On the contrary, there are several passages in ancient Jewish literature indicating that "black is beautiful." The well-known verse in the Song of Solomon (1:5), which the authorized version, following the Latin, renders "I *am* black, but comely, O ye daughters of Jerusalem," reads, in the original Hebrew and unequivocally in the earliest Greek translations, both Jewish and Christian, "I am black and comely." The "but" (*sed* in the Vulgate) appears to be the contribution of Saint Jerome. In Numbers 12, where Moses' sister Miriam denounces his marriage with an Ethiopian woman, she is punished by God for this offense. The punishment is leprosy—"Behold, Miriam became leprous, *white* as snow" (Numbers 12:10). Moses pleaded for his sister, who was let off with the lesser punishment of seven days' banishment from the camp, after which she returned, was forgiven, and, presumably, resumed her normal color.

The discoloration of Ham occurs, in rabbinic literature, only in this rare and curious story in which he is associated with the dog and the raven. It does not occur anywhere else in the Talmud, and it is not linked with the curse of servitude. In the Babylonian Talmud—and in most of the few midrashic texts that contain the story—there is no explicit reference to any hereditary change of color. Nevertheless, on the basis of this single, equivocal reference, J. R. Willis has concluded that "though the 'Curse of Ham' had its genesis in the Old Testament, its forcing bed was the Babylonian Talmud" (*Slaves and Slavery in Muslim Africa,* vol. 1 [London, 1985], p. 8; reprinted from "Islamic Africa: reflections on the servile estate," *Studia Islamica* 52 [1980], p. 194).

The earliest explicit reference to blackness as part of the curse inflicted on Ham for his offense against his father would appear to be a passage in the Bible commentary ascribed to the Syrian church father Saint Ephrem of Nisibis, according to whom Noah said: "Accursed be Canaan, and may God make his face black," whereupon the face of both Canaan and Ham became black (Paul Lagarde, *Materialen zur Kritik und Geschichte des Pentateuchs,* vol. 1 [reprinted Osnobrück and Wiesbaden, 1967], pp. 86–87, cited by M. Grünebaum, *Neue Beiträge zur Semitischen Sagenkunde* [Leiden, 1893], p. 86). This passage occurs in a late Arabic translation of some passages in Saint Ephrem's writings, and there may therefore be some question about its authenticity. No Syriac original for this passage has so far come to light; and the story may well be a later interpolation in the Arabic version, reflecting the current notions of that time. The idea also occurs in a later midrash (*Bereshit Rabbah,* 37, 7; English translation by H. Freeman, *The Midrash Rabbāh,* vol. 1, *Genesis* [London, 1977], pp. 292–93), where, for the first time in a Jewish text, the curse included the words "and therefore his seed will be ugly and black [*mefuḥam*]." Saint Ephrem died in 373 A.D.; the anonymous *Bereshit Rabbah* was probably compiled in the sixth century A.D., with later accretions of which this may be one. By that time the Canaanites were no more than a remote historic memory. Neither version mentions Kush, who in biblical, rabbinic, and most Christian versions, is the ancestor of the dark-skinned peoples of Africa.

The Qur'ān tells the story of Noah and his Ark, and speaks of one of Noah's sons who had separated himself from his family and therefore perished (XI:42ff.). There is, however, no reference to Ham or to his curse, whether of servitude or of blackness, and of course no descendants. The story of Ham appears, however, at an early date in Islamic literature and is widely cited by historians, commentators, and traditionists. Their versions vary considerably. While most indicate that Ham offended against his father Noah, not all specify his offense; and those who do so differ. In some versions, Noah withholds his blessing from Ham; in others, he curses him. In some versions, the curse consists only of servitude; in others, of both servitude and blackness. The earliest explicit statement of the latter (a mention by Jāḥiẓ [see above, p. 32] of the idea of blackness as a curse or punishment may be an allusion to this story) would appear to be a passage in Ibn Qutayba (828–89), who says:

> Wahb ibn Munabbih said: Ḥām the son of Noah was a white man, with a handsome face and a fine figure, and Almighty God changed his color and the color of his descendants in response to his father's curse. He went away, followed by his sons, and they settled by the shore, where God increased and multiplied them. They are the blacks. Their food was fish, and they sharpened their teeth like needles, as the fish stuck to them. Some of his children went to the West [Maghrib]. Ḥām begat Kūsh ibn Ḥām, Kan'ān ibn Ḥām, and Fūṭ ibn Ḥām. Fūṭ settled in India and Sind and their inhabitants are his descendants. Kūsh and Kan'ān's descendants are the various races of blacks: Nubians, Zanj, Qarān, Zaghāwa, Ethiopians, Copts, and Berbers. (*Kitāb al-Ma'ārif,* ed. Tharwat 'Ukāsha, 2d ed. [Cairo, 1969], p. 26)

Ibn Qutayba cites as source for this story Wahb ibn Munabbih, to whom many dubious stories are attributed. Wahb was a South Arabian convert to Islam, according to some, from Judaism, according to others, from Christianity. As he is also quoted as an authority on stories about Jesus, the latter seems more likely (see, e.g., Ibn Hishām, *Kitāb al-Tījān fī Mulūk Ḥimyar* [Haydarabad, 1347/1928–29], p. 27). He remains, in any case, a very problematic figure, and traditions ascribed to him are regarded, in Islamic religious literature, with reserve. In another version of the story (Muḥammad b. ʿAbdallāh al-Kisāʾī, *Vita prophetarum,* ed. I. Eisenberg [Leiden, 1923], pp. 98–99), because Shem covered his father's nakedness, his descendants would be prophets and nobles (*sharīf*), while those of Ham would be bondsmen and bondswomen until the Day of Judgment. Japhet's descendants would be tyrants (*jabābira*), Chosroes (*akāsira*), and kings (*mulūk*).

These Islamic versions depart in two significant respects from the biblical and rabbinic versions: first, that Ham, who is stricken by the curse, is presented primarily as the ancestor of the dark-skinned peoples; second, that the curse consists of the double burden of servitude and blackness. The curse of Ham also figures in medieval popular romances about the Arab expansion in Africa, notably the story of Sayf ibn Dhī Yazan, telling how he led the Muslim Arabs to victory against the infidel Ethiopians and blacks (*Sīrat Saif ibn Dhī Yazan* [Cairo, 1322/1904–5], and other editions).

As noted above, this story was by no means generally accepted by Muslim authors, and it was refuted in socio-historical terms by Ibn Khaldūn and with legal arguments by Aḥmad Bābā of Timbuktu. But the curse was too useful to disappear. The enslavement and displacement of vast numbers of blacks continued—and indeed increased after the gradual extinction of the traffic in white slaves from the North. For the sellers and buyers of black slaves, the curse of Ham provided both an explanation and a justification. When sugar and cotton and the black slave to cultivate them were transplanted, via the Iberian Peninsula and the Atlantic islands, to the new lands in the Americas, the moral problem and the mythical solution came with them, and Christian defenders of black slavery found justification in this amended version of the biblical tale. A whole literature appeared to reassure pious Christian slaveowners of the moral rightness and biblical sanction of the enslavement of the blacks. More recently, a similar school of para-scholarly literature has emerged, the purpose of which, this time, is to shift the blame for the enslavement of black Africans from Islam and Christendom to the Jews. For a discussion, see Ephraim Isaac, "Genesis, Judaism, and the 'Sons of Ham,' " *Slavery and Abolition* 1 (1980), pp. 3–17, also published, in a slightly different version, in Willis, *Slaves and Slavery,* vol. 1, pp. 75–91; Ephraim Isaac, "Concept biblique et rabbinique de la malediction de Noe," *Service international de documentation judéo-chretienne* 11, no. 2 (1978), pp. 16–35. On the whole question of the use of the Curse of Ham story, see David Brion Davis, *Slavery and Human Progress* (New York and Oxford, 1984), pp. 86–87, 337, n. 144. The Jewish sources will be examined in detail and in depth in a forthcoming study by David Goldenberg, to whom I am indebted for some of the information cited above.

10. See, for example, E. W. Lane, *An Arabic English Lexicon,* vol. 1, pt. 5 (London, 1874), p. 1935a: "*ʿAbd* is now generally applied to a male black slave; and *mamlūk* to a male white slave." J. B. Belot, *Vocabulaire arabe-français* (Beirut, 1893), p. 469, defines *ʿabd* as "Homme. Esclave, serf, serviteur. Nègre"; E. A. Elias, *Elias' Modern Dictionary, Arabic-English,* 2d ed. (Cairo, 1925), p. 369, as "Slave, bondman; bondsman. Man. Negro, black"; *Vocabulario Arabo-Italiano,* vol. 2 (Rome, 1969), p. 879, as "Schiavo, servo, servitore; negro (adibito a lavori servili)"; cf. Kh. K. Baranov, *Arabsko-Russkiy slovar* (Moscow, 1957), p. 629: "*ʿabīd:* negri." See also Simone

Delesalle and Lucette Valensi, "Le Mot 'Nègre' dans les dictionnaires français d'ancien régime: histoire et lexicographie," *Langue française* 15 (1972), pp. 79–104. From stories in *Kitāb al-Aghānī,* Abu'l-Faraj al-Iṣfahānī (20 vols. [Būlāq, 1285/1868–69]; ibid. [Cairo, 1927]—hereafter *Aghānī* [1868] and *Aghānī* [1927]) e.g., in the pages devoted to Nuṣayb, it is clear that black slaves, even after being manumitted, were still referred to as *ʿabd.* On the use of *ʿabd* in medieval Egypt, see S. D. Goitein, "Slaves and slavegirls in the Cairo Geniza records," *Arabica* 9 (1962), p. 2; idem, *A Mediterranean Society: The Jewish Communities of the Arab World as Portrayed in the Documents of the Cairo Geniza,* vol. 1, *Economic Foundations* (Berkeley and Los Angeles, 1967), p. 131. For a striking modern example of this usage, see L. C. Brown, "Color in North Africa," p. 471. This ethnic connotation of *ʿabd* does not seem to have been carried over from Arabic into Persian or Turkish. Ironically, in Ottoman Turkish and also in late Greek and in Russian, the word "Arab" acquires the meaning of black man or blackamoor and is applied to Negroes and Ethiopians. Some Turkish authors distinguish between *kara Arab,* "black Arab," and *ak Arab,* "white Arab," the former referring to the black peoples of Africa, the latter to the Arabs properly so called.

11. R. Dozy, *Supplément aux dictionnaires arabes,* 2d ed., vol. 1 (Paris, 1927), p. 355b, where other sources are cited. In classical Arabic usage, however, the word *khādim* does not, as has sometimes been stated, connote blackness. Its normal meaning is "eunuch," irrespective of race or color. See D. Ayalon, "On the eunuchs in Islam," *Jerusalem Studies in Arabic and Islam* 1 (1979), pp. 88–89. There are numerous other terms for "slave" in Arabic, Persian, Turkish, and other languages. Common euphemisms include *fatā* and *ghulām,* both meaning "youth" or "young man"; *usta* or *ustādh* (lit. "master") for a eunuch; *jāriya* (lit. "runner") for a slave girl. *Raqīq* and *waṣīf* are common Arabic terms for "slave"; the abstract form of the first-named, *riqq,* is the commonest term for slavery. Persian and Turkish use the Arabic terms and add some others—Persian *banda* (lit. "bondman") and *keniz* ("slavewoman"). The Turkish terms are *kul* and *köle,* but the former came to be used, in a quasi-metaphorical sense, for the officers and other members of the sultan's household and establishment. By the nineteenth century, the common Turkish term was *esir,* from an Arabic word meaning "captive."

12. For examples, see A. Mez, *Die Renaissance des Islams* (Heidelberg, 1922), pp. 153–54 (in English, *The Renaissance of Islam* [London, 1937], pp. 157–58); E. Ashtor, *Histoire des prix et des salaries dans l'orient médiéval* (Paris, 1969), pp. 57ff., 88 ff., 111, 208ff., 258, 360ff., 437ff., 463, 498ff. There may be exceptions. According to the tenth-century Byzantine emperor Constantine Porphyrogenitus (*De administrando imperio,* ed. Gy. Moravcsik, trans. R. J. H. Jenkins [Budapest, 1949], p. 94), the daily tribute paid to the Byzantine emperor by the Caliph ʿAbd al-Malik included, as well as money, "one purebred horse and one black slave" (the Greek *Aethiops* was not limited to Ethiopians *stricto sensu.*) The collocation of these two items would seem to imply that a black slave, like a purebred horse, was rare and precious, at least in Byzantine eyes, and that both were seen as valued products of the caliph's realm. According to the same source (p. 86), an earlier agreement between the emperor and Muʿāwiya provided for the annual delivery of fifty purebred horses but makes no reference to black slaves.

13. Jāḥiẓ, *Rasāʾil al-Jāḥiẓ,* ed. ʿAbd al-Salām Muḥammad Hārūn, vol. 2 (Cairo, 1385/1965), p. 177; edition and translation by A. F. L. Beeston, *The Epistle on Singing Girls by Jāḥiẓ* (Warminster, England, 1980). German translation in O. Rescher, *Excerpte und Übersetzungen aus der Schriften des Philologen Gahiz* (Stuttgart, 1931), p. 98; cf. G. Rotter, *Die Stellung der Negers* (Bonn, 1967), pp. 58–59, and C. Pellat, *The Life and Works of Jāḥiẓ* (London, 1969), pp. 259ff.

14. *Aghānī* (1868), vol. 5, p. 9; *Aghānī* (1927), vol. 5, pp. 164f.

15. Ibn Buṭlān, *Risāla,* p. 352; Bernard Lewis, *Islam from the Prophet Muhammad to the Capture of Constantinople,* vol. 2, *Religion and Society* (New York, 1974), pp. 247ff.

16. Yaʿqūbī, *Kitāb al-Buldān,* ed. M. J. de Goeje, 2d ed., *Bibliotheca geographorum arabicorum,* vol. 7 (Leiden, 1892), p. 334; French translation by G. Wiet, *Les Pays* (Cairo, 1937), p. 190; L. E. Kubbel and V. V. Matveev, eds., *Arabskiye istočniki VIII–X vekov po etnografii i istorii Afriki yužneye Sakhari* (Moscow and Leningrad, 1960), p. 41.

17. Ibn Baṭṭūṭa, *Voyages (Tuḥfat al-nuẓẓar),* ed. and trans. C. Defrémery and B. R. Sanguinetti, vol. 4 (Paris, 1969), p. 441; English version in Ibn Baṭṭūṭa, *Travels in Asia and Africa, 1325–1354,* trans. H. A. R. Gibb (London, 1929), p. 336, and in N. Levtzion and J. F. P. Hopkins, *Corpus of Early Arabic Sources for West African History,* trans. J. F. P. Hopkins (Cambridge, 1981), p. 302.

18. The slave revolt of the Zanj in Iraq was first studied by T. Nöldeke in his *Orientalische Skizzen* (Berlin, 1892), pp. 153–84; in English, *Sketches from Eastern History,* trans. John Sutherland Black (London, 1892), pp. 146–75. Later literature includes an Arabic monograph (Fayṣal al-Sāmir, *Thawrat al-Zanj* [Baghdad, 1954]); a critical analysis of the Arabic sources (Heinz Halm, *Die Traditionen des "Herrn des Zang": Eine Quellenkritische Untersuchung* [Bonn, 1967]); and a comprehensive study (A. Popovic, *La Révolte des esclaves en Iraq au iii*e*/ix*e *siècle* [Paris, 1976]). For an analysis of the place of the Zanj rebellion in the larger context of opposition movements, see Fārūq ʿUmar, *Al-Khilāfa al-ʿAbbāsiyya fi ʿAṣr al-Fawḍā al-ʿAskariyya* (Baghdad, 1974), pp. 106–18. Ghada Hashem Talhami ("The Zanj Rebellion reconsidered," *International Journal of African Historical Studies* 10, no. 3 [1977], pp. 443–61) attempts to prove, mainly on the basis of modern secondary literature in English and Arabic, that in classical Abbasid usage the term "Zanj" did not denote a specific place or people and that the Arab slave trade in East Africa is largely the invention of English and French writers concerned to defend their own colonial records. On the use of the term "Zanj," see above, pp. 50ff. On the East African slave trade, see UNESCO, *African Slave Trade* (Paris, 1979). The major Western studies on the revolt of the Zanj were written by two Germans and a Yugoslav.

19. Nāṣir-i Khusraw, *Safar-nāma,* ed. and trans. (into French) C. Schefer (Paris, 1881), text p. 82, trans. p. 227.

20. Aḥmad al-Wansharīsī (d. 1508), *Kitāb al-Miʿyār al-mughrib,* vol. 9 (Fes, 1313/1895–96), pp. 71–72; French translation by E. Amar, in *Archives Marocaines* 13 (1909), pp. 426–28. See below, p. 148.

21. *EI*², s.v. "ʿAbd" (by R. Brunschvig), p. 32a; Rotter, *Die Stellung des Negers,* pp. 44f., 49ff.

22. Mahmoud A. Zouber, *Ahmad Baba de Tomboktou (1556–1627): Sa vie et son oeuvre* (Paris, 1977), pp. 129–46. For an edition and translation, with commentary, of this text see Bernard Barbour and Michelle Jacobs, "The Miʾrāj: A legal treatise on slavery by Ahmad Baba," in *Slaves and Slavery in Muslim Africa,* ed. J. R. Willis, vol. 1 (London, 1985), pp. 125–59. In this work, Aḥmad Bābā quotes from an earlier jurist, Makhlūf al-Balbalī (d. 1533 A.D.), who said: "The origin of slavery is non-belief, and the black kāfirs are like the Christians, except that they are *majūs,* pagans. The Muslims among them, like the people of Kano, Katsina, Bornu, Gobir, and all of Songhai, are Muslims, who are not to be owned. Yet some of them transgress on the others unjustly by invasion as do the Arabs, Bedouins, who transgress on free Muslims and sell them unjustly, and thus it is not lawful to own any of them. . . . If anybody is

known to have come from these countries, he should be set free directly, and his freedom acknowledged" (pp. 130–31).

23. Al-Nāṣirī, *Kitāb al-Istiqsā'*, vol. 5 (Casablanca, 1955), pp. 131ff. This passage is translated in J. O. Hunwick, "Black Africans in the Islamic world," *Tarikh* 5, no. 4 (1978), pp. 38–40.

24. Ṭabāri, *Ta'rīkh,* ed. M. J. de Goeje, vol. 3 (Leiden, 1881), pp. 950–51; Hilāl al-Ṣābiʿ, *Rusūm Dār al-Khilāfa,* ed. Mikhā'īl ʿAwād (Baghdad, 1964), p. 8, cf. p. 12. For medieval Arabic accounts of castration, see Jāḥiẓ, *Kitāb al-Ḥayawān,* vol. 1 (Cairo, 1356/1958), pp. 106ff.; Spanish translation by Miguel Asin Palacios, *Isis* 14 (1930), pp. 42ff.; Al-Muqaddasī, *Aḥsan al-taqāsīm,* ed. M. J. de Goeje, 2d ed., *Bibliotheca geographorum arabicorum,* vol. 3 (Leiden, 1906), p. 242; French translation by C. Pellat, *Description de l'occident musulman au IVe–Xe siècle* (Algiers, 1950), pp. 57–58. Other sources in Rotter, *Die Stellung des Negers,* pp. 33–35. Descriptions of the procedures used in Egypt for castrating black boys are given by European observers at the beginning of the nineteenth century; see above, pp. 76–77. On eunuchs, see Mez, *Die Renaissance,* pp. 332ff. (*The Renaissance,* pp. 353ff.); M. F. Köprülü, in *Türk Hukuk ve Iktisat Tarihi Mecmuası* 1 (1931), pp. 208–11; Italian translation, idem, *Alcune osservazioni intorno all'influenza delle istituzioni bizantine sulle istituzioni ottomane* (Rome, 1953).

25. Jeremy Bentham, *The Correspondence of Jeremy Bentham,* vol. 3 (January 1781 to October 1788), ed. Ian R. Christie (London, 1971), p. 387.

26. See *EI*², s.v. "Ḥabshīs" (by J. Burton-Page).

27. The first poem is cited in the translation of A. J. Arberry, *Poems of al-Mutanabbī* (Cambridge, 1967), pp. 112–14. The second is translated from the original in al-Mutanabbi, *Dīwān,* ed. ʿAbd al-Wahhāb ʿAẓẓām (Cairo, 1363/1944), p. 460. On al-Mutanabbī's "racism," see J. Lecerf, "La Signification historique du racisme chez Mutanabbī," in *Al-Mutanabbī: Recueil publié à l'occasion de son millénaire* (*Mémoires de l'Institut français de Damas*) (Beirut, 1936), pp. 33–43.

28. The most famous was the Egyptian-born mystic Dhu'l-Nūn al-Miṣrī (ca. 796–861), the son of a freed Nubian slave. See *EI*², s.v. (by M. Smith); above, p. 114, n. 16.

Chapter 9

1. C. A. Plassart, "Les Archers d'Athènes," *Revue des études grecques* 26 (1913), pp. 151–213; O. Jacob, *Les Esclaves publiques à Athènes* (Liège, 1928), chap. 2; M. I. Finley, *Ancient Slavery and Modern Ideology* (New York, 1980), p. 85.

2. William L. Westermann, *The Slave Systems of Greek and Roman Antiquity* (Philadelphia, 1955), pp. 15–16, 37, 61; on the use of armed slaves as bodyguards, ibid., p. 67.

3. Wāqidī, *Kitāb al-Maghāzī,* ed. Marsden Jones (London, 1966), p. 91; Balādhurī, *Ansāb al-Ashrāf,* ed. Muḥammad Ḥamīdullah, vol. 1 (Cairo, 1959), p. 367.

4. *Akhbār al-Dawla al-Abbāsiyya,* ed. ʿA. ʿA. Dūrī and A. J. al-Muṭṭalibī (Beirut, 1971), p. 280; Ṭabarī, *Ta'rīkh,* ed. M. J. de Goeje, vol. 2 (Leiden, 1879–1901), pp. 1968–69; Julius Wellhausen, *The Arab Kingdom and Its Fall* (Calcutta, 1927), p. 534. When reproached by their masters, and even by some of his own supporters and companions, Abū Muslim replied: "If any slave comes willingly to join our cause, we shall accept him and he shall have the same privileges and the same duties as we." Speaking of a certain slave, belonging to one ʿĀṣim, Abū Muslim remarked: "It was God who liberated him, and God has a better claim than ʿĀṣim." A garbled version of

these events seems to have reached as far as Byzantium, where the historian Theophanes, in recording the events of the year of Creation 6240 (748 A.D.), reports that the slaves in Khurāsān, incited by Abū Muslim, killed their masters in a single night and equipped themselves with their arms, horses, and money. See Theophanes, *Chronographia* (Bonn, 1839), pp. 654–55; German translation by Leopold Breyer, *Bilderstreit und Arabersturm in Byzanz* (Graz, 1957), pp. 66–67, 70.

5. Balādhurī, *Futūḥ al-Buldān,* ed. M. J. de Goeje (Leiden, 1866), p. 458; discussed in David Ayalon, "Preliminary remarks on the mamluk military institution in Islam," in *War, Technology, and Society in the Middle East,* ed. V. J. Parry and M. E. Yapp (London, 1975), pp. 45–46.

6. The chronicle attributed to Dionysus of Tell-Mahre: J.-B. Chabot, ed., *Chronique de Denys de Tell-Mahre* (Paris, 1895), pp. 84f. of Syrian text (= p. 72, French trans.).

7. See O. S. A. Ismail, "Muʿtaṣim and the Turks," *Bulletin of the School of Oriental and African Studies* 29 (1966), pp. 12–24; David Ayalon, "The Military Reforms of Caliph al-Muʿtaṣim" (paper presented to the International Congress of Orientalists, New Delhi, 1964). On the origins and development of Islamic military slavery, see Patricia Crone, *Slaves on Horses: The Evolution of the Islamic Polity* (Cambridge, 1980), and the by-now classic articles of David Ayalon, collected in three volumes published in the Variorum Series: *Studies on the Mamlūks of Egypt (1250–1517)* (London, 1977), *The Mamlūk Military Society* (London, 1979), *Outsiders in the Lands of Islam: Mamluks, Mongols, and Eunuchs* (London, 1988). On Ottoman military slavery, see I. Metin Kunt, *The Sultan's Servants: The Transformation of Ottoman Provincial Government, 1550–1650* (New York, 1983), esp. chaps. 3, 4; idem, "Kulların Kulları," *Boğaziçi Üniversitesi Dergisi—Hümaniter Bilimler* 3 (1975), pp. 27–42; Halil Inalcik, *The Ottoman Empire: The Classical Age* (London, 1973), pp. 68ff., 77ff., 84ff.

8. Ibn Khaldūn, *Kitāb al-ʿIbar wa-dīwān al-mubtadā wa'l-khabar,* vol. 5 (Būlāq, 1284/1867), p. 371; English translation in Bernard Lewis, *Islam from the Prophet Muhammad to the Capture of Constantinople,* vol. 1 (New York, 1974), pp. 97–99.

9. On these, see Daniel Pipes, "Black soldiers," *International Journal of African Historical Studies* 13, no. 1 (1980), pp. 88–90, where references to sources are given. Dr. Pipes's careful examination of these sources has yielded a meager haul.

10. G. Rotter, *Die Stellung des Negers* (Bonn, 1967), pp. 65ff. On the "Aḥābīsh" of Mecca see EI^2, s.v. (by W. Montgomery Watt). For a more recent discussion of early black, slave soldiers, see Jere L. Bacharach, "African military slaves and the medieval Middle East: The cases of Iraq (869–955) and Egypt (868–1171)," *International Journal of Middle Eastern Studies* 13 (1981), pp. 471–94. In discussing the struggles between different ethnic and racial groups of soldiery, Bacharach is concerned to prove two propositions: that race was not the sole cause and that it was never of any great importance. He has no difficulty with the first, and as far as I am aware no one has ever claimed otherwise. He is rather less convincing on the second. The article does, however, offer a very useful collection of evidence and references.

11. The list of Ibn Ṭūlūn's treasures and possessions is given in al-Qāḍī al-Rashīd ibn al-Zubayr (attrib.), *Kitāb al-Dhakhā'ir wa'l-tuḥaf,* ed. Muḥammad Ḥamīd Allāh and Ṣalāḥ al-Dīn al-Munajjid (Kuwait, 1959), p. 227. See, further, C. H. Becker, *Beiträge zur Geschichte Ägyptens unter der Islam,* vol. 2 (Strassburg, 1903), pp. 192–93. On the participation of Tulunid black troops in the sack of Thessalonica in 904 A.D., see B. Christides, "Once again Caminiates' 'Capture of Thessaloniki,' " *Byzantinische Zeitschrift* 74 (1981), p. 8.

12. Maqrīzī, *Kitāb al-Mawā'iz wa'l-i'tibār fi dhikr al-khiṭaṭ wa'l-āthār* (hereafter Maqrīzī, *Khiṭaṭ*), vol. 1 (Būlāq, 1270/1854), p. 315; Abu'l-Maḥāsin Ibn Taghrī Birdī, *Al-Nujūm al-zāhira,* vol. 3 (Cairo, 1351/1932), p. 15. Even among the Zanj rebels, we are told, whites and blacks were segregated. Whites had separate houses, blacks did not; whites were allowed to drink wine, blacks were not (Ṭabarī, *Ta'rīkh,* vol. 3, pp. 1760, 1959; Rotter, *Die Stellung des Negers,* pp. 109–10).

13. Ibn Taghrī Birdī, *Nujūm,* vol. 3, p. 59.

14. Ibid., p. 137; Maqrīzī, *Khiṭaṭ,* vol. 1, p. 322.

15. 'Arīb ibn Sa'd al-Qurtubī, *Ṣilat Ta'rīkh al-Ṭabarī,* ed. M. J. de Goeje (Leiden, 1897), pp. 148–50. Other accounts in Muḥammad ibn 'Abd al-Malik al-Hamadānī, *Takmilat ta'rīkh al-Ṭabarī,* ed. Albert Yūsuf Kan'ān, 2d ed. (Beirut, 1961), p. 63; Miskawayh, *Kitāb Tajārib al-Umam,* ed. H. Amédroz, vol. 1 (Oxford and Cairo, 1332/1914), pp. 202–3 (English translation by D. S. Margoliouth, *The Eclipse of the Abbasid Caliphate,* vol. 4 [Oxford, 1920], pp. 227–28); Ibn al-Athīr, *Kāmil,* anno 318, ed. Tornberg, vol. 8 (Leiden, 1862), pp. 159–60; ibid., ed. 'Abd al-Wahhāb al-Najjār, vol. 8 (Cairo, 1353), p. 208 (hereafter Ibn al-Athīr, *Kāmil* [Tornberg] and Ibn al-Athīr, *Kāmil* [Cairo]). Cf. H. Bowen, *The Life and Times of 'Alī ibn 'Isā "The Good Vizier"* (Cambridge, 1928), p. 290.

16. The fullest account is that of Ibn al-Ṣābi' (d. 1056), cited by Ibn Taghrī Birdī, *Nujūm,* vol. 4, pp. 180–83. Cf. Muḥammad 'Abdallah 'Inān, *Al-Ḥākim bi 'amr illāh . . . ,* 2d ed. (Cairo, 1379/1959), pp. 207–8; S. Lane-Poole, *A History of Egypt in the Middle Ages,* 2d ed. (London, 1914), p. 133. Another atrocity story is recorded under the year 428 of the Hijra, corresponding to 1036–37, the time of the great famine in Cairo: "The blacks used to wait in the alleys, catch women with hooks, strip off their flesh and eat them. One day a woman passed through the Street of the Lamps in old Cairo. She was fat, and the blacks caught her with hooks and cut a piece off her behind. Then they sat down to eat and forgot about her. She went out of the house and called for help, and the chief of police came and raided the house. He brought out thousands of bodies and killed the blacks" (Ibn Taghrī Bīrdī, *Nujūm,* vol. 5, p. 17). There are other stories of cannibalism, especially in times of famine, without any racial implication. See Bacharach, "African military slaves," p. 494, n. 55, where examples are cited.

17. Ibn al-Athīr, *Kāmil,* anno. 564 (Tornberg), vol. 9, pp. 228–93; ibid. (Cairo), vol. 9, p. 103.

18. Abū Shāma, *Kitāb al-Rawḍatayn,* ed. Muḥammad Ḥilmī Muḥammad Aḥmad, vol. 1, pt. 1 (Cairo, 1962), p. 452; cf. Maqrīzī, *Khiṭat,* vol. 2, p. 3.

19. The chief Arabic sources are Ibn al-Athīr; Abū Shāma, *Kitāb al-Rawḍatayn,* vol. 1, pt. 1, pp. 450–55; Maqrīzī, *Khiṭat,* vol. 2, pp. 2–3, 19; Ibn Wāṣil, *Mufarrij al-kurūb,* ed. Jamāl al-Dīn al-Shayyāl, vol. 1 (Cairo, 1953), pp. 176–78. See, further, S. Lane-Poole, *Saladin and the Fall of the Kingdom of Jerusalem* (New York, 1898), pp. 101–3; H. A. R. Gibb, "The rise of Saladin," in *A History of the Crusades,* ed. K. M. Setton, vol. 1, *The First Hundred Years,* ed. M. W. Baldwin, 2d ed. (Madison, 1969), pp. 565; N. Elisséeff, *Nūr ad-Dīn, un grand prince musulman de Syrie au temps des Croisades,* vol. 2 (Damascus, 1967), pp. 642–44; 'Abd al-Mun'im Mājid, *Ẓuhūr khilāfat al-Faṭimiyyīn wa-suqūṭuhā* (Cairo, 1968), pp. 482–83.

20. Maqrīzī, *Khīṭaṭ,* vol. 2, p. 19.

21. D. Ayalon, *Gunpowder and Firearms in the Mamluk Kingdom* (London, 1956), pp. 66ff.

22. Maqrīzī, *Kitāb al-Sulūk,* ed. Muḥammad Muṣṭafā Ziyāda, vol. 1 (Cairo, 1934),

p. 440 (French translation in E. Quatremère, *Histoire des sultans mamlouks de l'Egypte,* vol. 1, pt. 1 [Paris, 1837], pp. 122–29). See, further, A. N. Poliak, "Les Révoltes populaires en Egypte à l'époque des mamelouks et leurs causes économiques," *Revue des études islamiques* (1934), pp. 241–73, esp. 254–72.

23. Slightly variant accounts in Ibn Taghrī Bīrdī, *Ḥawādith al-Duhūr,* ed. W. Popper, vol. 8, pt. 1 (Berkeley, 1930), pp. 19–20; al-Sakhāwī, *Al-Tibr al-masbūk fī dhayl al-Sulūk* (Cairo, 1896), p. 126; Ibn Iyās, *Badā'iʿ al-zuhūr,* vol. 2 (Būlāq, 1311/1893–94), p. 28. See also Poliak, "Les Révoltes populaires," pp. 272–73; I. M. Lapidus, *Muslim Cities in the Later Middle Ages* (Cambridge, MA, 1967), pp. 171–72.

24. Anṣārī, cited and translated from an unpublished manuscript by D. Ayalon, "Gunpowder," p. 70.

25. Andrew Handler, "The *ʿabīd* under the Umayyads of Cordova and the *mulūk al-ṭawā'if,*" in *Occident and Orient: A Tribute to the Memory of Alexander Scheiber,* ed. Robert Dán (Budapest and Leiden, 1988), pp. 229–39. M. Brett, "Ifriqiya as a market for Saharan trade from the tenth to the twelfth century A.D.," *Journal of African History* 10 (1969), pp. 354–56. On black slaves in medieval Tunisia, see also H. I. Idris, *La Berbérie orientale sous les Zirides: Xᵉ–XIIᵉ siècles* (Paris, 1962), pp. 575–76, 684–85; M. Talbi, *L'Emirat aghlabide 184–296/800–909: histoire politique* (Paris, 1966), pp. 193–247.

26. Ramón Lourido Díaz, "La rebelion de los ʿAbīd, en 1778, y su desintegración como milicia especial," *Cuadernos de historia del Islam* 5 (1973), pp. 99–149; Nicola Ziadeh, "Al-Mawlāy Ismāʿīl Sulṭān al-Maghrib, 1082–1139/1672–1727," *Al-Abḥāth* 17 (1964), pp. 155ff.; Allan R. Meyers, "Class, ethnicity, and slavery: The origins of the Moroccan ʿAbīd," *International Journal of African Historical Studies* 10 (1977), pp. 427–42; Henri Terrasse, *Histoire du Maroc,* vol. 2 (Casablanca, 1950), pp. 256–57; Ch.-André Julien, *Histoire de l'Afrique du Nord,* 2d ed. (Paris, 1961), pp. 229–30. The relevant passages from Nāṣirī's chronicle were translated into French by Eugène Fumey and published in *Archives marocaines* 9 (1906), pp. 74–78, 94–96.

27. David Hume, "Of parties in general," in *Essays.* My thanks are due to E. Kedourie for drawing my attention to this passage.

28. Fumey, *Archives marocaines,* pp. 330–33.

29. W. G. Browne, *Travels in Africa, Egypt, and Syria from the Year 1792 to 1798,* 2d ed. (London, 1806), p. 54; Louis Frank, *Mémoire sur le commerce des nègres au Kaire et sur les maladies auxquelles ils sont sujets en y arrivant* (Paris, 1802), pp. 37–38.

30. On this curious episode, see Raverat and Dellard, "Historique du bataillon nègre égyptien au Mexique (1863–1867)," *Revue d'Égypte* 1 (1894–95), pp. 42–53, 104–23, 176–85, 230–45, 272–86; ʿUmar Ṭūsūn, *Buṭūlat al-Ürṭa al-Sūdāniyya al-Miṣriyya fī ḥarb al-Maksīk* (Cairo, 1352/1933).

31. R. R. Madden, *Travels in Turkey, Egypt, Nubia, and Palestine . . .* , 2d ed., vol. 1 (London, 1833), pp. 145–46.

32. Bernard Lewis, "Slade on the Turkish Navy," *Journal of Turkish Studies* 2 (1987), p. 10. The report was written by Adolphus Slade, a British naval officer attached at that time to the Turkish Navy and known as the author of a number of important books about the Ottoman Empire.

33. The Turkish is *kapı kulu,* lit. "slave of the Gate." On the Gate, or entrance to a building, as a metaphor of sovereignty, see B. Lewis, *The Political Language of Islam* (Chicago, 1988), pp. 20–21. The term "Sublime Porte," which came into European usage at a later date, refers to the office of the grand vizier, to which the effective conduct of government had been transferred.

Chapter 10

1. W. G. Browne (*Travels in Egypt, Syria, and Africa (in 1793)*, 2d ed. [London, 1806]) offers considerable information on the slave routes in Africa. For the nineteenth-century slave trade, see J. L. Burckhardt, *Travels in Nubia,* 2d ed. (London, 1822), esp. pp. 290ff.; T. F. Buxton, *The African Slave Trade and Its Remedy* (London, 1840), esp. pp. 39ff., 90ff., 192ff.; Captain Colomb, R. N. *Slave-Catching in the Indian Ocean* (London, 1873). For some modern studies, see J. B. Kelly, *Britain and the Persian Gulf 1795–1880* (Oxford, 1968), pp. 441–51; Reginald Coupland, *The Exploitation of East Africa 1856–1890: The Slave Trade and the Scramble* (London, 1939); A. Adu Boahen, *Britain, the Sahara, and the Western Sudan 1788–1861* (Oxford, 1964); Esmond B. Martin and T. C. I. Ryan, "A quantitative assessment of the Arab slave trade of East Africa, 1770–1896," *Kenya Historical Review* 5 (1977), pp. 71–91; Glauco Ciammaichella, *Libyens et français au Tchad (1897–1914): La Confrérie senoussie et le commerce transsaharien* (Paris, 1987); G. Baer, *Studies in the Social History of Modern Egypt* (Chicago, 1969), pp. 161–89; Terence Walz, "Black slavery in Egypt during the nineteenth century as reflected in the *Mahkama* archives of Cairo," in *Slaves and Slavery in Muslim Africa,* ed. J. R. Willis, vol. 2 (London, 1985), pp. 137–60; Terence Walz, *Trade between Egypt and Bilād as-Sudan, 1700–1820* (Cairo, 1978), pp. 173–221 (chap. 6, "Trading in Slaves"); Allan G. B. Fisher and Humphrey J. Fisher, *Slavery and Muslim Society in Africa* (London, 1970); on the Sudan, see, further, R. Hill, *Egypt in the Sudan 1820–1881* (London, 1959), pp. 24ff., 62ff., and passim; R. Gray, *A History of the Southern Sudan 1839–1889* (London, 1961); P. M. Holt, *A Modern History of the Sudan,* 2d ed. (London, 1963), pp. 14, 35, 61–72, and passim; Gabriel Warburg, "Slavery and labour in the Anglo-Egyptian Sudan," *Asian and African Studies* 12 (1978), pp. 221–45.

2. Cheykh Muḥammad ibn ʿAlī ibn Zayn al-ʿĀbidīn, *Le Livre du Soudan,* trans. Marcel Grisard and Jean-Louis Bacqué-Grammont (Paris, 1981), pp. 8–9. The Arabic original of this work is lost; the translation was made from a Turkish version published in Istanbul in 1846. On the slave trade, see, further, R. S. O'Fahey, "Slavery and the slave trade in Dār Fūr," *Journal of African History* 14 (1963), pp. 29–43.

3. See Alan Fisher, *The Crimean Tatars* (Stanford, 1978), pp. 15–16, 26–29, 42; idem, *The Russian Annexation of the Crimea, 1772–1783* (Cambridge, 1970), pp. 19–21.

4. Ettore Rossi, *Storia di Tripoli e dalla Tripolitania della conquista araba al 1911* (Rome, 1968), pp. 316–19 (based mainly on Italian consular reports). Sometimes over-successful slave raiding produced a glut of slaves, and lowered prices. At the market in Bagirmi, at the southern end of Lake Chad, in 1878, an old man could be bought for two to three dollars; a woman, young or old, for five dollars. A child, age six to eight, could be bartered for a locally made shirt, valued at seventy-five cents. See Fisher and Fisher, *Slavery and Muslim Society in Africa,* p. 165. On African slaves in Ottoman Europe, see Richard Pankhurst, "Ethiopian and other African slaves in Greece during the Ottoman occupation," *Slavery and Abolition* 1 (1980), pp. 339–44. A British visitor to Crete in 1834 noted that "in the principal towns there are slaves in the families of every gentlemen. The price of labour is everywhere very high, the difficulty of obtaining labourers in many cases amounting to an absolute impossibility, and the markets of Khania and Megalo-Kastron are as regularly furnished with human flesh as they are with bullocks, the supply of both being chiefly drawn from the same place, Bengazi" (Pankhurst, "Ethiopian and other African slaves," p. 341, citing Robert Pashley, *Travels in Crete,* vol. 2 [Cambridge and London, 1837], p. 104). Pankhurst cites numerous other sources on this topic.

5. See below, pp. 161ff.

6. Enver Pascha, *Um Tripolis* (Munich, 1918), p. 90. My thanks are due to Michel Le Gall for this reference.

7. See documents in Lewis Hertslet, ed., *A Complete Collection of the Treaties and Conventions, and Reciprocal Regulations, at Present Subsisting between Great Britain and Foreign Powers, etc.*, vol. 10 (London, 1859), pp. 1011–12, 1014–17, 1097–1100; vol. 11 (1861), pp. 551–53.

8. See C. Snouck Hurgronje, *Mekka,* vol. 2 (The Hague, 1888–89), pp. 12–23, 132–37; in English, C. Snouck-Hurgronje, *Mekka in the Latter Part of the Nineteenth Century* (London, 1931), pp. 10–20, 106–10; R. F. Burton, *Peronal Narrative of a Pilgrimage to al-Madinah and Mecca* (London, 1924), vol. 1, pp. 47, 49, 59–61; vol. 2, pp. 12–13, 233, 251–52.

9. Quoted in M. Kaya Bilgegil, *Ziya Paşa üzerinde bir Araştırma,* 2d ed., vol. 1 (Ankara, 1979), p. 399.

10. Rudolf C. Slatin, known as Slatin Pasha, who was a captive of the Mahdi for two years, wrote a vivid account of the slave trade—the capture and transportation of the slaves and the central slave market at the Mahdist capital, Omdurman (*Fire and Sword in the Sudan* [London, 1897], pp. 557ff.).

11. Browne, *Travels,* p. 76. *Bouza* or *buza* is a kind of beer.

12. E. W. Lane, *An Account of the Manners and Customs of the Modern Egyptians,* 5th ed., vol. 1 (London, 1871), pp. 168–69, 233–34.

13. Arnold Kemball to Lt. Col. H. D. Robertson (officiating resident, Kharaq), July 8, 1842 (enclosed in H. D. Robertson to Willoughby [chief secretary to the government in Bombay], July 9, 1842 [No. 116 Secret Dept.]), enclosure to Secret Letter 106 of Sept. 30, 1842, *Enclosures to Bombay Secret Letters,* vol. 50, India Office Records, London. Cf. Kelly, *Britain and the Persian Gulf,* pp. 411ff. See below, Document 5, pp. 157–59. On the slave trade from Africa to the Persian Gulf, see, further, Charles Issawi, ed., *The Economic History of Iran 1800–1914* (Chicago, 1971), pp. 124–28.

14. I am indebted to Shaun Marmon's study, in preparation, on the eunuch custodians of the Prophet's tomb. For a contemporary comment on the quasi-sacerdotal status of certain eunuchs, see Alfred von Kremer, *Aegypten: Forschungen über Land und Volk während eines zehnjährigen Aufenthalts,* vol. 2 (Leipzig, 1863), p. 88.

15. On the Ottoman court eunuchs, see H. A. R. Gibb and Harold Bowen, *Islamic Society and the West,* vol. 1, *Islamic Society in the Eighteenth Century,* pt. 1 (London, 1950), pp. 76f., 329ff.; N. M. Penzer, *The Harem* (London, 1936), pp. 125–51, 233; Ismail Hakkı Uzunçarşılı, *Osmanlı devletinin saray teşkilâtı* (Ankara, 1945), pp. 172–83; Çağatay Uluçay, *Harem II* (Ankara, 1971), pp. 117–31 and passim. For an earlier comment, see Paul Rycaut, *A History of the Present State of the Ottoman Empire,* 4th ed. (London, 1675), pp. 66–67. On the modern period, see chapter 1, n. 34.

16. A. Ubicini contrasts the brilliant careers open to white slaves, both male and female, with the domestic drudgery that is the universal fate of the blacks: "Only one path is open to them [black males] to reach high honor, that of the mebeyn [palace staff]; but one knows on what condition" (*La Turquie actuelle* [Paris, 1855], p. 294).

17. Louis Frank, *Mémoire sur le commerce des Négres au Kaire* (Paris, 1802), pp. 13–14; Gabriel Baer, *Studies in the Social History of Modern Egypt* (Chicago, 1969), p. 164.

18. J. L. Burckhardt, *Travels in Nubia* (London, 1819), pp. 294–96. See, further, Prince von Pückler-Muskau, *Aus Mehemed Ali's Reich,* vol. 3 (Stuttgart, 1844), pp. 158–59 (in English, Prince von Pückler-Muskau, *Egypt under Mehemet Ali,* vol. 2

[London, 1845], p. 251); H. von Maltzan, *Meine Wallfahrt nach Mekka,* vol. 1 (Leipzig, 1865), pp. 48–49. Maltzan notes that many of the castrated black boys died, and that the survivors were sold at twenty times their previous price.

19. See above, p. 101.

20. Baer, *Studies,* p. 166 (citing a British consular report); cf. other sources quoted pp. 165–68.

Chapter 11

1. "O you who believe! Do not forbid the good things which God has permitted to you" (Qur'ān V:87). On this, the commentator Fakhr al-Dīn al-Rāzī (*al-Tafsīr al-Kabīr,* vol. 12 [Cairo, 1938], p. 71) observes: "It is clear that just as one may not permit what God forbids, so one may not forbid what God permits." The same point was made by the sultan of Morocco in a letter of April 1842 written in reply to an enquiry from the British consul general concerning the slave trade. See below, p. 156.

2. There is an extensive literature on the Western, largely British, anti-slavery movement. For a detailed survey of abolitionism and abolition in the Muslim states, see Murray Gordon, *Slavery in the Arab World* (New York, 1989), pp. 208–38, and sources cited there.

3. M. Bompard, *Législation de Tunisie* (Paris, 1888), p. 398. An important and interesting statement of views on slavery is contained in a letter sent by Ḥusayn Pasha, head of the Tunis municipal council, to Amos Perry, the U.S. consul general in Tunis, in the last decade of Jumādā I, 1281 = late October 1864, in answer to his enquiry about Tunisian experience of slavery and abolition and their effects. Ḥusayn Pasha, while conceding that Islamic law allows slavery, nevertheless argues on both practical and moral grounds in favor of abolition and commends this choice to the American republic (Amos Perry to Ḥusayn Pasha, November 12, 1863, Record Group No. 84, pp. 178–80, U.S. National Archives; Ḥusayn Pasha to Amos Perry, October 1864, in *Kanz al-Raghā'ib fi Muntakhabāt al-Jawā'ib,* vol. 6 [Istanbul, 1871–80], pp. 46–51, and in Ra'īf al-Khūrī, ed., *Al-Fikr al-ʿArabī al-Ḥadīth: Athar al-thawra al-Faransiyya fī Tawjīhihi al-Siyāsī wa'l-Ijtimaʿi* [Beirut, 1943], pp. 223–28 [it was first published, in Arabic, in the Istanbul Arabic newspaper *Al-Jawā'ib*]; English translation by Iḥsān ʿAbbās, *Modern Arab Thought: Channels of the French Revolution to the Arab East* [Princeton, NJ, 1983], pp. 152–57).

4. On abolition in the Ottoman Empire, see Ehud R. Toledano, *The Ottoman Slave Trade and Its Suppression* (Princeton, NJ, 1982); Ismail Parlatır, *Tanzimat Edebiyatında Kölelik* (Ankara, 1987). This book is concerned with slavery in nineteenth-century Turkish literature. The introduction, based on documents in the Turkish archives, deals with the practice and abolition of slavery in the Ottoman Empire. On Egypt, see Gabriel Baer, "Slavery and its abolition," in his *Studies in the Social History of Modern Egypt* (Chicago, 1969), pp. 161–89.

5. G. Young, *Corps de droit ottoman,* vol. 2 (Oxford, 1903), pp. 171–72.

6. Ibid., pp. 172–74, 180–81.

7. Ibid., pp. 175ff. For some Turkish documents, see Hamdi Atamer, "Zenci Ticaretinin Yasaklanması," *Belgelerle Türk Tarihi Dergisi* 3 (1967), pp. 23–29, partially translated in Documents 6 and 7, below, pp. 160–61.

8. A detailed account of these events in the Ḥijāz, including the texts of the documents cited, is given in Cevdet Paşa, *Tezakir 1–12* (Ankara 1953), pp. 101–52. Other contemporary accounts may be found in the reports of the British and French

consuls in Jedda. For modern studies, see Bernard Lewis, "The Tanzimat and social equality," in *Économie et sociétés dans l'Empire Ottoman,* ed. Jean-Louis Bacqué-Grammont and Paul Dumont (Paris, 1982), pp. 47–54; William Ochsenwald, *Religion, Society, and the State in Arabia: The Hijaz under Ottoman Control, 1840–1908* (Columbus, OH, 1984), pp. 117–27, 138–41; Toledano, *Ottoman Slave Trade,* pp. 129–35.

9. I owe this image to Lord Shackleton; see his speech of July 14, 1960, in the debate cited in note 10.

10. For a discussion of the slave trade between Africa and Arabia in 1960, see *Hansard Parliamentary Debates* (House of Lords), 5th ser., vol. 225 (1960), col. 335.

11. C. Snouck Hurgronje, "Über seine Reise nach Mekka," *Verhandlungen der Gesellschaft für Erdkunde zu Berlin* 14 (1887), pp. 150–51; for a more extensive treatment, idem, *Mekka,* vol. 2 (The Hague, 1889), pp. 12ff.; in English, C. Snouck Hurgronje, *Mekka in the Latter Part of the Nineteenth Century,* trans. J. H. Monahan (Leiden and London, 1931), pp. 10ff.

12. T. F. Keane, *Six Months in Mecca* (London, 1881), pp. 94–100.

13. Ludwig Stross, "Sclaverei und Sclavenhandel in Ost-Afrika und im Rothen Meere," *Oesterreichische Monatsschrift für den Orient* 12 (December 15, 1886), pp. 211–15.

14. For estimates of the numbers of slaves sent from black Africa to North Africa and the Middle East, see L. C. Brown, "Color in Northern Africa," *Daedalus* 96 (1967), pp. 467, 479; Charles Issawi, ed., *The Economic History of Iran, 1800–1914* (Chicago, 1971), pp. 124–26; Raymond Mauny, *Les Siècles obscurs de l'Afrique noire* (Paris, 1970), pp. 240ff.; UNESCO, *African Slave Trade* (Paris, 1979), contributions by I. B. Kakc and Bethwell A. Ogot. In about 1839, T. F. Buxton gave, as a "conservative estimate," a figure of twenty thousand black slaves a year transported by the desert routes to the Arab lands (*The African Slave Trade* [London, 1839], pp. 46ff., cited by Brown). Estimates of slaves exported by sea routes from Zanzibar, in the same period, vary between twenty and thirty thousand a year. Esmond B. Martin and T. C. I. Ryan ("A quantitative assessment of the Arab slave trade of East Africa, 1770-1896," *Kenya Historical Review* 5 [1977], pp. 71–91) conclude that in the 125 years covered by their study, fewer than one million slaves were exported to destinations outside East Africa and about another one million were absorbed by local demand on the East African coast. In an admittedly rough estimate, Mauny puts the total drain of African slaves to the Muslim lands at fourteen million. See also above, p. 10, and below, pp. 157ff.

15. Louis Frank, *Tunis, description de cette régence,* p. 119, edited and annotated by J. J. Marcel, in *L'Univers pittoresque* (Paris, 1850).

16. Bowring, cited by Buxton, *African Slave Trade,* p. 193, cf. 108ff.

17. The position of these black communities in Arab and Turkish cities still awaits scholarly investigation. One of the few black ghettoes in Arab cities to be studied is that of the old city of Jerusalem, which, owing to special circumstances, has been opened to scholarly research. See Adriana Destro, "Habs el ʿAbid: Il Quartiere Africano di Gerusalemme," *Africa* (Rome) 29, no. 2 (1974), pp. 193–212.

Chapter 12

1. *EI*[2] s.v. "Kafā'a" (by Y. Linant de Bellefonds); Y. Linant de Bellefonds, *Traité de droit musulman comparé,* vol. 2 (Paris, 1965), pp. 171–81; F. J. Ziadeh, "Equality (*Kafā'ah*) in the Muslim law of marriage," *American Journal of Comparative Law* 6

(1957), pp. 503–17; cf. G. Rotter, *Die Stellung des Negers* (Bonn, 1967), pp. 131ff., and the standard treatises on Muslim law, esp. those by Ḥanafī and Shāfiʿī jurists, e.g., Shams al-Dīn al-Sarakhsī, *Kitāb al-Mabsūṭ* (Cairo, 1324/1906), pp. 22ff. The Mālikīs interpret *Kafāʾa* in religious, not social, terms, while the Shīʿa do not recognize the doctrine at all. The quotation from Mālik is from *Al-Mudawwana al-Kubrā,* vol. 4 (Cairo 1323/1905), pp. 13–14. For a Shiʿite view, see Shaykh Muḥammad Hādī al-Yūsufī, "Mafhūm al-Kafāʾa," *Al-Hādī* 4, pt. 6 (Qumm, 1396), pp. 59–64.

2. On the *Mawālī,* see above, pp. 37ff. and 44ff.

3. G. Levi Della Vida, "Un'antica opera sconosciuta di controversia Šī ʿita," *Annali dell'Istituto Universitario Orientale di Napoli,* n.s., vol. 14 (1964), p. 236.

4. Summarized by L. P. Harvey, "Arabs and Negroes," in *Encounter* (London), February 1971, pp. 91–94. The text of this story may be found in Abu'l-Layth Naṣr al-Samarqandī, *Tanbīh al-Ghāfilīn* (Cairo, 1306/1888–89), pp. 226–27.

5. Muttaqī, *Kanz al-ʿUmmāl,* vol. 8 (Haydarabad, 1313/1895–96), p. 248.

6. Ibn ʿAbd al-Raʾūf, "Risāla," in *Thalāth Rasāʾil Andalusiyya,* ed. E. Lévi-Provençal (Cairo, 1955), p. 80; French translation by R. Arié, *Hespéris-Tamuda,* vol. 1 (Morocco, 1960), p. 27.

7. Masʿūdī, *Murūj al-dhahab,* ed. C. Pellat, vol. 4 (Beirut, 1973), p. 126. Ibn Akwaʿ was a Companion of the Prophet.

8. Ibn Ḥabīb, *Wāḍiḥa,* as cited by Ibn ʿAbd al-Raʾūf, "Risala," p. 81 (Arié, *Hespéris-Tamuda,* p. 29).

9. Abu'l-Faraj al-Iṣfahānī, *Kitāb al-Aghānī,* 20 vols. (Būlāq, 1285/1868–69); ibid. (Cairo, 1927–)—hereafter *Aghānī* (1868) and *Aghānī* (1927); Ignaz Goldziher, *Muhammedanische Studien,* vol. 1 (Halle, 1888), p. 128 (*Muslim Studies,* vol. 1 [London, 1967] p. 121); U. Rizzitano, "Abū Miḥǵan Nuṣayb b. Rabāḥ," *Rivista degli studi orientali* 20 (1943), pp. 428–29. On Nuṣayb's daughters, see *Aghānī* (1868), vol. 1, p. 138, *Aghānī* (1927), vol. 1, p. 347; cf. Ibn Qutayba, *ʿUyūn al-akhbār,* vol. 3 (Cairo, n.d.), p. 126; Rizzitano, "Abū Miḥǵan," p. 456; Khayr al-Dīn al-Ziriklī, *Al-Aʿlām,* 2d ed., vol. 7 ([Beirut?], 1376/1956), p. 355, where further sources are cited.

10. Abu'l-ʿAlāʾ, *The Letters of Abu'l-ʿAlaʾ of Maʿarrat al-Nuʿmān,* in *Anecdota Oxoniensia,* ed. and trans. D. S. Margoliouth (Oxford, 1898), text p. 55, trans. p. 61. Zubayr ibn Bakkār (d. 870), a qadi of Mecca, is quoted as telling a relevant anecdote: "A woman came to Ibn al-Zubayr to complain about her husband, who, she claimed, was sleeping with her maidservant. Ibn al-Zubayr summoned the man and questioned him about his wife's complaint. He replied: 'She is black and her maidservant is black and my eyesight is weak. When night falls I grab whichever is nearest to me' " (Ibn ʿAbd Rabbihi, *Al-ʿIqd al-Farīd,* vol. 8 [Cairo, 1953], p. 132).

11. See H. Lammens, *Le Berceau de l'Islam,* vol. 1 (Rome, 1914).

12. Ibn Durayd, *Al-Ishtiqāq,* ed. F. Wüstenfeld (Göttingen, 1854), p. 183; ibid., ed. ʿAbd al-Salām Hārūn (Cairo, 1387/1959), p. 302; cf. Goldziher, *Muhammedanische Studien,* vol. 1, p. 118 (*Muslim Studies,* vol. 1, pp. 112–13).

13. See the biography of Ibrāhīm ibn al-Mahdī in Ibn Khallikān, *Wafayāt al-aʿyān,* vol. 1 (Būlāq, 1299), pp. 9–10; English translation by MacGuckin de Slane, *Ibn Khallikān's Biographical Dictionary,* vol. 1 (Paris, 1843), p. 18. Astonishingly, this episode is quoted by Arnold as evidence that "the converted Negro at once takes an equal place in the brotherhood of believers, neither his colour nor his race nor any association of the past standing in the way" (T. W. Arnold, *The Preaching of Islam,* 3d ed. [London, 1935], pp. 358–59).

14. See, further, Goldziher, *Muhammedanische Studien,* vol. 1, pp. 121ff. (*Muslim Studies,* vol. 1, pp. 115ff.); Rotter, *Die Stellung des Negers,* pp. 75ff., 132ff.

15. Ḥassān ibn Thābit, *Dīwān* (Cairo 1347/1929), p. 61; ibid. (Beirut, 1381/1961), p. 36; ibid., ed. Walid N. ʿArafat, vol. 1 (London, 1971), p. 364 (cf. vol. 2, p. 266). In the Cairo edition the word *mawdūna,* "short-necked," is replaced by *Nūbiyya,* "Nubian." See, further, Rotter, *Die Stellung des Negers,* p. 133, n. 4.

16. Ibn Rashīq, cited in Ibn Nājī, *Maʿālim al-Aymān fi maʿrifat ahl al-Qayrawān* (Tunis, 1320/1902), p. 15.

17. Ibn Sahl al-Andalusī, *Dīwān,* vol. 10 (Cairo, 1344/1926), p. 108.

18. For a striking example of this attitude, from contemporary Egypt, see Mohamed Heikal, *Autumn of Fury: The Assassination of Sadat* (New York, 1984), pp. 8–9, 11–12, 25, 181. According to Heikal's extremely hostile account, Sadat's mother was the daughter of a black slave imported from Africa, from whom both she and her son inherited Negroid features. Heikal comments repeatedly on these features, and on the problems—and anxieties—which they allegedly brought.

19. John Lewis Burckhardt, *Travels in Arabia: Comprehending an Account of Those Territories in Hedjaz which the Mohammedans Regard as Sacred* (1829; reprint, Beirut, 1972), pp. 182–87.

20. W. G. Palgrave, *Personal Narrative of a Year's Journey through Central and Eastern Arabia* (London, 1883), pp. 270–72; Charles M. Doughty, *Travels in Arabia Deserta,* vol. 1 (Cambridge, 1888), pp. 553–55; C. Snouck Hurgronje, *Mekka,* vol. 2 (The Hague, 1889), pp. 10–24.

21. Alois Musil, *Arabia petraea,* vol. 3, *Ethnologischer Reisebericht* (Vienna, 1908), pp. 224–25; R. P. Antonin Jaussen, *Coutûmes des Arabes au pays de Moab* (Paris, 1948), pp. 60–61, cited in Patricia Crone, *Roman, Provincial, and Islamic Law* (Cambridge, 1987), p. 137.

22. J. O. Hunwick, "Black Africans in the Islamic world: An understudied dimension of the black diaspora," *Tarikh* 5, no. 5 (1978), p. 35.

23. *EI*[2], s.v. "Hutaym" (by G. Rentz). But cf. Doughty, *Travels in Arabia Deserta,* vol. 1, p. 553.

24. Several of the travelers attest the higher price of white slaves, which they attribute to scarcity and, for women, to sexual preference. One observer, in an extensive treatment of slavery in late-nineteenth-century Egypt, offers another reason for preferring and marrying white women; that they wear better: "white girls . . . wear much longer than either native Egyptian ladies or Abyssinians, retaining their fine physique to thirty-five or even forty years of age, while the latter are generally withered and *passées* before five-and-twenty" (J. C. McCoan, *Egypt as It Is* [London, 1877], p. 319).

Chapter 13

1. In an earlier treatment of this topic I tried to suggest how some of these stereotypes might have arisen and referred in particular to the overwork and undernourishment to which the slave was often subject. A reviewer in a French journal (Geneviève Bedoucha, review of B. Lewis, *Race et couleur en pays d'Islam* [Paris, 1982], *Cahiers d'Études Africaines* 22, nos. 3, 4 [1987–88], pp. 534–35) found these suggestions "sociologically naive" and also potentially dangerous, in that they could open the way to believing in "the real foundation of the stereotype." The more usual view among sociologists is that stereotypes always contain a modicum of truth, without which they would be neither viable nor usable. In the words of the anthropologist Clyde Kluckhohn: "There is almost always a grain of truth in the vicious stereotypes

that are created, and this helps us swallow the major portion of untruth" (*Mirror for Man: The Relation of Anthropology to Modern Life* [New York, 1949], p. 138).

2. Abu'l-Faraj al-Iṣfahānī, *Kitāb al-Aghānī,* 20 vols. (Būlāq, 1285/1868–69), vol. 7, p. 20; ibid. (Cairo, 1927–), vol. 7, p. 269.

3. Ibn Buṭlān, *Risāla fī Shirā' al-Raqīq,* ed. ʿAbd al-Salām Hārūn (Cairo, 1373/1954), pp. 374–75, where there are similar or even worse comments on other African groups. Among whites, Ibn Buṭlān most dislikes the Armenians.

4. Shihāb al-Dīn Aḥmad al-Abshīhī, *Kitāb al-Mustaṭraf fī kull shay' mustaẓraf* vol. 2 (Cairo, 1352/1933), pp. 75–77; French translation by G. Rat, *al-Mostatraf,* vol. 2 (Paris, 1902), pp. 151–57.

5. Fazıl Bey, *Huban-name* and *Zenan-name* (Istanbul, 1255/1839), pp. 11–12, 62–64. On Fazıl Bey and his works, see J. Hammer-Purgstall, *Geschichte der Osmanischen Dichtkunst,* vol. 4 (Pest, 1838), pp. 428–53, esp. 435; E. J. W. Gibb, *A History of Ottoman Poetry,* vol. 4 (London, 1905), pp. 220–42; *EI*², s.v. "Fāḍil bey" (by J. H. Mordtmann). A somewhat inaccurate French translation of the *Zenan-name* was published by J. A. Decourdemanche, *Le Livre des femmes* (Paris, 1879).

6. Masʿudī, *Murūj al-dhahab,* vol. 1, pp. 166–67; Charles Pellat, *Les Prairies d'or,* vol. 1 (Paris, 1962), p. 70.

7. Ibn Buṭlān, *Risāla,* p. 374.

8. For examples, see Muḥammad ibn Ṣaṣrā, *A Chronicle of Damascus 1389–1397,* ed. and trans. W. M. Brinner (Berkeley and Los Angeles, 1963), pp. 211ff. 278ff.; G. Rotter, *Die Stellung des Negers* (Bonn, 1967), pp. 179–81.

9. See Fatna A. Sabbah, *Women in the Muslim Unconscious* (New York, 1984), pp. 37–43; Rotter, *Die Stellung des Negers,* pp. 178–79.

10. Jāḥiẓ, *Rasā'il al-Jāḥiẓ,* vol. 1 (Cairo, 1385/1965), p. 214 (O. Rescher, *Beiträge zur arabische Poesie,* sec. 6 [Istanbul, 1956–58], p. 175); variants in Ibn ʿAbd Rabbihi, *Al-ʿIqd al-farīd,* vol. 7 (Cairo, 1953) p. 89, and Ibn Abī ʿAwn, *Kitāb al-Tashbīhāt,* ed. M. Abdul Muʿid Khan (Cambridge, 1950), p. 235; cf. Rotter, *Die Stellung des Negers,* p. 173. Ibn Abi ʿAwn gives other examples of erotic verse about black women (*Kitāb al-Tashbīhāt,* pp. 235ff.). A short collection of Arabic verses on the merits of whites, blacks, and browns is mainly concerned with the attractions of black women (Jalāl al-Dīn al-Suyūṭī, *Nuzhat al-ʿUmr fi'l-tafḍīl bayna'l-Bīḍ wa'l-Sūd wa'l-Sumr* [Damascus, 1349/1930–31]). For a discussion of this work and a translation of Suyūṭī's somewhat equivocal preface, see Akbar Muḥammad, "The image of Africans in Arabic literature: Some unpublished manuscripts," in *Slaves and Slavery in Muslim Africa,* vol. 1, *Islam and the Ideology of Slavery,* ed. J. R. Willis (London, 1985), pp. 59–60.

11. Rotter, *Die Stellung des Negers,* pp. 165, 173–74. For some modern parallels on Jewesses, see E. Kedourie, *The Chatham House Version* (London, 1970), pp. 334–35.

12. But, it may be noted, a fourteenth-century Egyptian author (Qalqashandī, *Ṣubḥ al-aʿshā,* vol. 2 [Cairo, 1331/1913], pp. 8–9) cites it, in the course of a discussion of colors, to prove his point that white is good and black is bad. He goes on to remark that many people, nevertheless, have begun to find beauty in the blacks and "incline toward them." For an earlier assertion of the presumed superiority of whiteness over blackness, see Sharaf al-Zamān Ṭāhir Marvazī (ca. 1120 A.D.), *Sharaf al-Zamān Ṭāhir Marvazī on China, the Turks, and India,* ed. and trans. V. Minorsky (London, 1942), pp. 54–55. Marvazī, however, allows that "blackness, though a defect, has its use in some instances; (such as) its physical utility, through its usefulness for sight, for it collects light and narrows the opening of the eye, and consequently does not allow light

to spread: (such as) its political and moral utility, as when the government agents dress in black in order to inspire the subjects with awe and fear."

13. For a discussion of these, see Minoo Southgate, "The negative images of blacks in some medieval Iranian writings," *Iranian Studies* 17, no. 1 (1984), pp. 3–36.

14. See Rudi Paret, "*Sīrat Saif ibn Dhi Jazan,*" *ein Arabischer Volksroman* (Hanover, 1924).

15. Examples in R. W. Hamilton, *Khirbat al Mafjar, an Arabian Mansion in the Jordan Valley* (Oxford, 1959), pls. 44, nos. 2, 4, 5; 53, no. 2; R. Ettinghausen, *Arab Painting* (Cleveland, OH, 1962), pp. 82, 93, 108, 121, 151; B. Gray, *Persian Painting* (Cleveland, OH, 1961), pp. 119, 131; E. J. Grube, *The Classical Style in Islamic Painting* (Venice, 1968), pls. 31, nos. 1, 6; 32; 36, nos. 1, 3; 37; 59; 66; 73; idem, *Muslim Miniature Painting* (Venice, 1962), pl. 58; Ivan Stchoukine, *Les Peintures des manuscrits Timurides* (Paris, 1954), pl. 76; A. U. Pope, *Survey of Persian Art,* pls. 889, 891, 912; B. W. Robinson, *Persian Miniature Painting* (London, 1967), pl. 28; Rachel Arié, *Miniatures hispano-musulmanes* (Leiden, 1969), pl. 41, fol. 71, verso of Ibn Ẓafar al-Siqillī, *Kitāb al-Sulwānāt fī musāmarāt al-khulafā' wa'l-sādāt* (Ms. Monastery St. Lawrence of Escurial, no. 528); O. Löfgren, *Ambrosian Fragments of an Illuminated Manuscript Containing the Zoology of Al-Gahiz* (Uppsala, 1946), pls. 3, 6, 9, 10.

Chapter 14

1. Alfred von Kremer, *Aegypten: Forschungen über Land und Volk während eines zehnjährigen Aufenthalts* (Leipzig, 1863), pp. 82–110.

2. C. Snouck Hurgronje, *Mekka in the Latter Part of the Nineteenth Century* (Leiden and London, 1931), p. 14 (German original, *Mekka* [The Hague, 1889], pp. 15–16). The Soviet scholar I. P. Petrushevsky (*Islam in Iran,* trans. Hubert Evans [Albany, NY, 1985], p. 155) observes with obvious disapproval that "not a few Western orientalists, scholars and travellers—Edward Lane, Snouck Hurgronje and J. L. Burckhardt among them—have been prone to expatiate on the mildness and humanity of Muslim slavery" and then goes on to paint a somewhat somber picture of reality.

3. Report from the British Consulate, Baghdad. April 28th 1847. Published in Charles Issawi, *The Fertile Crescent 1800–1914: A Documentary Economic History* (New York and Oxford, 1988), pp. 192–93.

4. See Gabriel Baer, *Studies in the Social History of Modern Egypt* (Chicago, 1969), pp. 161–89 (chap. 10, "Slavery and Its Abolition").

5. Snouck Hurgronje, *Mekka* (1931), p. 11 (*Mekka* [1889], p. 12).

6. See B. Lewis, "Gibbon on Islam," *Daedalus* 105 (1976), pp. 89–101; idem, *Islam in History* (London, 1975), pp. 133ff. For a modern example of such use, see Claude Lévi-Strauss, *Race et histoire* (Paris, 1961), pp. 47–50.

7. E. W. Blyden, *Christianity, Islam, and the Negro Race* (London, 1888); T. W. Arnold, *The Preaching of Islam,* 3d ed. (London, 1935), pp. 356ff.

Documents

List of Documents

1. A Discussion of National Character (Late Tenth Century). Translated from Abū Ḥayyān al-Tawḥīdī, *Kitāb al-Imta' wa'l-Mu'ānasa,* ed. Aḥmad Amīn and Aḥmad al-Zayn, vol. 1 (Cairo, 1939), pp. 70–80.
2. The Rights of the Slave (Late Eleventh to Early Twelfth Century). Translated from Muḥammad al-Ghazālī, *Iḥyā' 'Ulūm al-Dīn,* vol. 2 (Cairo, 1387 A.H./1967), pp. 279–91.
3. A Legal Ruling (Fifteenth Century). Translated from Aḥmad al-Wansharīsī, *Kitāb al-Mi 'yār al-Mughrib,* vol. 9 (Fes, 1313 A.H./1896), pp. 171–72.
4. Correspondence Concerning Slavery between Consul General Drummond Hay and the Sultan of Morocco (1842). Public Record Office, London, Foreign Office 84/427.
5. Report on Slavery from the Persian Gulf (1842). *Enclosures to Bombay Secret Letters,* vol. 50, India Office Records, London L/P&S/5/412.
6. Letter from the Sultan to the Vizier Mehmed Nejib Pasha, Governor of Baghdad (9 Safar 1263 A.H./January 27, 1847). Translated from Hamdi Atamer, "Zenci Ticaretinin Yasaklanması," in *Belgelerle Türk Tarihi Dergisi* 3 (1967), p. 24.
7. Draft of a Letter from the Grand Vizier Mustafa Reshid Pasha to the Governor of Tripoli (Libya) (21 Muḥarrem 1266 A.H./November 28, 1849). Translated from Hamdi Atamer, "Zenci Ticaretinin Yasaklanmasi," in *Belgelerle Türk Tarihi Dergisi* 3 (1967), pp. 24–25.
8. Letters from Benghazi Concerning the Traffic in Slaves (1875). Public Record Office, London, Foreign Office 195/1082.
9. Instructions Concerning the Trade in Slaves (1936). Translated from *Umm al-Qurā* (Mecca, 16 Rajab 1355 A.H./October 2, 1936).

1.
A Discussion of National Character (Late Tenth Century)

He said: Which do you consider superior, the foreigners or the Arabs?

I said: Scholars take account of four nations: the Byzantines, the Arabs, the Persians, and the Indians. Three of these are foreigners, and it would be hard to say that the Arabs alone are superior to all three of them, with all that they have and all their diversity.

He said: I just mean the Persians.

I said: Before I give my own judgment, I shall relate what was said by Ibn al-Muqaffaʿ,[1] a noble Persian and a distinguished foreigner, outstanding among men of culture. . . . Shabīb ibn Shabba said . . . We were received by Ibn al-Muqaffaʿ, who asked us: "Which is the wisest of nations?" We thought he meant the Persians, so we said, trying to ingratiate ourselves with him: "Persia is the wisest of nations." "Certainly not," he said, "they cannot claim this. They are a people who were taught and learned, who were set an example and copied it, who were given a start and followed it, but they have neither originality nor resource." We suggested the Byzantines, and he said, "No, it is not with them either. They have firm bodies, and they are builders and geometers. They know nothing else, and excel in nothing else."

"The Chinese," we said. "People of furnishings and handicrafts", he replied, "with neither thought nor reflection." "The Turks," we said. "Wild beasts for the fray," he replied. "The Indians," we said. "People of fantasy," he said, "of legerdemain and conjuring and tricks." "The Zanj," we said. "Feckless cattle,"[2] he replied.

So we turned the question back to him; and he said: "The Arabs," at which we exchanged glances and whispers. This made him angry with us. He turned pale and said: "You seem to suspect me of trying to flatter you. By God, I dearly wish that you did not have this privilege; but even if I have lost this privilege, I would disdain to lose the truth as well. . . . The Arabs are the wisest of nations because of their sound character, balanced physique, precise thought, and keen understanding."

He said: How well Ibn al-Muqaffaʿ spoke, and how well you relate it. And now give as your own version, both what you have heard and what you have thought of yourself.

I said: What [Ibn al-Muqaffaʿ] said is sufficient. To add to it would be superfluous, to repeat it useless.

He said: . . . This question—I mean the relative merits of nations—is one of the main topics about which people contend and argue and on which they never reach agreement.

I said: Inevitably, since it is not in the nature or custom or innate qualities of the Persian to admit the merit of the Arab, nor is it in the character or usage of the Arab to affirm the merits of the Persian, and likewise the Indian, the Byzantine, the Turk, the Daylami, and the rest. Recognition of merit and honor depends on two things: one is that which distinguishes one people in its prime from others, in the choice between good and evil and in sound or faulty judgment and in study from beginning to end. On this basis, every nation has merits and defects; and every people has committed good and evil deeds; and every community of men, in its works and in its doing and its undoing, has both perfection and shortcoming. In consequence, good and bad qualities are spread among the whole of mankind and implanted in all of them.

The Persians have statecraft, civility, rules, and etiquette; the Byzantines have science and wisdom; the Indians have thought and reflection and nimbleness and magic and perseverance; the Turks have courage and impetuosity; the Zanj have patience and toil and merriment; the Arabs are intrepid, hospitable, loyal, gallant, generous, protective, eloquent, and cogent.

These qualities are not found in every individual of these nations but are widespread among them. Some, however, may be bereft of all these qualities or even marked by their opposite. Thus there are Persians who are ignorant of statecraft, lacking in civility—ruffians and rabble; there are Arabs who are cowardly, boorish, fickle, miserly, and tongue-tied; and likewise with the Indians, the Byzantines, and the others. And so, if the people of merit and excellence among the Byzantines are compared with those among the Persians, they meet on the Straight Path and differ only in the dimensions of merit and extent of excellence; and this does not distinguish but unites them. Likewise, if the flawed and vicious of one nation are compared with the flawed and base of another, they meet on one track; and they differ only in the magnitude and scope of their defects. . . . It is clear that all nations have their share of merits and defects, by both innate compulsion and intellectual choice. The rest is mere argument among people, according to their places of origin, their inherited customs, and their aroused passions.

There is another point, of prime importance, which we cannot omit from this discussion.

Every nation has a time when it prevails over its rivals. This becomes clear if you direct your imagination to Greece and to Alexander, who conquered and governed and reigned and led and ripped apart and joined together and prescribed and disposed and aroused and restrained and erased and recorded. And if you consider the story of Chrosroes Anushirvan,[3] you will find precisely the same circumstance. . . . When Abū Muslim . . . was asked: Which people do you find the bravest? he replied: "All people are brave when their power is rising." He spoke truth, for every nation at the beginning of its felicity is worthier, bolder, braver, more glorious, more generous, more munificent, more eloquent, more articulate, more judicious, and more veracious; and this derives from something that is common to all nations . . . and shows the abounding generosity of Almighty God to all His creatures.

On Languages

We have heard many languages (even if we did not understand them) of all nations, such as the languages of our friends the Persians, Indians, Turks, Khwarezmians, Slavs, Andalusians, and Zanj; and we have found nothing in these languages like the limpidity of Arabic. . . . This will be recognized by any healthy person who is free from passion or tribal bigotry and who is devoted to equity and to fairness. . . . Indeed, I would be astonished if any man of wide knowledge, sound mind, and extensive culture, would disagree with what I say.

Reply to al-Jayḥānī

I am greatly astonished by al-Jayḥānī,[4] who in his book abuses the Arabs and says that they eat jerboas and lizards and rats and snakes, denounce and attack each other, and excite and commit obscenities with each other, as if they had cast off the qualities of humanity and donned the hides of swine. That, he said, is why Chosroes used to call the king of the Arabs *Sagānshāh,*[5] that is to say, the king of the dogs. . . . He (al-

Jayḥānī) did not realize that if every Chosroes who was in Persia, and every Caesar who was in Rome . . . and every Khaqan who was among the Turks came into this desert and desolation and emptiness, they would not have acted otherwise, since he who is hungry eats what he finds and drinks what he can in order to survive. If Anushirvan had found himself in the deserts of the Banu Asad . . . the rocks of Ṭība, the sands of Yabrīn, or the wastes of Habīr and if he were hungry and thirsty and naked, then would not he, too, eat jerboas and rats? Would not he, too, drink camel's urine and well water? Would not he, too, wear rough and tattered garments? . . . To say such things is ignorance, to repeat them injustice, because the Arabs are the finest of mankind.

Notes

1. Ibn al-Muqaffaʿ (ca. 720–ca. 756), a Persian convert to Islam, an adviser to the caliphs, and one of the founders of classical Arabic prose literature.

2. Reading *bahā'im hāmila,* as suggested by the editors of the text. The ms. reads *ha'ila,* "fearsome," which does not accord with *bahīma* (pl. *bahā'im*), a term normally used of cattle or domestic animals.

3. Chosroes Anushirvan (531–79 A.D.), a Sasanid emperor of Iran. Because of his celebrity, his name, in the Arabized form Kisrā, was used in Islamic literature as the title of the sovereign of Persia, the equivalent of Caesar in Rome and Byzantium.

4. Presumably one of a well-known family of viziers and scholars of that name, in the service of the Samanid princes who reigned in eastern Iran and Central Asia. See *EI*[2] suppl. s.v., "al-Djayḥānī" (by C. Pellat).

5. From the Persian *sag,* "dog." The epithet is a mocking parody of the Persian imperial title *shāhanshāh,* "king of kings."

2.
The Rights of the Slave (Late Eleventh to Early Twelfth Century)

Know that the rights of ownership by marriage have already been treated above in the section on marriage. As for ownership by slavery, this too entails rights in social relations which must be respected. Among the final injunctions of the Prophet of God, may God bless and preserve him, he said: "Fear God concerning those whom you own [literally, 'those whom your right hands possess']. Feed them with what you eat and cover them with what you wear, and do not set them tasks which they cannot perform. Those whom you like, keep; and those whom you dislike, sell. Do not torment God's creatures. God made you their owner; and had He wished, He could have made them your owners."

He also said, may God bless and save him: "The slave is entitled to his food and clothing, as is appropriate; and he should not be set tasks which he cannot perform."

ʿAbdallah, the son of ʿUmar, may God be pleased with them both, said: "A man came to the Prophet of God and said: 'O Prophet of God, how many times shall we pardon a slave?' And the Prophet was silent, and then he said: 'Forgive him seventy times every day.' "

ʿUmar, may God be pleased with him, used to go to al-Awālī every Saturday; and when he saw a slave with a task beyond his power, he would lighten his task. It is related on the authority of Abū Ḥurayra, may God be pleased with him, that he saw a man riding a steed and his slave running behind him; and he said to the man: "Slave of God, mount him behind you, for he is your brother and his soul is as your soul."

. . . A slave girl of Abu'l-Dardaʿ said to him: "For a year I have been poisoning you, but nothing happens to you." He said: "Why do you do this?" She said: "I want to be rid of you." He said: "Go, you are free for the sake of God."

Al-Zuhrī said: "If you say to a slave: 'May God punish you,' then he is free." Someone said to al-Aḥnaf ibn Qays: "From whom did you learn magnanimity?" He said: "From Qays ibn ʿĀṣim." It was said: "How far did his magnanimity reach?" He replied: "Once when he was sitting in his house a slavewoman came with a roast on a spit. The spit fell from her hand on his son, who was wounded and died. The slave girl was horrified, and he said: 'Nothing will calm this slave girl but manumission.' He therefore said to her: 'You are free, don't be afraid.' "

ʿAwn ibn ʿAbdallah used to say, when his slave disobeyed him: "You are like your master. Your master disobeys his master, and you disobey your master." One day he made him angry, and he said: "What you want is to make me beat you. Go, you are free."

Maymūn ibn Mihrān had a guest with him, and he told his slave girl to make haste in bringing dinner. She came hurrying, with a full dish; but she stumbled and emptied in on the head of her master Maymūn. He said: "Slave girl! You have scalded me." She said: "You who teach what is good and punish people, return to what God said." "And what did God say?" he asked. She replied: "He said 'Those who hold back their anger.' " He said: "I have held back my anger." She said: "And those who forgive others." He said: "I have forgiven you." She said: "And more, for God also said: 'God loves those who do good' " (all from Qur'ān XXX:128). He said: "You are free for the sake of God."

Ibn al-Munkadir said: "A man who was one of the Companions of the Prophet of God struck a slave of his, and the slave began to cry out: 'I ask you for the sake of God, I ask you for the sake of God'; but he did not pardon him. The Prophet heard the cry of the slave and went to him; and when the man saw the Prophet of God, he withheld his hand. And the Prophet of God said: 'He asked you for the sake of God and you did not forgive him, but when you saw me you withheld your hand.' And the man said: 'He is free for the sake of God, O Prophet of God.' And the Prophet of God said: 'Had you not done this, hellfire would have scorched your face.' "

The Prophet of God also said: "The slave who is loyal to his master and faithful in the service of God will have a double reward." When Abū Rafīʿ was manumitted, he wept and said: "I used to have two rewards, and now one of them has gone."

The Prophet of God said: "I was shown the first three to enter Paradise, and the first three to enter Hell. The first three in Paradise were the martyr [who falls in the holy war], the owned slave who is faithful in his service to God and loyal to his master, and the chaste and moral man with children. The first three to enter Hell are an oppressive ruler, a rich man who does not give God's share, and a pauper braggart."

It is related on the authority of Abū Masʿūd al-Anṣārī, who said: "I was beating one of my slaves when I heard a voice behind me saying: 'Know this, O Abū Masʿūd!' The voice said this twice. I turned around, and there was the Prophet of God. I threw the whip from my hand, and he said: 'By God, God has more power over you than you have over this man.' "

The Prophet of God said: "If one of you buys a slave, the first food he gives him should be something sweet, for this will be the most soothing for him." This was related by Maʿādh.

Abū Hurayra said that the Prophet of God said: "If one of you has his slave bring him food, he should seat him and let him eat with him, and if he does not do this, he should at least give him a mouthful." . . .

A man came to see Salmān, who was kneading dough; and the man said to him: "O Abū ʿAbdallāh, what is this?" And Salmān replied: "I sent my servant on some task, and I did not wish to double his work."

The Prophet of God said: "If anyone has a slave girl and he respects her chastity and treats her well and then manumits her and marries her, then he has two rewards." He also said: "Every one of you is a shepherd and every one of you is responsible for his flock."

In sum, the right of the slave is that his master should share his food and clothing with him, not give him tasks beyond his strength, not look upon him with the eye of arrogance and disdain, forgive him for his trespasses, and when he is angry with him for some lapse or offense, think of his own sins and offenses against Almighty God and his shortcomings in obedience to God, and remember that God's power is greater over him than his power over his slave.

3.
A Legal Ruling (Fifteenth Century)

I have been asked about slaves who come from the land of Abyssinia and who profess monotheism and accept the rules of holy law; is it lawful or not to sell and buy them? If they are converted to Islam while subject to the ownership of their masters, have the masters the right to sell them or not? And if the Sunna allows the sale of slaves, how is it that the profession of the monotheistic creed, which saves [an infidel prisoner] from death and from punishment in the other world, does not save from the humiliation and the suffering of slavery? Indeed, ownership is an enslavement and diminution of the individual ennobled by the faith. And what is the meaning of the saying of the doctors of the holy law: "Slavery is unbelief [*kufr*]"? Does this apply after one has become a believer?

I reply: If it is proved that a slave was originally an unbeliever of one kind or another—unless he is of Quraysh—and if on the other hand it is not proved that he adopted Islam when he was in his own country and a free agent, then once his captors have laid hands on him after conquest and victory, it is lawful for them to sell or buy him, without hindrance. The profession of the monotheistic creed by these slaves does not prevent the continuance of their status as slaves, since slavery is a humiliation and a servitude caused by previous or current unbelief and having as its purpose to discourage unbelief. That is why the slave is deemed "absent" for himself but "present" for his master. When he is liberated, he acquires legal identity and becomes master of his own person. He is then able to own property, to be a judge or witness, or to hold public office.

As to those who profess monotheism and observe the rules of holy law among the slaves arriving from Abyssinia and from other countries of unbelievers and of the House of War, their profession of monotheism does not hinder their sale and their purchase on the basis of their original unbelief and uncertainty, whether their conversion to Islam is previous or subsequent to the establishment of a right of ownership by their master. The doubt is about the hindrance, and doubt about hindrance is of no effect.

Certainly, if it is known that a whole section or community of the inhabitants of a region have adopted Islam or been conquered by Islam, in such a case the way to avoid error would be to prohibit the possession of these slaves.

But if conversion to Islam is subsequent to the establishment of a right of ownership [over the slaves], then Islam does not require freedom, because slavery has been caused by unbelief. This state of servitude continues after the cessation of the unbelief, because of its past existence and in order to discourage unbelief.

4.
Correspondence Concerning Slavery between Consul General Drummond Hay and the Sultan of Morocco (1842)

Consul General Drummond Hay
Slave Trade No. 2
Four Inclosures
Received Mar 30
By Sea via Gibraltar
Correspondence with the Moorish Government regarding the traffick in Slaves.

Tangier 12th March 1842

My Lord [Earl of Aberdeen],

Having made application to the Sultan of Marocco, in pursuance of the directions in your Lordship's Circular of the 27th last December, marked Slave Trade No. 4, as mentioned in my Despatch of the 29th January, marked Slave Trade No. 1,—I received an Answer from the Potentate, of which—and my own letter to which it replies—I do myself the honor of presenting herewith the English Versions. [Inclosure 1.]

The Sultan's Answer being far from satisfactory, and His Majesty having distinctly asked for information on the subject of my communication,—whereon, as regarding other nations than his own, he appeared entirely ignorant,—I considered the occasion convenient for transmitting to this Potentate, (so soon as the sickness of our Interpreter permitted him to prepare the Arabic translation) a second Letter and this in considerable detail: that Translation was completed and despatched yesterday to the Sultan, who is now at Meknas,—and thereof also I beg leave to present herewith my English original. [Inclosure 2.]

If much time had not elapsed since receipt of your Lordship's instructions, I would yet wait the Moorish Sultan's reply to my second Letter; but, as that may not arrive till after the departure of several mails, I am unwilling to lay any longer under the possible imputation of not having used my best efforts to forward the views of your Lordship,—by endeavouring to obtain, as promptly as possible, the desired information regarding the Slave Trade in this country.

Having addressed myself on the subject to Her Majesty's Vice Consuls at the outposts of Marocco, I have not collected from their replies a single fact worthy relation: the little that I have myself been able to obtain, through another channel, of matter illustrative in some degree of Laws and Regulations respecting Slavery and the Slave Trade in this country, is presented herewith to your Lordship in the original Arabic, with accurate Translations, (Inclosures Nos. 3 and 4).

The mere circumstance of the Thaleb, from whom I obtained the documents in the Inclosure No. 3, having assured me, that his head would be endangered, if I made known to any one in this country that I had gotten from him such documents,—will show (though I believe he greatly exaggerated his pretended fear) how difficult it is to obtain authentic information in Marocco, on any subject, wherein an inquirer may be suspected of trenching on the religious prejudices of its most bigoted people.

It will be agreeable for your Lordship to know, that the Slaves in this country are not numerous and, according to all my own observation and every report, are kindly treated by their masters, who—at their decease—frequently emancipate their Slaves.

During nearly thirteen years of residence in Marocco, I do not remember a single instance of Slaves having been exported from this country; and the last case of the kind, of which I have information, occurred about twenty four years ago,—when five hundred Black men were purchased by the late Algerine Consul Hadj Abd-al-crim Ben-Thaleb for the Dey of Algiers, to which place they were sent by sea and were formed—as I am told—into a Body-guard of the Dey.

I have the honor to be,

with the highest respect,
My Lord,
Your Lordship's most obedient
very humble Servant
E. W. A. Drummond Hay

Letters to and from the Sultan of Marocco

[Inclosure No. 1, in Despatch marked Slave Trade No. 2 of 12th Mar. 1842 from Cons. Gen. Drummond Hay to the Earl of Aberdeen, etc.]

To His Imperial Majesty Mulai Abd Errachman Ben Heesham,[1] Sultan of Marocco, etc. Her Britannic Majesty's Agent and Consul General Drummond Hay—with profound respect.

In consequence of instructions from the principal Secretary of State for Foreign Affairs of the Queen my Gracious Sovereign, I do myself the high honor of requesting Your Imperial Majesty to be pleased to cause me to be informed, if any Laws or any administrative Acts have emanated from your Majesty or your Majesty's Royal Predecessors, or from any Governors of Districts or from any Municipal Officers under the Imperial authority,—for the purpose of regulating, restraining or preventing the traffic in Slaves; and, if there have been any such Acts or Laws promulgated, I am to beg of Your Majesty to be pleased to direct that, I be furnished with authenticated copies of all such documents, whether they may have been of a temporary or of a permanent character.

I would add, in exemplification of this application to your Imperial Majesty that it is desirable that your Majesty may be pleased to cause me to be instructed, if there be any Law or Regulation in any part of Your Majesty's Dominions, whereby the traffic in Slaves—if not wholly prohibited—is in any degree moderated or kept within certain bounds; as for example, if there be prohibition against any merchant purchasing man, woman or child of any colour whatsoever, for exportation as Slaves, and if they can or cannot be legally exported from out Your Majesty's dominions by land or Sea.

Dated at Tangier the 22nd of January in the year of Jesus Christ the Messiah 1842
(signed) E. W. A. Drummond Hay

Translation of the Sultan's Answer to the foregoing letter.

N.B. Although this letter, (which appears a production of great haste) is addressed on the face of it to "The Consul of the French," it was on the Envelope addressed to "The Consul of the English"

In the name of the Most Merciful God!
There is no power or strength but in God the High and Almighty

To the Employed who manifests in our Sheriffian Service attention and Solicitude, Drummond Hay Consul of the French [*sic*] Nation residing in Tangier.

which premised:

We have received the Letter you have addressed to our presence exalted of God, wherein you state that the Minister for Foreign Affairs of the Queen of your Nation has called upon you to make inquiry regarding the Trade in Slaves, if it be lawful by our beloved Law or no.

Be it known to you, that the Traffic in Slaves is a matter on which all Sects and Nations have agreed from the time of the sons of Adam, on whom be the Peace of God, up to this day—and we are not aware of its being prohibited by the Laws of any Sect, and no one need ask this question, the same being manifest to both high and low and requires no more demonstration than the light of day: But if there be any peculiar event which has occurred, inform us about it particularly, in order that the answer may be apposite to the question.

Ended the 23rd Doolhadja 1257 (4 Feb 1842)

True Copies
Henry John Murray
Vice Consul

[Inclosure No. 2]

To the Noble Prince exalted of the Lord Mulai Abd Errachman Ben Heesham Sultan of Marocco, etc., etc. Her Britannic Majesty's Agent and Consul General E. W. A. Drummond Hay—with profound respect.

I have had the honor to receive Your Imperial Majesty's Letter dated the 23rd Doolhedja, purporting to be an Answer to that addressed by me to Your Majesty on the subject of the Slave-trade; but, it would appear from some expressions in Your Majesty's Letter, that Your Majesty has not clearly apprehended the sense of the application made therein, on the part of the Government of Her Majesty my Gracious Sovereign.

That wise and enlightened Government is fully aware, that, Slavery and Trading in Slaves are not prohibited by the Law of Islam, any more than by the more ancient Law of the tribes of Israel, nay indeed Slavery and the Slave trade were not—until a comparatively very recent period—prohibited by the Laws of even any Christian state.

Your Imperial Majesty having deigned to express a desire that if any peculiar event have occurred, I should inform Your Majesty about it particularly in order that the answer may be apposite to the question,—I now do myself the honor of presenting to Your Imperial Majesty, in as short a form as so large a subject may admit, a general view of the progress made—within some thirty four years past—in favor of suffering humanity, with regard to Slavery and the Slavetrade, which will clearly show, that many nations—and these of various religious persuasions—have disapproved and have modified and some have entirely abolished the traffic in Slaves.

The Government of Great Britain had the high honor of taking the lead in Europe for this righteous work of charity, in abolishing the traffic by British Subjects in Slaves; of whom it is computed that, for a long course of years, upward of 300,000 in all have been carried off annually by various Nations from the Coasts of Africa, conveyed thence in frightful bondage across the ocean and sold as Slaves in numerous distant lands.

Ultimately between six and seven years ago, the British Government abolished also *Slavery itself* throughout the vast extent of its Empire, at the cost of Twenty Millions Sterling or about $100,000,000 Dollars, for indemnification of all British Subjects possessors of Slaves; thus emancipating more than seven hundred and fifty thousand of our fellow men from Slavery; and it is not unworthy the contemplation of Your Imperial Majesty's exalted mind, that, while this glorious work of charity was performed by the British Government on a scale of munificence never heard of before in the history of mankind, the said vast sum of treasure—paid in such compensation—present the most admirably striking instance of a liberal and just resolution to vindicate and maintain the rights of property.

Upon this grand event in British legislation, it was enacted that any Subject of the British Crown or any individual residing in any part of the British dominions, who shall engage in the Slave-trade or in the conveyance of Slaves upon the sea, shall be held guilty of the crime of Piracy—involving the punishment of death; and that anyone who shall knowingly embark capital or lend other aid of any kind to the traffic, although not personally engaged in it, shall be held guilty of felony—the punishment whereof is exile to a penal settlement.

More than 26 years ago the efforts of Great Britain, in combination with corresponding efforts on the part of her Allies, had already succeeded so far as to have induced the Representatives of Eight of the greatest Powers of Europe—assembled in Congress at Vienna—to declare unanimously, after a solemn deliberation, that the Slave-trade is repugnant to the principles of humanity and universal morality,—and that it was the earnest desire of their Sovereigns to put an end to a scourge, which has so long afflicted humanity, degraded those European Nations which have exercised that traffic and desolated Africa.

Subsequently, almost all the Powers of Europe have given practical effect to the humane principles, proclaimed in that memorable Declaration, by their Legislative enactments and by Treaty engagements; and in the same generous purpose have concurred a very large portion of the great States of America, both North and South.

But it is with yet additional pleasure, I acquaint Your Imperial Majesty, that—according to information I have recently received, which, although not official seems to be perfectly authentic,—the Rulers of several Mooslem States—those namely of Muscat, of Egypt and of Tunis—have already exhibited a generous disposition to follow the Christian Governments in the same march of beneficence. Circumstances indeed are understood to have—for the present—delayed fulfilment by the Pasha Mohamed Ali of his purpose in this matter, as expressed some time since to Agents of the British Government but the Prince Imaum of Muscat, who, as Your Majesty is doubtless aware, rules over important possessions on the East Coast of Africa, as well as over a large territory in South Arabia, has abolished the external Slave-trade of his dominions;—and the Bey of Tunis has, within a few months past, taken measures for abolishing the Slave-trade within his Regency. There may be also other Mooslem Princes, who have entered the same glorious career for alleviating the afflictions of our fellow man,—but I have not at present further notices regarding them for Your Majesty's information on this most interesting subject; there do yet however remain circumstances in the present history of the World, that cannot fail to be highly gratifying to the benevolent mind of Your Imperial Majesty; namely that, a convention was just half a year since entered into with the British Government by the King of Bonny, one of the Southern regions of Soodan, not only to abolish the Slave-trade totally within his dominions,—but, as that potentate's realm occupies some extent of sea coast, the stipulation is added, that, no Slaves shall ever again be permitted to pass through or be exported from his dominions. The value of this Convention to the common cause of Charity will be better appreciated, when it is considered that—until lately—no less than 20,000 Slaves were annually exported from the Kingdom of Bonny alone.

About the same time also Treaties were concluded, by Officers of the Queen my Gracious Sovereign, for the total abolition of the Slave-trade within their dominions by the Kings of Eboe and of Iddah,—regions also of Soodan through which the great river Quorra runs to the North of Bonny, where it joins the ocean: the kingdoms of Eboe and Iddah have, as did Bonny, afforded for ages hitherto vast markets for the dealers in Slaves.

Having made these statements in order to comply to the best of any power at present with Your Majesty's desire,—I would beg leave to observe to Your Imperial Majesty, that, although the Prophets and other Legislators of ancient nations had not, on account of the uncultivated times wherein they lived, held it expedient to frame any Laws for the prohibition of the traffic in Slaves; yet in no age nor in any Country of the world (except in cases indicated as of punishment for the wicked) has the Enslaving of Human Beings been prescribed as a praiseworthy usage or as one that can be grateful to the ONE All-Beneficent God,—but it appears to have been merely a practice permitted, as arising out of rude habits.

In conclusion, I crave Your Majesty's condescending attention, while I repeat this, I am commissioned—as Agent near your Majesty for the Queen my Gracious Sovereign—to inquire if (although the Law of Islam has not prohibited the trading of Slaves) there have been put forth at any time by Your Majesty or by any of Your Majesty's predecessors or by any Officers under your own or their Imperial Authority any Ordinance or Regulation, whereby that traffic was or is in any degree limited or modified and, if there have been any such ordinances or Regulations promulgated, I am to request Your Majesty to be pleased to cause me to be supplied with authenticated copies of the same.

I rely on Your Majesty's respect for the Queen my Sovereign and for the great Empire, with the care of which Her Majesty is entrusted by the Divine Grace, to accept this communication in the same spirit of friendliness, with which it is addressed to Your Imperial Majesty for a more mature consideration.

The Queen's Government, I may be allowed to add, feel so great anxiety to see the Slave-trade extinguished in every part of the World, that they are unwilling to let pass any occasion, which offers a hope of being able to mitigate that evil in any Country where it continues to exist; and the present appeared a favorable period for this inquiry with regard to the Institutions, usage and Regulations in force and affecting Slavery and the Slave-trade in West Barbary; while this fine Country is happily under the Government of a Prince so enlightened as Your Majesty, and one whose rule over his dominions exhibits Your Imperial Majesty as the kind father of a grateful People.

Dated at Tangier this 26th day of February in the Year of Jesus Christ the Messiah 1842—(16th Moharrem the first month of the year 1258)

Drummond Hay
Her Britanic Majesty's Agent and
Consul General in Marocco.

[Arabic documents from the Thaleb Hamed Ben Yahia regarding Slavery and the Slave Trade in Morocco.
Inclosure No. 3, in Despatch marked "Slave-trade No. 2 of 12th.March..1842 from Cons. Gen. Drummond Hay to the Earl of Aberdeen]

[English translation of Arabic documents from the Thaleb Hamed Ben Yahia regarding: Slavery and Slave-trade in Marocco. Inclosure No. 4, in Despatch marked "Slave-trade No. 3 of 12th Mar 1842 from C. G. [Consul General] Drummond Hay to the Earl of Aberdeen.]

Translation of Arabic documents received by Consul General Drummond Hay at Tangier 2nd March 1842 from the Thaleb Hamed Ben Yahia of that place.

(No. 1) Praise be to the One God!

In as much as the Consul General Agent for the Queen of the English Nation, at this present time in Tangier, has asked me what are the ordinances of the Law regarding Slaves or Bond-servants, and if there be anything in our Law which alleviates their condition of bondage: I replied in the words of the Shehk, the Imaum, the most learned Seeyed Mohamed Ben Ismael al-Bokhary, in his book entitled *Jamea E'Sahih*[2]

"The Apostle of God, upon whom be the blessing of God said—(a class of) your brethren are given to you for doing service, God has set them beneath you. To him whom God has placed beneath his brother let the same meat and drink be given of which he partakes himself and let the same clothing be given as that with which he himself is clothed, let him (the master) fear God in respect to him (the slave) and not force him to do more than he can." Peace.

(No. 2) Praise be to the One God!

Be it known to you that, as to the question regarding the sale of Slaves or Bond-servants no Sultan of the Gharb nor any other Authority has enacted any ordinance respecting them, except that which is ordained by the Religion of the Apostle of God, on whom be the Blessing of God, since he was in life now 1258 years,—as said the Shehk, the Imaum, the most learned Aboo Abd Allah Seeyed Mohammed Ben Ismael al Bokhary in his book entitled *Jamea E'Sahih*

"The Apostle of God, on whom be the Blessing and the Peace of God, hath said—whosoever sets any person free God will set his soul free from the fire (of Hell)."

(No. 3) (Extracts from the work of Shehk Khalil wuld Isaac, called *Moktassar Khalil* or Khalil's compendium.)[3]

The Shehk Khalil, to whom God be propitious, states the following in his abridgement of the chapter regarding Sales.

"It has been prohibited to sell a Mooslem, the sacred *misshaf* [Qur'ān] and a young person to a disbeliever; that is to say, to any who do not profess the Faith of Islam, whether Christian, Jew or Majoosy:[4] to make a present (of the same) or to give as in alms is held in the same light as a sale"

Praise be to the One God!

The Said Shehk Khalil states in his aforesaid compendium, in a section of the chapter regarding Emancipation, that—

"(A Slave) is emancipated by the Law if illtreated: that is to say if he (the master) intends to illtreat the Slave or actually does so. Whether he (the Slave) can take with him what he may possess of property or no, is a matter yet undecided by the Doctors of the Law" Peace!

true translation from the Said Arabic documents as certified to me.

E. W. A. Drummond Hay
Her Majesty's Agent and Consul General in Marocco

* * *

[Consul General Drummond Hay
Slave Trade No. 3
One Inclosure
Received 11 Apr.
by Sea via Gibraltar
Inclosing the Translation of a Letter from the Sultan of Marocco]

Slave Trade No. 3
Tangier 27th March 1842

My Lord

I have the honor to inclose a translation of a Letter I have received from the Sultan of Marocco, in reply to that dispatched upon the 11th instant to this potentate on the subject of Slavery and the Slave Trade; of which my Letter I sent your Lordship the English version in a Dispatch marked "Slave Trade No. 2" and dated the 12th instant.

I have the honor to be, with the highest respect, My Lord, Your Lordship's most obedient very humble servant,
E. W. A. Drummond Hay

Translation of a letter received from the Sultan of Marocco on 23rd March 1842, in reply to the last of Consul General Drummond Hay, respecting Slavery and the Slave Trade.

In the name of the Most Merciful God! There is no strength or power but in God the High and Almighty!

To the Employed who has in our Sheriffian Service diligence and solicitude, Drummond Hay, Consul for the English nation residing in Tangier the Protected.

which premised:

We have received your Letter explaining the object of the Minister of the potentate of your Nation, with reference to his inquiries respecting Slaves,—and we have made ourself acquainted with the proceedings had in that matter, as well as with the expenditure incurred in the purchase from their Masters of all those in your dominions; (we learn) also that, in Soodan and other parts that example had been followed.

Be it known to you that the religion of Islam—may God exalt it—has a solid foundation, of which the corner stones are well secured and the perfection whereof has been made known to us by God—to whom belongs all praise—in his book *Forkan*[5] which admits not either of addition or diminution.

As to what regards the making of Slaves and Trading therewith, it is confirmed by our Book as also by the *Sunna* of Our Prophet, on whom be the blessing and the peace of God—and furthermore there is not any controversy between the *Oolamma*[6] on that subject, and no one can allow what is prohibited or prohibit that which is made lawful.

By whomsoever innovation be attempted contrary to it (the Law) the same shall be rejected, inasmuch as our sacred religion is not regulated by mens' counsel or deliberation, for it proceeds out of Inspiration from the Lord of all creatures, through the tongue of our Faithful Prophet, on whom be the Peace and Blessing of God!

Ended the 5th Safar 1258 (18th March 1842)

True Translation as certified to me

EWA Drummond Hay

Notes

1. Mawlāy ʿAbd al-Raḥmān ibn Hishām (reigned 1822–59). See *EI*², s.v. (by Ph. de Cossé Brissac).
2. *Al-Jāmiʿ al-Ṣaḥīḥ,* the standard collection of *ḥadīth*s, by al-Bukhārī.
3. The *Mukhtaṣar,* "Abridgement," a standard legal work by Khalīl ibn Ishāq.
4. *Majūsī,* "Magian." Originally used of the Zoroastrians, later also of the Vikings and other pagans.
5. Furqān = Qur'ān.
6. ʿUlamā'.

5.
Report on Slavery from the Persian Gulf (1842)

To

Lieutenant Colonel Robertson
Off[iciatin]g Resident, Persian Gulf
Harrack 8th July 1842

Sir,

Agreeably to your wishes, that I should frame full answers, to the Questions on the subject of Slaves, conveyed in Colonel Sheil's letter dated June 30, I beg now to offer the result of my endeavours in collecting the required information.

Before entering respectively into the answers to each [of the] questions, It maybe as well to premise,

1st That Slaves imported into the South of Persia, are of two kinds, Seedee or African, from the Coast of Zanzibar, principally the territory of the Imaum of Muscat; and Hubshee or Abyssinian, from the shores of the Red Sea.

2[d] That slaves are seldom kidnapped by the crews of Boats or by the slave Merchants but by Men employed for that purpose in the interior. A proportion are prisoners made in their petty war.

3d That Muscat and Soor are the principal, if not only primary ports, to which all slaves, from whencesoever shipped, whether Zanzibar, or the Red Sea, are brought, and whence they are eventually carried into Turkey, Persia, Scinde, the Arab States, and even our own territories, the Western Coast of India, by boats belonging chiefly to the Eastern Coast of Arabia, which are not bound for any particular ports, but make coasting voyages selling as they touch. Of the above Countries, Turkey consumes by far the greater proportion. Bussorah and Bagdad being the largest Marts, of the Persian ports send vessels direct to Zanzibar, with the exception of Lingah—whence three or four boats are annually dispatched, each returning with about 70 slaves.

The season for the Gulf Traffic in slaves is from the 1st August to 1st December.

In Bushire, and the other Persian ports, there are no places established as Markets or days fixed for the Sale of Slaves. But on the arrival of a Boat, the owner takes his Cargo to a hired dwelling, where they are either sold privately, or whence they are taken and publicly exposed for Sale, at one of the caravanceries of which there are several. Should the Market be overstocked, and thus the owner be unable expeditiously to gain his profits, they are re-shipped and taken either to Bussorah, Mohumra, or Bagdad at any of which places there is a certainty of a ready sale.

The answers to the first and Second Questions must of necessity be somewhat vague, from the want of time and opportunity for making a reference to the Custom House registers of the several Ports on the Persian Coast of the Gulf. The statements of those, the best informed, with whom I have been able to communicate, agree pretty nearly, differing in no material points. The conclusions from them are as follows. Average number of African slaves sold annually at

Bushire	250
Lingar	350
Gombroom or Bunder Abbas	300
Congoon	150

of Hubshees at

Bushire	25
Lingar	15
Congoon	10
Bunder Abbas	20

Allowing an importation of 100 or 150 of the former, and 10 of the latter, to Asseloo, and the other numerous small ports, would give a total of 1000 and 80 respectively, annually imported into Persia, through the Ports in the Gulf, but this by no means forms the whole number that find their way into the interior of that Country, from the South; for Bussora and Bagdad are the largest Marts whereby far the greater proportion is carried, the actual number from which places however I have been unable to ascertain or even to form a guess at.

The large number of Pilgrims that go annually from Persia to Mecca and to Kerbela etc. return with slaves averaging rich and poor, one to each Pilgrim.

Of African Slaves imported the number of Males bears somewhat a greater proportion to the females—six to five.

Of Hubshees By far the greater number are females—two to one.

Price of Africans	at Zanzibar
Boys from 7 to 10 years of age --	7 to 15 Dollars
---"--- 10 to 20 ----------------------	15 to 30 "
Full grown Men -------------------	17 to 20 "

The females are somewhat more valued than the Males. A good stout lass will sell for 35 dollars. The profit on the above at Muscat is 20 per cent and at Bussorah and Bushire never less than 50 per cent.

The Hubshee females are much prized for their beauty and Symmetry of figure. Their value [is] from 300 to 1000 koronies or indeed to any amount. The Males also are much valued—their price from 200 to 600 and upwards.

After 20 the slaves of both sexes whether Hubshee or Africans deteriorate much in value, from their being at that mature age less tractable, and taking less kindly to the language religion, and customs of their Masters.

The treatment of the slaves is at no time either severe or cruel, but they are most compelled to rough it during the sea voyage when they are very scantily clothed and supplied with but sufficient food, and that coarse, to keep them alive. From the moment of purchase at their eventual destination however their condition is materially changed for the better, (the purchasers in general feeding and treating them almost as kindly as the Members of their own families, they in return work hard, willingly and well & appear to be happy and contented) unless indeed they become the property of other slave Merchants from the Interior when the condition remains much the same. In travelling from one place to another, they are supplied with Mules. In the boats they are not bound or manacled.

The Men are employed in all hard and out door work, the women in cooking, bringing water etc. and but very rarely as concubines except by the poorer and lower classes.

Children born in bondage are free but are nevertheless provided for by the owners of their parents and with them entitled to the same rights and privileges.

The Hubshee Slaves of both sexes are at all times much cared for well clothed and well fed. The Males are early sent to school and having learnt to read and write are employed in the performance of house duties as Peish khidmuts etc. etc. and very frequently if intelligent in the most trustworthy situations as supercargos of ships, stewards and superintendents.

The Females are most generally retained as concubines or employed in the lightest duties as attendants in Harems, bringing Kaleeons etc. The intelligence and honesty of Hubshee slaves are almost proverbial. The children by these concubines are heirs equally to the Estate of the Father with their legitimate offspring.

Nubian and Hubshee Eunuchs are very high priced and only to be seen in the service of the King, Nobles and very rich Merchants.

In forwarding the above account I trust it may not be considered an act of Superogation my giving the accompanying short statement of the policy that has been hitherto pursued, and a summary of those portions of the Several treaties that have been entered into with the Imaum of Muscat and the Principal Arab Tribes with regard to the traffic in slaves, as a knowledge of our Political powers by treaty in this Quarter may tend to elucidate the subject and facilitate the attainment of so great an end as the suppression of a traffic, so contrary to the best feelings of humanity.

A treaty was first entered into with the Imaum of Muscat in 1822, by which a Right of Search was granted to British Cruizers for all vessels belonging to the subjects of His Highness, suspected of having slaves on board, intended for sale rendering the same liable to confiscation on conviction, if found eastward of a line drawn from Cape Delgade passing 60 miles to Seaward of the island of Socotra, and ending at Deer Head unless they should happen to have been driven beyond the line specified by stress of weather.

In December 1839 three articles were framed in supercession to the above, and agreed to by the Imam. By the two first of which all vessels belonging to his subjects are liable to search and seizure etc. if found Eastward of a line drawn from Cape Delgade passing 2 degrees Seaward of Socotra to Pusseenor on the Mekran Coast, with a reservation that the vessels have not been driven beyond the line by stress of weather or other case of necessity. The 3rd Article provided that the sale of any individual of the Soomonlee tribe (inhabiting the country opposite to Aden and bordering on Abyssinia) who are considered Hoor or Free, shall be considered as Piracy, and that those who may be convicted in such an act, shall be treated as pirates. In the same year these said three articles formed the treaty which was entered into with all the Shaiks except those of Bahrein and Koweit. This treaty greatly extended our right of search etc. and prohibits the importation of slaves under any circumstances into Scinde, Cutch etc.

In 1820 a treaty was entered into with all the chiefs on the Arabian Coast, except the Imam of Muscat and the sheikh of Koweit, an article of which prohibits the *carrying off* of slaves and renders any vessels having such on board liable to be treated as pirates.

In 1838 an agreement was entered into with all the chiefs on the Arabian Coast with the exception of the Shaiks of Koweit and Bahrein, which authorizes the Government Cruizers to detain and search any vessels belonging to those chiefs, or their subjects, suspected of having any individuals whom the crews may have *kidnapped, on board,* and renders them liable to be confiscated on conviction. Whatever may have been the intention in framing these two Articles (the latter being merely a modification of the former at the expiration of nearly 20 years) certain it is that not a single seizure has been made for their meaning has not hitherto been held to preclude those (parties to them) from purchasing slaves from others although they may have been Kidnapped and carrying them on board their vessels with the intention of selling them.

I have the honor to be etc.
/Sig. of A. B. Kemball
Asst. Resident, Persian Gulf

6.
Letter from the Sultan to the Vizier Mehmed Nejib Pasha, Governor of Baghdad (9 Safar 1263 A.H./January 27, 1847)

Whereas special agreements were made between the British government and certain rulers on the African continent, to prevent the transportation of black slaves from the said African continent to America and other places, it has been observed that certain merchant ships are still approaching the African coasts, stealing slaves, and transporting them elsewhere. Since, for this reason, it has not been possible to enforce the provisions of these agreements, the British government has requested that we help them in this and initiate the appropriate measures.

The treatment accorded to slaves who are stolen and transported to those parts is harsh and bereft of humanity and mercy, to a degree not comparable with the treatment of slaves coming to these parts. Since, for this reason it is in accordance with justice and compassion to prohibit the slave trade, henceforth it is totally prohibited for merchant ships flying the flag of my state to engage in this traffic of slaves. If any of them violate this prohibition, then with God's help they will be seized by our warships to be sent to those waters or by British warships cruising in those parts. The ships will be surrendered to the officers in our ports on the Gulf of Basra, and their captains will be arrested and punished.

7.

Draft of a Letter from the Grand Vizier Mustafa Reshid Pasha to the Governor of Tripoli (Libya) (21 Muharrem 1266 A.H./ November 28, 1849)

The Sultan has received, with sorrow, the shocking and evil news that a caravan which set out from Bornu in June with a great number of black slaves, bound for Fezzan, ran out of water on the way, so that 1,600 blacks perished.

It is a well-known fact, which there is no need to state, and which was indeed sent in writing to your province in the time of your predecessor as governor, Raghib Pasha, that while our Holy Law permits slavery, it requires that slaves be treated with fatherly care; those who act in a contrary manner will be condemned by God.

Those people whose practice it is to bring such slaves from inside Africa and make commerce with them, if they wish to bring thousands of God's creatures from such far places and bring them through such vast deserts, then it is their human duty to procure the necessary food and drink for the journey, and ensure that these unfortunates suffer as little as possible on the way. When these people in no way accept this duty, and cause the death of so many human beings in misery and suffering, they are behaving in a way that is not compatible with humanity.

The Sultan can neither condone nor forgive such cruel conduct, and such inhumane behavior is categorically and emphatically forbidden. It will be announced and clearly conveyed to them personally, that if the people engaged in this trade in these regions treat their slaves in a manner contrary to humanity and justice, and if slaves thus perish on the way from thirst and hunger, they will be subjected to various severe punishments. Since it is an obligation of the official duties of a holder of authority to give no scope to such cruel persons and actions, you will be held responsible and reprimanded for the slightest negligence on your part. You will therefore henceforth give this matter your close and personal attention, so that slavedealers known to have acted in this cruel way and notorious in this regard will be brought before the courts and subjected to condign and exemplary punishment. This is required by the Sultan's exalted command.

8.
Letters from Benghazi Concerning the Traffic in Slaves (1875)

Bengazi 31 December 1875

His Excellency
the Right Honorable Sir Henry Elliot ACB

I have the honor to acknowledge receipt of your Excellency's Dispatch No. 5 of the 11th October last with Inclosure.

I inclose herewith a copy of a report I have made to the Secretary of State by his request, on the Slave Trade at Ozla and Jalo from which Your Excellency will gather how far the reports of Moustapha Pasha to the Sublime Porte are in accordance with the truth.

His Excellency cannot plead ignorance of the real state of affairs as the Kaimacam of Jalo (whom I know very well) has reported to him the extent to which the trade in slaves is being carried on, and when I was in Jalo in November last the Kaimacan [*sic*] informed me of the purport of a Dispatch which he had then addressed to His Excellency on this very subject and which I myself forwarded to him through Mr. Drummond Hay.

I would not accuse His Excellency of Wilful misrepresentation but his Dispatch to the Minister of Foreign Affairs must have been written under a very great misapprehension or without having taken any pains to ascertain the truth. When I was at Jalo the Kaimacam and myself verified the arrival of 118 slaves by a caravan which had arrived at Jalo the day before me and I handed the names of the forty three owners of the slaves to the Mutasariff of Bengazi on my return. The caravan arrived here some time ago but I only succeeded in liberating three of the one hundred and eighteen slaves and that after such opposition that I have been obliged to abandon all hope of liberating any others.

With reference to Hadi Hamed Mehduai. I can only state that he was caught by my own cavass[1] in the very act of shipping five slaves for the Levant and the then Governor imprisoned his two servants for four months; and during the time they were in prison Hamed Mehduai paid them a dollar a day each and they were only liberated after he had paid the usual hush money to the Pasha.

I have the honor to be, with great respect, Your Excellency's most obedient humble servant,

P. Henderson

P.S. I would request that the name of the Kaimacam of Jalo should not be mentioned as the person from whom I derived my information as I fear, were it known, it might be prejudicial to him. P.H.

Copy
No. 3
Slave Trade
Bengazi 24 December 1875
The Right Honorable the Earl of Derby

My Lord

With reference to Mr. Lister's No. 1 Slave Trade of the 31st of August last I have the honor to report to your Lordship that, availing myself of the sanction contained therein to visit the slave entrepot in Jalo I accomplished this journey last month Mr. Kirri having acted for me during my absence.

At the last moment many obstacles were put in the way to prevent my making the journey and the Governor much to my surprise and disappointment declined to accompany me, as he had volunteered to do alleging the road to be too dangerous, the season to be unfavorable and various other excuses too frivolous to be worth a moments consideration, but promising if I would postpone my journey for a month or two to accompany me without fail.

I determined to go without him as a favorable opportunity presented itself for enabling me to meet a large caravan which had arrived at Koffra from Wadai and which was expected to arrive at Jalo about the same time as I had calculated I would arrive at that place myself and it was to prevent my attaining this object that so many difficulties were placed in my way. When the Pasha found that his refusal to accompany me in no way changed my determination he formally protested against my going, refused to give me the usual escort and hinted at detaining me by force. I however provided my own escort and left Bengazi on the 28th of October. After my departure the Pasha thinking better of his refusal sent an escort after me, and although it increased the expense of my journey considerably was very useful to me.

I was most desirous to inspect this caravan from Wadai in order to see and judge for myself if the various accounts which had reached me, of the deplorable condition of the negroes on their arrival and the excessive cruelty of their masters were exaggerated or not. The Slave dealers at Jalo considered my presence there as a most unwarrantable intrusion on a locality sacred to slavery and previous to my arrival had held a meeting at which it was resolved that I should not be permitted to enter the oasis at all. On my arrival however their resolution quite failed them and after reading my firman to the principal sheiks all opposition ceased and they received me hospitably and placed every facility at my disposal for visiting the different villages in the Oasis.

The caravan had arrived five days before me and I was unable therefore to verify by personal observation the exact number of slaves it brought but I saw and learnt quite enough to convince me of the magnitude and atrocity of the Slave trade at this place.

I was informed that two hundred and fifty two slaves had arrived with this caravan but I can only assert that it brought one hundred and eighteen as I was enabled to verify this latter number myself.

I quite believe that the former number is in no way magnified but owing to the shortness of the time at my disposal and the unwillingness of the people to give me any information on this subject I could not verify their number. I therefore confine myself to the smaller number as I am adverse to making a statement of this kind unless I am satisfied of its accuracy.

Two hours before entering the oasis we met four slaves in charge of an Arab on their way to Ozla and as we entered the palm groves we met another Arab leading a female slave by a rope tied around her waist. These slaves had arrived by the caravan. A little further on some ten or twelve were crouching round a well. I went up and examined them; they had also arrived on the caravan and could not speak a word of Arabic. They were emaciated to mere skeletons, their long thin legs and arms and the apparently unnatural size and prominence of their knees and elbows and hands and feet giving them a most repulsive and shocking appearance and I have never seen in all my life a more disgusting spectacle than they presented. I have seen the slaves in Cuba and in Brazil but their very value in those countries ensures their being well fed and well treated.

The poor creatures who are brought to Jalo from the interior do not fetch more than Ten or Twelve Pounds and if one out of every three reaches Jalo alive the owner still realizes a profit which amply repays him for all his risks as the cost of a slave in Wadai is from three pieces of calico upwards.

Twenty three degrees these miserable beings traverse on foot, naked, under a burning sun with a cup of water and a handful of maize every twelve hours for their support. For fourteen days between Tukkru and Jahuda not a drop of water is found and the caravan pursues its weary journey depending for its very existence on the gerbas which have been filled up at the wells of Tukkru. Thirst and hunger in vain lessen the numbers of the exhausted negroes, in vain they drop down way worn and fainting on the dreary journey to die a frightful death in the desert. The market at Jalo must be supplied and supplied it is but at what a cost of human life.

The journey from Morah, the capital of Wadai, to Jalo is one of unparalleled hardship and fatigue and cannot be accomplished under three months, two being consumed in actual travel. In Koffra the distance is about fifty days journey.

The distance in days journey between the intermediate resting places on the route are, as described to me by the courier, as follows

	Days journey
From Morah, the capital of Wadai, to Arada	3
Arada to Kashmar	2
Kashmar to Umashaluba	3
Umashaluba to Swalla	5
Swalla to Millumdam	3
Millumdam to Wayta	2
Wayta to Arraggia	2
Arraggia to Bedale	4
Bedale to Hayjanco	3
Hayjanco to Tukkru	3
Tukkru to Jahuda	14
Jahuda to Gebabo	2
Gebabo to Sbatea	5
Sbatea to Koffra	2

and from Koffra to Jalo is 8 days journey without water over a trackless desert. The caravans during this part of the journey are obliged to travel day and night, the guide alone receiving from sixty to one hundred dollars for the single journey.

Jalo is the most important oasis in this group. Its population cannot number less than eight thousand. The inhabitants are a fanatical and intollerant [*sic*] sect of Berber origin retaining to this day in language and appearance a marked distinction from the surrounding Bedouin tribes.

The oasis being the starting point and terminus of the numerous caravans to and from Wadai and Bornoo, is the centre of a large and valuable trade and the inhabitants are all well to do and many of them very wealthy. Last year a Maltese trader joined an Arab in a speculation to Wadai. They sent goods to the value of Two thousand Pounds and after fourteen months they realized Eighteen thousand Pounds by the sale of the ostrich feathers and ivory for which they bartered their goods.

During the past four months six large caravans have left for Wadai and as the route becomes better known its difficulties will be more easily overcome and a corresponding development of this lucrative trade will doubtless take place. The trade is in the hands of the Arabs and its ever increasing proportions will certainly cause a relative increase in the traffic in slaves. If one or two good examples were made and the whole of the slaves seized at Jalo on the arrival of the caravan the Arabs would find out to their cost that it neither paid nor was safe to bring them and that ostrich feathers and ivory neither died during the journey nor necessitated an additional provision of water and maize and that in the end they yielded a much more certain profit than negroes.

The caravans usually remain at Jalo for a month or two in order that the Arabs and Slaves may recover from the effects of their long journey. During the interval the slaves improve in condition, they are taught a few sentences of Arabic and receive an outfit of a Ma'raka or white cotton skullcap and a long blue cotton sourieh or shirt with long sleeves. Many are bought by the brothers at Jalo who send them on to Bengazi in lots of eight or ten at a time and thus are sent on to Egypt via Siwah. The greater number at present are brought here as the Egyptian Government act more energetically and has greater means at its disposal for checking the traffic than the Governor of such a remote Turkish province as that of Bengazi.

I was fortunate enough to procure the names of the owners of the one hundred and eighteen slaves already mentioned as having arrived from Wadai and immediately on my return to Bengazi I handed the list of Forty three names to the governor who promised to take steps to capture them on their arrival here. Many have been smuggled into the town during the last fortnight but only three have as yet been captured and liberated. The difficulty when many are captured and liberated at [the] same time is what to do with them.

It is impossible to turn the poor creatures out in the Streets to be again kidnapped and sold and I have hitherto maintained them at my own cost till I could find employment for them.

The Turks as a rule treat them well; they are well clothed and well-fed and if torn from their own country they are at least removed from its idolatries and ignorance, as the first care of a Moslim (who in this respect is infinitely superior to his more highly educated and polished fellow of the Western Hemisphere) is to teach them a religion which assures them that there is a God and that men of all colours are alike his children and equal in his eyes. When I say this I do not mean that it in any way mitigates the horrors of the Slave trade or lessens the privations to which the slaves are exposed before reaching this comparative state of happiness. The Arabs on the other hand treat their slaves badly and no matter what obligations they may enter into to pay liberated slaves wages they take the first opportunity to sell them.

I have had several long conferences with the Pasha since my return and we have agreed that the only way to check this traffic is to station a small military force which need not consist of more than one hundred men at Jalo; this would only be a temporary measure until the great changes which are taking place in the interior become accomplished facts and until a neighbouring potentate is in a position to check the traffic at its very fountain head.

The Pasha informed me, verbally however, that he has proposed this measure to his own Government and expressed to me his belief that the Porte would at once assent to the proposal were it seconded and supported by Her Majesty's Ambassador at C[onstantino]ple.

Sir H[enr]y Elliot is much more competent than I am to form an opinion as to the expediency of recommending this course, at present, and I only repeat the suggestion as it was put into my mouth.

I would mention to your Lordship a circumstance which may probably be of some interest taken in connection with the slave trade.

For some time past large quantities of gunpowder have been brought to Bengazi and there has been much speculation here as to its destination. I found out at Jalo that this gunpowder is being regularly and expeditiously conveyed to Wadai and the natives made no secret of the purpose for which it was intended.

This purpose is one with which we can have no sympathy and it is remarkable that the local authorities here are tolerating the introduction of this powder notwithstanding the severe prohibitory laws and its being contraband by treaty.

If I have been unable to altogether stop the traffic in slaves at Bengazi, I have at least succeeded in wresting the trade to the Levant out of the hands of the Arabs and this of itself is a step in the right direction because as I have before said the Turks treat their slaves far more humanely than the Arabs and although the trade is still carried on by the Turks it is not accompanied with the same cruelty nor I am glad to say to the same extent as formerly.

I have put the local Gov^{t} in possession of the names of the slavedealers, of the positions of the slave depots and in short of the whole particulars and organization of this trade to its minutest detail. I have now accomplished my by no means agreeable task and I venture to hope that my unremitting efforts may meet with Y.L. approval I have etc.

signed P. Henderson

Note

1. An Ottoman term for an armed guard who escorted consular officials and other dignitaries.

9.
Instructions Concerning the Trade in Slaves (1936)

Part I

ARTICLE I

Inasmuch as the provisions of the noble Sharīʿa preclude the enslavement or purchase of the subjects of countries in treaty relationships,[1] it is accordingly absolutely forbidden

1. to import slaves from any country to the Kingdom of Saudi Arabia by sea
2. to import slaves to the Kingdom of Saudi Arabia by land, unless the slavedealer has a government document attesting that the person imported was recognized as a slave in the country from which he was imported at the time when this statute was promulgated
3. to enslave free persons in the Kingdom of Saudi Arabia
4. to purchase or own any person imported or enslaved, in a manner in violation of the foregoing provisions, after the promulgation of this statute.

Any violation of the foregoing provisions shall require the punishment of the perpetrator, as follows:

1. the liberation and release of the slave
2. the application of the current customs regulations to the smugglers
3. severe imprisonment for a term not exceeding one year.

Part II

ARTICLE II

The rights of the slave against his owner or possessor[2] are that he (1) feed, clothe, and lodge him; (2) treat him decently and employ him compassionately and without cruelty; (3) care for him in sickness and pay the cost of his treatment; (4) in general he has the same rights as the man's family and household, as is laid down in the laws of the noble Sharīʿa.

ARTICLE III

If any slave complains of ill-treatment by his owner or possessor, both parties shall be summoned to appear before the competent authority. If the validity of the complaint is proven, on the first occasion the authority shall give the owner or possessor a warning and allow him a period of grace not exceeding two months, to reconsider the situation of the complainant. If it is proven on a second occasion that the causes of the complaint are still present, the authority shall order the owner or possessor to remove the complainant from his ownership or possession, by sale or otherwise. If the owner or possessor fails to present the complainant to the authority within the period which it has specified, he shall be punished the first time with a fine not exceeding one pound. If he persists in this refusal, his fine shall be doubled; and he may be sentenced to a term of imprisonment for a period not exceeding one week.

Article IV

Any slave who can prove that he was born free, or that he was enslaved in a manner contrary to Sharīʿa, during the period that has passed since the establishment of His Majesty's government in the year 1344 [= 1925],[3] has the right to claim his manumission. The competent authority must agree to examine the case and pronounce a just judgment.

Article V

While respecting any rights reserved by the owner or possessor in a manner recognized by the Sharīʿa and recorded in writing at the time of the marriage, the owner or possessor may not separate two slaves between whom a marriage has been contracted in accordance with the Sharīʿa, except as provided in the Sharīʿa.

Article VI

An owner or possessor may not part children from their mother before they come of age.

Article VII

A slave may request a contract to purchase his freedom[4] from his owner or possessor, who must respond to this request. If there is a disagreement between the owner or possessor and the slave as to the amount, then the fixing of the amount and the dates of payment shall be settled with the knowledge of the competent authority. The existence of such a contract shall not be deemed to annul the application of the rules in Article III above.

Article VIII

Any slave born outside the Kingdom of Saudi Arabia shall, in the event of his manumission in accordance with the terms of this statute or in any other way recognized by Sharīʿa, have the right to choose his place of domicile.

Article IX

All existing slaves shall be registered in a special register to be kept by the competent authority; and every slave shall be given an identity document containing his description and, for males, a photograph. Identity documents shall be prepared in three copies, one to be kept by the competent authority, one for the owner or possessor, and one for the slave. The document shall record all transactions relating to the slave. The owner or possessor must complete the registration procedures within one year from the promulgation of this statute.

Article X

Any slave whose owner has not registered him as set forth in the foregoing article, may request the competent authority to give him a certificate of freedom.

Article XI

When slaves change hands, they must be submitted to a doctor of the public health department, for a certificate on their state of health.

Article XII

A slave may not be employed as an agent or broker without written authorization issued by the competent authority.

Article XIII

A special official shall be appointed for slave affairs. He shall be called the Inspector of Slave Affairs, and he shall have a deputy who shall be mobile as required.

Article XIV

The local competent authorities shall present a half-yearly report on the enforcement of this statute, containing a summary of transactions that have occurred. The half-yearly reports shall be submitted, with the observations of the Inspector of Slaves, to the Minister of the Interior, during the two months following the end of the six-month period covered in the report.

Article XV

The competent authorities mentioned in this statute shall be the Ministry of Internal Affairs in the capital and the governors' offices elsewhere. For the inspection of cases in accordance with the provisions of this statute, the competent authority shall form a body composed of its own representative, a representative of the police administration, and a member of the administrative council to examine the case and adjudicate.

Article XVI

This statute shall enter into effect from the date of its promulgation.

Notes

1. On the significance of this term, see *EI*², s.vv. "Dār al-'Ahd" (by Halil Inalcik) and "Dār al-Ṣulh" (by D. B. MacDonald and A. Abel).

2. Literally, "one who disposes of him." Islamic law, like Roman law, distinguishes between absolute ownership and possession with the right of use.

3. In 1925, ʿAbd al-ʿAzīz Ibn Saʿud was proclaimed king of Najd, Ḥijāz, and their dependencies. In 1932 the name of the kingdom was changed to Saudi Arabia.

4. On the contract to purchase freedom, see above, p. 8.

Sources of Illustrations

1. Al-Ḥarīrī, *Maqāmāt*
   Illustrated by al-Wāsiṭī
   Ms. Arabe 5847, f. 105
   Bibliothèque Nationale, Paris
   Previously published in W. Walther, *Die Frau im Islam* (Leipzig, 1980), p. 25., pl. 11

2. Al-Ḥarīrī, *Maqāmāt*
   Ms. Arabe 6094, p. 16
   Bibliothèque Nationale, Paris

3. Farīd al-Dīn ʿAṭṭār, *Manṭiq al-Ṭayr*
   Add. 7735, f. 84a
   British Library, London

4. Firdawsī, *Shāhnāme,* in Turkish translation
   Treasure 1519, f. 141b
   Topkapı Saray Museum, Istanbul
   Previously published in Nurhan Atasoy, "1510 Tarihli memluk şehnamesinin minyatürleri," *Sanat Tarihi Araştırmaları* 2 (n.d.), p. 57

5. Jalāl al-Dīn Rūmī, *Maṣnavī*
   Add. 27263, f. 29a
   British Library, London

6. *Shāhanshāhnāme*
   B. 200, vol. 2, f. 82b
   Topkapı Saray Museum, Istanbul

7. *Shāhanshāhnāme*
   B. 200, vol. 2, f. 83a
   Topkapı Saray Museum, Istanbul

8. *Shāhanshāhnāme*
   B. 200, vol. 2, f. 146a
   Topkapı Saray Museum, Istanbul

9. Vehbī, *Sūrnāme*
   Illustrated by Levnī
   A. 3593, f. 173b
   Topkapı Saray Museum, Istanbul

10. Vehbī, *Sūrnāme*
    Illustrated by Levnī, ca. 1720–32
    A. 3593, f. 63
    Topkapı Saray Museum, Istanbul

11. Firdawsī, *Shāhnāme*
    Houghton, *Shahname,* f. 435v
    Previously published in Martin Bernard Dickson and Stuart Cary Welsh, *The Houghton Shahnameh* (Cambridge, MA, 1981), vol. 2, pl. 202

12. Niẓāmī, *Khamse*
    Or. 1363, f. 237a
    British Library, London

13. Abū Ṭāhir Tarasūsī, *Dārābnāme*
    Or. 4615, f. 29b
    British Library, London

14. Abū Ṭāhir Tarasūsī, *Dārābnāme*
    Or. 4615, f. 33a
    British Library, London

15. Abū Ṭāhir Tarasūsī, *Dārābnāme*
    Or. 4615, f. 33b
    British Library, London

16. Al-Wāqidī, *Siyer-i Nebi,* in a Turkish translation prepared by order of Murad III
    Treasure (Hazine) 1221, f. 377a
    Topkapı Saray Museum, Istanbul

17. Al-Wāqidī, *Siyer-i Nebi,* in a Turkish translation prepared by order of Murad III
    Treasure (Hazine) 1222, f. 194a
    Topkapı Saray Museum, Istanbul

18. Al-Wāqidī, *Siyer-i Nebi,* in a Turkish translation prepared by order of Murad III
    Treasure (Hazine) 1222, f. 263a
    Topkapı Saray Museum, Istanbul

19. Mīr ʿAlī Shīr Nawāʾī, *Dīwān*
    Sup. Turc. 316, f. 447v
    Bibliothèque Nationale, Paris
    Previously published in Basil Gray, *Persian Paintings* (New York, 1961), p. 131

20. The Album of Mehmed II, the Conqueror
    Treasure (Hazine) 2152–53 and 2160
    Topkapı Saray Museum, Istanbul
    Previously published in UNESCO, *Turkey: Ancient Miniatures,* World Art Series (Paris, 1960), pl. 10

21. Abū Ṭāhir Tarasūsī, *Dārābnāme*
    Or. 4615, f. 118b
    British Library, London

22. Jalāl al-Dīn Rūmī, *Ma͟snavī*
    Add. 27263, f. 298a
    British Library, London

23. Saʿdī, *Būstān*
    Add. 27262, f. 129a
    British Library, London

24. Fāzıl Enderūnī, *Zenānnāme*
    Or. 7094, f. 12a
    British Library, London

Index